Repeatedly since 1945, and on average about once every two and a half years, Britain has been obliged to review and often drastically to revise her defense policy. Slow economic growth, rising domestic expectations, rapid technological change, a multiplicity of external challenges posed by the Soviet Union and by Afro-Asian nationalists have all combined to present British defense planners with an almost impossible task. The development of the British nuclear deterrent and the debates provoked by it, the Anglo-American special relationship and the defense of western Europe, the various efforts to defend British interests outside Europe, the controversy over Britain's role east of Suez, the successes and failures of Britain's weapon-procurement policies are all fundamental themes running throughout the book. Particular crises such as the Korean War, Suez, "Confrontation with Indonesia", the cancellation of "Blue Streak", TSR-2 and of new aircraft-carriers are also analyzed. Controversy over defense policy has cut across party lines, and created divisions between and within the Services themselves. Often the debates have been emotional rather than constructive. The author's aim has been to analyze, as dispassionately as possible in the light of available evidence, this complicated and controversial period, and to provide a comprehensive guide to the many changes in British defense policy since 1945.

C. J. Bartlett is Reader in International History at the University of Dundee. He is the author of *Great Britain and Sea Power, 1815–53* and *Castlereagh,* and the editor of *Britain Pre-eminent.*

THE LONG RETREAT

The Long Retreat

A Short History of British
Defence Policy, 1945–70

C. J. BARTLETT

MACMILLAN
ST MARTIN'S PRESS

First published 1972 by
THE MACMILLAN PRESS LTD
London and Basingstoke
Associated companies in New York Toronto
Dublin Melbourne Johannesburg and Madras

Library of Congress catalog card no. 79-177925

SBN 333 03118 0

Printed in Great Britain by
BUTLER AND TANNER LTD
Frome and London

To Shirley

Contents

'Now *here,* you see, it takes all the running *you* can do, to keep in the same place. If you want to get somewhere else, you must run at least twice as fast as that!'

The Red Queen, in *Through the Looking-Glass* by Lewis Carroll

Preface

Instant history, commented Sir William Hayter, is as 'widespread as instant coffee, and nearly as tasteless'. Instant coffee has the advantage of being consumed instantly, and not overtaken by the passage of events while the author's typescript is in the hands of the printer. Fortunately a more sympathetic reviewer once wrote: 'A work dealing with the most recent past often gives a useful service merely by setting down a factual account laboriously gathered from the mass of ephemeral materials which are the bones of contemporary history.' It seems fitting that such an exercise should be attempted as the first post-war generation of British defence policy draws to a close.

Buffeted by Britain's economic problems, and by rapidly changing circumstances – political and technical – British defence policy since 1945 presents a confused and bewildering picture. Major changes of direction or emphasis have occurred at least ten times between 1945 and 1970 – an average of one every two and a half years (one notes apprehensively that another change is about due!). In the space of a single generation a host of well-established ideas, institutions and instruments have been challenged or overthrown. The pace of technological change has been breathtaking, with nuclear power, jet and rocket propulsion, and a host of electronic developments creating new dimensions in space and time. As one Minister of Defence rather plaintively told the House of Commons on 4 November 1960: 'If we could lock up all the scientists for five or six years, we might possibly have a consistent defence policy.' Yet the pace of political change in the world has been almost as giddy, with the emergence of nationalists and revolutionaries throughout Africa and Asia. That awakening, facilitated by radio, the printed word and modern small arms, has presented the armed forces with a host of problems undreamed of in 1945.

The British, despite their passion for war stories, have never been noted for their interest in defence. They have bewailed its cost in general, but have shown little detailed concern for the expenditure of some £40 billion between 1946 and 1970. Defence experts and a few politicians have regularly lamented this lack of interest, which often extended to Parliament itself. The quality of its debates, admittedly, has been further diminished by governmental secrecy far in excess of that practised before 1939. Richard Crossman asserted on 29 February 1956: 'One of my difficulties today [is] that I am able to study the Army, not as a Member of Parliament, but only as a journalist.' Intelligent parliamentary critics sometimes incurred the Speaker's wrath by their constant interruption of government spokesmen, but persistent questioning was a natural response to the vague generalisations that issued from the front bench. Defence debates all too often degenerated into hair-splitting controversies, a game played even by some distinguished front-benchers with all the relish of raw but enthusiastic undergraduates first exposed to textual criticism. Occasional oases flourished in this desert, while outside Parliament there were always a few newspapers, journals and independent writers who did their best to master the key questions and discuss their implications as intelligently as government information would permit.

Crucial information and commentaries on British defence policy are to be found in *Brassey*, an annual publication; the *Royal United Service Institution Journal*; a variety of specialist journals such as *Aircraft Engineering* and *Flight International*; the varied productions of the Institute for Strategic Studies and the Royal Institute of International Affairs, and the perennial *Jane's All the World's Fighting Ships* and *Aircraft*. If Liddell Hart remained the doyen of British defence analysts until his death, an encouraging number of new names have emerged in this field since the Second World War. Few memoirs relating to the period since 1945 have given much space to defence, though the sum total of information to be gathered from such sources, reinforced by the speeches, lectures, articles and books by leading political,

service, scientific and industrial figures, is not unimpressive.
Some comparison of the evidence becomes possible, so that
one can begin both to check and supplement the official story.
The reports of various parliamentary Select Committees are
of great value on some questions, notably the difficulties of
aircraft procurement. Quite apart from the vast American
literature on defence and related questions, the studies and
memoirs of a number of leading American statesmen and
their advisers likewise throw some light on British defence
policy. All too often, of course, the available evidence does
no more than heighten one's awareness of the lacunae. But
equally the non-specialist reader may be surprised to find how
much can be established – however tentatively in places.

I wish to express my gratitude to the University of Dundee
for financial assistance in the preparation of this book, to the
University's library staff for their unfailing efforts to track
down the material I required, and to Professor D. F.
Macdonald and the other members of the History Department in Dundee for their unfailing interest, and for pointing
out newspaper and similar references that I would otherwise
have missed. My wife has patiently read draft after draft,
clarifying style and content as far as I would allow, and assisting with the typing and indexing.

C. J. B.

1 In Search of a Defence Policy: 1945-7

'Well, it certainly is a great day; a great historic day . . .' wrote a distinguished British scientist, Sir Henry Tizard, in his diary on 8 May 1945 on the defeat of Hitler's Germany. But he went on thoughtfully: 'It is hard to realise now, but we shall know better later on. I feel rather like a patient coming round after a severe but successful operation. Deep down there is a feeling that all is well . . . but other feelings are not so pleasant, and the nurse who pats one on the arm and shouts that all is over is excessively exasperating.' His forebodings were justified, for among the many problems that Britain was to face in the post-war world was the staggering cost of defence as new challenges to her security and interests, and new and revolutionary weapons, emerged. Given the development of nuclear weapons, more powerful bombers and submarines, and perhaps too of guided missiles, even a prosperous and powerful Britain could well prove more vulnerable than at any time in her previous history. For the clear-sighted there was the further realisation that Britain's strength would not easily be restored. In particular, power in Europe might soon become the prerogative of the Soviet Union alone.

In 1953 a distinguished British student of international affairs, Geoffrey Gathorne-Hardy, insisted that it was almost a truism for thoughtful Britons that the main issue for their country in the twentieth century was its adjustment to a greatly reduced position in the world. Yet for many people the nation appeared to be facing no more than a temporary period of post-war crisis and recuperation, not a permanent change in its economic and political position. As late as 5 March 1962 *The Times* could repeat with approval a sonorous Churchillian claim: 'Ask what you please, look where you will, you cannot get to the bottom of the resources of Britain . . . no strain is too prolonged for the patience of our people.' Later in the same year Dean Acheson's assertion that Britain had lost an empire and had yet to find a new role ignited widespread consternation and protest. But the truth of the matter, as some people had long been wholly or inter-mittently aware – according to Lady Violet Bonham-Carter, Churchill himself first really recognised it during the Teheran Conference in 1943 – was that Britain's resources and interests in the world had been increasingly out of balance since the late nineteenth century. The industrialisa-tion of the United States, Japan and other European powers had brought a triple economic, imperial and naval chal-lenge, ending the half-century or so that followed the Vienna Settlement of 1814–15 when Britain's ability to pursue her interests in the wider world had never been so untrammelled. True, Britain's ability to influence the politics of Europe and the Near East without a major ally had remained limited. But at sea, down to the 1870s, she had possessed the potential to maintain a three-power naval standard, had she been so minded, and until the spread of railways across Asia in the last years of the nineteenth century no power had been in a posi-tion to pose a serious land threat to her interests in the East.

Britain responded between 1895 and 1914 to this revolu-tion in the world balance of power with a series of agreements designed to limit the number of likely enemies to two – from 1907 to only one – and by beginning to transform the Indian army from an essentially colonial force into one that might be of some value against a European power. When relative agreement with all the leading powers, save Germany, proved possible, Britain directed her main defence preparations to the command of the North Sea and the despatch of a small expeditionary force to France, relying heavily elsewhere for security on Japanese, American and French friendship, and on Russian preoccupations in eastern Europe. Sea power, the great imperial chain of strategic bases and the Indian army, nevertheless provided highly flexible means of redeployment if necessary.

The early years of the twentieth century also saw an im-pressive effort to rid Britain's armed forces of the obsoles-cence, amateurishness and lethargy that had crept into so much of their thinking and practice since the struggle against Napoleon. The Crimean and various colonial campaigns had been insufficient stimulants. The Boer War and the imperial scramble from the 1890s were needed to begin this transformation. The Committee of Imperial Defence was to provide the Cabinet with a notable instrument for the review of defence policy; a General and – more belatedly – a Naval War Staff were instituted; training and service equipment were modernised; Churchill and Fisher in dramatic if uneven fashion, Haldane more systematically, dragged navy and army into the modern era. The need for speedy mobilisation was recognised, though not the mounting evidence that any war between evenly matched industrial powers was likely to degenerate into long, slogging matches of attrition, in which plans and preparations for a complete mobilisation of the nation's resources would be as vital as the initial dash to the front. Nor were the capabilities of probable allies and enemies properly assessed, save for the remarkably perceptive analyses of the British and German battle-fleets by Admiral Jellicoe. Inter-service co-operation, especially in amphibious operations, was non-existent, and strategic thinking was often divorced from what was practicable. The tragic waste of Gallipoli was to be the penalty for imagination that was not backed by a grasp of the material problems. Nothing, however, brought the allied cause so near disaster as the French offensives of August 1914, and the latter's management of the opening phases of the war. Only the 'Miracle' on the Marne prepared the way for the great stalemate on the Western Front. Russia, too, contributed to this breathing-space that made possible the great British mobilisation of men and machines, while British sea power drew upon the resources of the extra-European world and denied them to the enemy.

The battles of the First World War have been fought twice over – first with blood and then with ink – but for Britain their lessons were abundantly clear. Against a great, disciplined and efficient industrial power such as Germany there were, failing some remarkable technological break-throughs in the art of war, no short-cuts. Railways, at least as far as Constantinople, largely negatived the mobility of sea power. Even tanks and aircraft, at their current state of development

The war was won by attrition and by overwhelming numbers; by a blockade that sapped the strength and morale of Germany; by offensives on all fronts, which by sheer weight, and only partially through improved arms, training and tactics, finally robbed the enemy of all hope of victory. It was a war in which Britain, for all her massive contribution of industry, finance, shipping, land and sea power, was heavily dependent upon her allies – even, in the later years, upon the loans of America. Although Britain had required land allies against Napoleon, she had emerged the paymaster of Europe and unquestioned mistress of the seas. By 1917–18 the United States had assumed the first role – at least in part – and the second was hers for the taking. Nor, by 1918, had so much been achieved as in the war against Napoleon. For all its harshness the Treaty of Versailles in 1919 still left Germany potentially the strongest of the western European powers. Furthermore, the revolutionary threat, so much feared in connection with France after 1815 and so much a stimulant to continued allied unity, came now not from Germany but from Russia, following the Bolshevik seizure of power in 1917. Germany thus possessed much more freedom to manœuvre in the post-war world, and was indeed to play with great effect upon this ideological divide. Given American isolation, the future peace of Europe rested upon German restraint, or eternal Anglo-French vigilance based upon a readiness to intervene before Germany recovered sufficient strength to defend herself. The latter policy was rejected by the British as unthinkable, impracticable and unjust. The alternative course – appeasement – required the corollary that Germany should throw up leaders who could be appeased.

Britain had fought the First World War to maintain the balance of power in western Europe. The outcome left the possibility that in the long run the balance would be even less favourable to her. In the wider world the British Empire, in appearance, had expanded, but in practice the balance between responsibilities and resources was worsening. The awakening of Asiatic nationalism from Cairo to Canton had been hastened by the war; the possible pretensions of her important ally, Japan, had been underlined; while overall the relative moral and material strengths of Britain in the face of all these challenges were lessening. Not only had the war struck heavy blows at Britain's physical strength, but it had left the mass of her people disillusioned with the old apparatus of power politics, appalled at war as an instrument of policy, and disposed to recite the liturgy of collective security in the innocent belief that this was somehow a substitute for power itself. The League of Nations was less than the sum of its parts, and indeed British governments hesitated to commit themselves to any positive international agreements since they recognised that a great part of the burden of enforcement would have to be borne by Britain herself.

Britain's security had been further eroded by the advance of weapon technology, and this deterioration had been compounded by national failures to adjust thinking and equipment to many of these changes. Most dangerous in 1914–18 had been the perfection of the ocean-going submarine, which had threatened to disprove Mahan's thesis that a great naval power could not be defeated by *guerre de course*. Belated introduction of the convoy system had averted disaster for the time being, only to breed a dangerous complacency at the Admiralty concerning the future. More dramatic and immediate for the people of south-eastern England had been their first taste of air-bombing. The damage had been emotional rather than material, but as one air record after another was broken in the 1920s, so to the existing horror of trench-warfare was added the potential horror of large-scale terror raids from the skies. Baldwin somberly declared that the bomber must always get through. It was fortunate that another scientific advance – the discovery and successful development of radar in the mid-1930s – should have provided Britain with a fighting chance to defend herself from within her own territory. Indeed, save in radar and Fighter Command, Britain was unable to establish a qualitative lead over Germany, an ironic outcome given the Air Staff's preference for offensive warfare. Meanwhile the British, having pioneered tanks and the theories of armoured warfare from 1915, had allowed this new arm to languish for want of funds, through service conservatism and preoccupation with im-

perial policing. Britain, having reverted to a small professional army after 1919, lacked even a proper mechanised
élite to throw into the scales of battle in Europe in 1939–40.[1]
A second time she put her trust in the army of France, but in
1940 there was to be no 'Miracle' of the Marne.

Indeed, so completely were the French out-fought and out-
generalled that it is difficult to hazard even a guess at the
qualitative and quantitative improvements that would have
been necessary to enable Britain's land and air forces to
redress the balance. To have made no more than a start
towards such forces would have demanded a revolution not
only in the thinking of the General and Air Staffs,[2] but also
in the nation as a whole. To have built more and better arms
would have required dynamic political, bureaucratic and
industrial management, reinforced by trade union co-opera-
tiveness and flexibility. Major balance of payments problems
would have arisen as imports increased. A whole book would
be needed to do justice to these hypothetical implications.
But what is clear is that there was no simple answer by the
later 1930s. No easy panacea was to be found in the management of foreign affairs (historians continue to debate whether
an alliance with Russia was realisable or not in 1939), by re-
adjustments to rearmament, or the mere expenditure of
money. Consequently in 1939–40 Britain possessed no more
than a half-equipped, half-trained expeditionary force, a
'paper' Bomber Command, and barely adequate naval and
air defence forces. Fortunately the navy had not lost the
'Nelson touch', while the youngest service was to discover a
magic all its own. Fortunately, too, the morale of the nation
as a whole seemed to find new strength in each disaster.

Long before the fall of France it had been clear that any
major allied defeat was likely to encourage the pretensions
of the egregious Mussolini in Italy and the confused but
ambitious xenophobic factions in Japan. British defence
planners had long been emphatic that Britain, in the foreseeable future, could not handle more than one major foe, and
that one preferably not until the 1940s. Despite the completion of Singapore in the late 1930s Britain lacked the means
to do more than stand upon the defensive against Japan. After
the disasters of 1940 there was little that could be spared even

for defence in the East. Since the 1920s the British had recognised their inability to win a war against Japan without American aid: but in 1941 and early 1942 even the Anglo-American combination was ineffectual, and the Japanese tide lapped towards both India and Australia. Pessimistic as British defence experts had often been in the 1930s, they had never in their worst moments conceived such disasters. Of the pre-war assumptions few had withstood the havoc of war. The air defence of Britain had held – by a narrow margin; the Atlantic sea routes were being kept open – just. But France had fallen when she should have bought time while Britain mobilised such strength as would be necessary to exploit the numbing effects of allied bombing and the blockade. Economic warfare was nullified by German victories, and by their ability to trade with the Soviet Union until the summer of 1941. As yet British bombing was proving a mere pin-prick, while the advance of the Axis was menacing Britain's traditional positions of strength in the Middle East.

Fortunately the uncontrollable ambitions of the Axis powers were to bring about their downfall. In 1941 it was they who forged the reluctant alliance of Britain, Russia and the United States. Without America the industrial balance, and therefore the military balance, could not be swung decisively against the enemy. Failing Russia the maritime powers would almost certainly have found it impossible to fight their way back into Hitler's Europe without some such instrument as the atomic bomb to blast it open for them. Sea power could not land sufficient force until more than half the land strength of Germany was committed and ground to pieces in the East. Whatever the value of bombing and the blockade as weapons of attrition, Hitler might well have proved invincible had he chosen to fight on only one front at a time.

Such were the experiences, then, that filled, or should have filled, the minds of those entrusted with the formulation of British defence policy at the end of the Second World War. For the more perceptive the elation of victory was tempered by the realisation of the marginal escape from disaster in 1940–2, by the enormous cost to Britain, by the deficiencies in her forces and industries, and by her overwhelming indebtedness to others. Many of the very landmarks that had guided their predecessors had been swept away. The European states system, whose internal checks and balances had favoured Britain so strongly as little as fifty years before, had gone. The United States had become the world's greatest industrial, naval and air power. Russia, more inscrutable even than in Tsarist days, had advanced into the very centre of Europe, and was displaying a disturbing interest in the affairs of Turkey, Iran and China; while from the eastern Mediterranean to the Indian Ocean and the Pacific a variety of peoples clamoured for independence and a say in world affairs in a manner that was not easily to be denied or controlled. Cast overall was the mushroom-shaped cloud of the atomic bomb, whose true military significance had yet to be properly assessed, but which seemed to threaten a type of war more sudden, short and terrible than anything conjured up by the German *Blitzkrieg*, or the Japanese strike on Pearl Harbour. Nor could modern weapon development be expected to rest there, especially in the air and beneath the sea, as new forms of propulsion and weapon guidance systems emerged.

Of what value in such circumstances would be the world's second largest navy? Of what value in this new world of Asiatic nationalists would be Britain's traditional eastern strategic reserve – the Indian army? What strategic bases could be held throughout the world in the face of such nationalism and Britain's weakened economy? How could Britain adopt her traditional policy of partial aloofness from the continent and reliance on the balance of power when Russia might soon prove to be the only real power in Europe? Should Russia prove hostile, how could one blockade that virtually self-sufficient land mass? Did either a continental strategy or one of limited liability promise any security against so formidable a force? Would even a second Battle of Britain prove feasible in the nuclear age? Could Bomber Command be developed into a viable instrument against so distant and huge a country, especially after its dependence on American assistance in its controversial contribution in the recent war? Any lingering self-confidence might be further shaken by the reflection that many of the basic assumptions in British defence policy of the 1930s had been

completely confounded between 1939 and 1942. Not surprisingly some who turned their minds to these problems
were disposed to feel that Britain was too small, too vulnerable, too weakened to survive as a great power for long in this
new age, but should disperse her energies and resources
among the white Dominions of the Commonwealth.

Britain faced this triple revolution – in the balance of
power, in her relationship with Afro-Asia, and in military
technology – with a limited number of assets and many weaknesses. The end of the war found her with the potential to
remain the world's third industrial power for some time at
least, with high levels of expertise in some key sectors of arms
manufacture, especially aircraft, aero-engines, shipbuilding
and electronics. Furthermore, her scientists, having made a
major contribution to the unleashing of nuclear power, gave
her the potential to produce atomic weapons within the foreseeable future. Overshadowed as she now was by the United
States and the Soviet Union, a wide gap nevertheless separated her from all other states. She had no close rival in western
Europe. Her distinguished array of war leaders – both political and military – were massively backed in depth by professional experts of all kinds. The war, indeed, had released
a remarkable range of talents, while quantitatively no less
than 9 million, or some 40 per cent of the nation's manpower,
had been mobilised for the services or their support.

On the other hand it had to be recognised that so great an
effort – with the dedication of about half the nation's
resources to the war – had been heavily dependent on
American economic assistance under Lend-Lease. Churchill
himself described his economic policy as one of 'reckless
abandon': John Maynard Keynes thought it 'financial impru-
dence which has no parallel in history'. Thus in the last year
of the war Britain was spending some £2000 million abroad,
yet was earning a mere £800 million. Her current reserves
equalled only one-sixth of short-term foreign debts. Much as
Britain had contributed to the allied cause, it is still instruc-
tive to compare it with that of the United States. By 1945 the
latter had mobilised some 12 million in the services compared
with roughly 5 million British. If Britain had supplied about
70 per cent of the munitions used by Commonwealth forces,

the United States had provided about a quarter of the extra
machine tools employed by her industries during the war. At
sea, for long the scene of Britain's greatest efforts, the United
States had also become the dominating partner, building six
times the tonnage of ocean-going merchant shipping, and adding three times as much to her navy.[3] All this had been done
without strain to her economy. In contrast that of Britain
would require several years of adjustment and capital re-
equipment – ideally, too, a massive improvement in industrial efficiency – before the nation could hope to pay its way in
the world, even by the standards of the 1930s, and make good
the overall losses in national wealth. Indeed, without further
American aid, the nation would be 'virtually bankrupt'.

True, no immediate major threat to the peace of the world
seemed very likely. Both Germany and Japan were prostrate,
though uncertainty was growing concerning Soviet intentions. Churchill's mounting apprehension from the closing
stages of the war in Europe is well known. Indeed, he was
temporarily to stop the reduction in the strength of the R.A.F.
in Europe in May 1945 as relations with the Soviet Union
reached one of their low points.[4] Eden, in July 1945, feared
the spread of Soviet influence as far afield as Egypt and
Tangier.[5] As early as September 1944 the Chiefs of Staff were
envisaging the possible co-operation of parts of western
Germany with Britain and other European states in some
future stand against Russia. This was too revolutionary for
the Foreign Office, though it also was showing interest in
some form of western European grouping to provide security
against a resurgent Germany and other unforeseen contingencies. Such a relationship might in any case act as a
counterweight to the super-powers, Russia and the United
States. But others, including Churchill, feared that the states
of western Europe would prove so weak after the war that
they would act as a drain on rather than a reinforcement to
British strength. Until a strong French army had been reconstituted, Britain should look for her security to the
Channel, and to her naval and air strength.[6] Just how far
Britain should commit land forces to the defence of western
Europe was to remain a major issue in defence planning in
the first post-war years, and there existed a strong school of

thought that such a commitment would prove futile and beyond the nation's resources – certainly outside the context of an alliance embracing the United States.

Many eyes were turned hopefully towards that power, despite its professed determination to withdraw its forces from Europe in the near future. A vain effort was made to prolong the intimate co-operation that had developed between their respective Chiefs of Staff organisations during the war years. All three services encouraged any hint of an American disposition to be more co-operative. Interest in a concerted Commonwealth defence policy was also running high, and in some instances led to very radical, even frenetic conclusions. Lord Alanbrooke and Sir Henry Tizard were so impressed by British vulnerability in the approaching nuclear era that they advocated the transfer of as much British manpower and industry as possible to the white Dominions. There exist reports that the Chiefs of Staff drew up a paper on these lines for the Commonwealth Conference of April– May 1946.[7] Less ambitiously, Clement Attlee was looking to Australia to develop as an industrial and military power, and take over an increasing proportion of Britain's responsibilities in the Far East. But hopes of a more integrated Commonwealth defence policy ran counter to the inclinations of the Dominions themselves, while Britain, the atomic threat notwithstanding, could not take seriously the proposal to disperse her resources overseas.

In default of quick and revolutionary solutions Britain's defence planners had to proceed more tentatively. Immediate problems in any case absorbed most of their attention. Defence had to be reviewed in the light of the nation's massive economic difficulties. Current exports could purchase no more than one-quarter of the pre-war volume of British imports. Given the decline in Britain's invisible earnings, through the loss of about half of her foreign investments and nearly one-third of her merchant shipping, a big expansion in exports compared with the 1930s was essential. A massive redeployment of the nation's resources had to be carried through before Britain could once again pay her way in the world. The ending of American Lend-Lease in August 1945, following the defeat of Japan, was a great blow; Keynes thought the nation faced a 'financial Dunkirk' that autumn. But optimism returned to some extent when negotiations in the winter of 1945–6 produced the American and Canadian loans, to the value of some £1000 million, that were intended to meet Britain's balance of payments deficits while the conversion from a wartime economy was taking place. If there was much dissatisfaction with the terms of these loans, the initial feeling was nevertheless one of considerable confidence concerning the future; sufficient breathing-space had been secured, it was felt, to enable Britain to demobilise in an orderly fashion, while at the same time both to maintain considerable forces overseas, and to make tentative plans for the provision of sizeable armed forces in the future.

Nor did the return to power of a Labour government with an overwhelming parliamentary majority in July 1945 bring any radical departures in defence policy.[8] Indeed, complaints were soon to be heard from Churchill and the Conservatives at the slow pace of demobilisation, as well as from the traditional critics of large armaments. Attlee replied on 4 March 1946 that the government was hoping to reduce personnel in the armed forces to about 1,200,00 by the end of the year, with some 500,000 in the supply industries. These figures should be contrasted with the 9 million engaged in the war effort in 1944, and the $1\frac{3}{4}$ million early in 1939, at which time, incidentally, only 477,000 were in the services.

Defence expenditure still stood at £1736 million in 1946, or one-fifth of the gross national product. The ultimate target was some £500 million, or perhaps 5 per cent of the gross national product, a level of defence spending roughly twice the inter-war average. Shades of appeasement[9] and pre-war unpreparedness influenced this thinking, and in particular it was intended that neither the army nor the R.A.F. should be allowed to languish as in the 1920s and early 1930s. Furthermore, if the forthcoming independence of India removed one imperial commitment, it also eliminated the Indian army, a vital element in British strength East of Suez. Lord Alanbrooke described Indian independence in 1947 as a crippling blow to British military power, while Air Vice-Marshal McCloughry, looking back in 1955, asked whether there should not have been a commensurate cut in Britain's

Far Eastern interests from 1947.[10] This, however, was easier said than done, given the state of the post-war world, and only imminent economic bankruptcy would have led to so drastic a reappraisal of British world interests at that time. As it was, the American loan, and subsequent economic expedients, made it possible for Britain to bear the heavy military burdens of a global power for many years to come.

Thus there was no lack of British military commitments at the end of the war, quite apart from the inescapable need for armies of occupation in much of Europe – Germany, Austria and Venezia Giulia. Disorder in Greece, and the fear of a Communist take-over there, tied down more British troops. Occupation forces were needed in ex-Italian colonies in Africa, and many parts of the East lately occupied by the Japanese. Apart from former British territories, such as Burma, Malaya, Singapore and Hong Kong, Anglo-Indian forces assisted in the reoccupation of the former French and Dutch colonies in Indo-China and the East Indies far into 1946.[11] India and Palestine were also weighty responsibilities, with their mounting political unrest. The historic strongpoints of the empire had to be garrisoned, from Gibraltar, Malta and Suez to Aden, not to mention air force contingents in Iraq. Suspicion of Soviet intentions in Iran in 1946 necessitated some precautionary moves, so that by the beginning of 1947 the extra-European responsibilities alone absorbed some 300,000 service personnel. Only with the coincidence of the 1947 economic crisis and the approaching independence of India, Pakistan, Burma and Ceylon did Attlee on 6 August 1947 announce that it was government policy to reduce the number of service personnel on all overseas posts from half a million to 300,000.

Long-term strategic considerations had only a limited influence on the distribution of British service personnel immediately after the war. The liquidation of occupation responsibilities took time, and the process was not finally completed until the mid-1950s. Nevertheless strategic priorities of a sort had to be drawn up. Plans for Commonwealth defence had to take account of the approaching independence of India and other states, which would entail the loss of the Indian army and a probable lessening of British interest in the Far East. Attlee hoped that Australia would assume more of the responsibilities in this area. She was in fact to take over Britain's occupation role in Japan from 1948, but in general both Britain and Australia were to be disappointed by each other's provision of forces in the East, and the unreadiness of each to meet the other half-way in defence talks. Australia had already witnessed the dramatic British defeats in Malaya and Singapore in 1941-2, and had been rescued from the power of Japan by the United States rather than by the Mother Country. Even while the British ruled in India the Commonwealth had been short of the local transport and industrial facilities needed to fight a really formidable foe, useful though the Commonwealth forces had proved in the war against Japan. It was true that after August 1945 no major power seemed likely to threaten the security of the East for many years to come, while Australia's recent champion, the United States, was displaying no real interest in the south-west Pacific. Anglo-Australian defence talks proceeded in a desultory fashion, with Australia's long-term hopes pinned on American support. Meanwhile British warships patrolled Chinese waters in an attempt to provide traders with some protection in that turbulent region; Hong Kong and Singapore re-emerged as bases; while, following the grant of independence to India, Pakistan and Ceylon, the British contented themselves in that region with naval and air bases in Ceylon – to be used at the discretion of Colombo – and the recruitment of Gurkhas in Nepal. The Chiefs of Staff abandoned their hopes of 1945-6 that India would become the centre of one regional Commonwealth defence grouping. It was only with the 1948 Communist rising in Malaya that the Far East began to have a major influence upon British defence policy.

Immediately after the Second World War the Middle East constituted a much heavier drain on British military resources. The war had led to a massive build-up of strength here and in the Mediterranean, firstly to defeat the Axis in North Africa and then in Southern Europe. The reopening of the Mediterranean route had saved much allied shipping space in the last years of the war. British strategists had viewed Egypt as the key to the routes to the East since the 1890s, but the Mediterranean and various parts of the Middle and Near East had loomed large in their thinking long before that. If the route had proved unusable for half the war it was nevertheless believed that allied control of the area had done much to weaken and later cripple the enemy. He had been denied Middle Eastern oil, and had been forced to disperse valuable forces over a wide area. As the allies advanced, so more enemy targets came within reach of their bombers. It was the scene of some of Britain's most cherished victories, and loomed large in the battle honours of all three services. The latter certainly had no doubt of the relevance of this great region, from Gibraltar to Habbaniyah, from Cyprus to Kenya, to future defence planning.

Historical and sentimental arguments, however, were not enough. The British presence was an elaborate and expensive one. The great Suez base was a cause of friction with the Egyptians; the Palestinian mandate, which was originally acquired in part for strategic reasons, had become an arena, with the British caught in the cross-fire of Zionists and Arabs. For a British strategy in the region to make sense it was necessary to think of the whole area as an entity from Malta to the Persian Gulf. It was inevitable that some should query the utility and practicability of a British effort to play a major role in the defence of this theatre. In 1918–19, intoxicated by victory, Britain had endeavoured to draw strategic lines in the deserts and wastes of Asia Minor until obliged by force of circumstance to retreat to a more modest position. At that time she had certainly been stronger, had had less cause to fear local nationalist reactions, and above all she had not been faced by a mighty power to the north. In 1946 there was the inscrutable yet potentially formidable presence of the Soviet Union, whose interests certainly extended to Iran and Turkey. Attlee, for one, felt that the traditional British policy could not be accepted without question. He raised the matter in September 1945, and again with some of his colleagues during a week-end at Chequers in mid-February 1946. Dalton recorded upon the second occasion:

Attlee is fresh-minded on Defence. It was no good, he thought, pretending any more that we could keep open the

Mediterranean route in time of war. That meant we could pull troops out of Egypt and the rest of the Middle East, as well as Greece. Nor could we hope, he thought, to defend Turkey, Iraq or Persia against a steady pressure of the Russian land masses. And if India 'goes her own way' before long, as she must, there will be still less sense in thinking of lines of Imperial communications through the Suez Canal. We should be prepared to work round the Cape to Australia and New Zealand. If, however, the U.S.A. were to become seriously interested in Middle Eastern oil, the whole thing would look different.[12]

Attlee pressed these views on the Chiefs of Staff and the Defence Committee, arguing that Britain should retreat to a line from Lagos to Kenya, with a major base in the latter, and rely heavily on geographical obstacles to protect this African Empire. These ideas were welcomed by Dalton, as he struggled with balance of payments problems: Cabinet interest seriously alarmed the Chiefs of Staff, especially Alanbrooke, who thought Kenya too remote as a base. As late as January 1947 the Chiefs of Staff felt obliged to intimate privately to the Prime Minister that they would resign unless the Middle East were held.[13] On 20 March 1947 the Minister of Defence found it necessary to justify a British presence in the Middle East against Labour back-bench critics.

The services were strongly supported by Bevin,[14] after some initial enthusiasm on his part for a retreat to Mombasa. Thus, although the Foreign Secretary was prepared to re-negotiate the Anglo-Egyptian treaty of 1936, and to withdraw all British forces from Egypt under certain conditions, he agreed with the Chiefs of Staff that no power vacuum should be allowed to develop in the Middle East. He was particularly impressed by British dependence on Middle Eastern oil, and argued that he for one was not prepared to endanger the living standards of the working man at home. Not surprisingly the Left wing of his party began to call him 'Lord Palmerston in a cloth cap'. Nevertheless Bevin was prepared to agree to a British withdrawal from Suez in return for a new, and as it transpired, a limited defence agreement with Egypt. By the autumn of 1946 the Foreign Office was ready to accept no more than a consultative treaty which would include discussion of Anglo-Egyptian policy in the event of an attack on Greece, Turkey or Iran. Anglo-Egyptian differences over the future of the Sudan, Egyptian nationalism and internal political rivalries prevented agreement even on these terms at the end of 1946, and the British continued their uneasy watch at Suez. It is worthy of note that the new Chief of the Imperial General Staff, Lord Montgomery, accepted a retreat from Suez in June 1946 (his predecessor, Alanbrooke, had also done so with great reluctance), providing the base was properly maintained, and the Egyptians agreed to its reoccupation in an emergency. He believed that in time of peace the British bases in Malta, Cyprus, Libya, Transjordan, the Sudan and Palestine provided sufficient security.

For a time, indeed, Britain sought alternatives to Suez as its main Middle Eastern base. Palestine was the first candidate, until the government grew tired of the impossible task of reconciling Zionist and Arab ambitions, and decided to abandon the mandate late in 1947. Plans that Kenya should succeed Suez as the main storage base were dropped in 1949. Worsening relations with the Soviet Union found the services determined to fight for the whole of the Middle East, however hopeless the task, and even if no more than a fighting withdrawal should prove possible. They argued too that allied control of North Africa would be invaluable should the Soviet Union succeed in overrunning much or all of Europe. Kenya was too far distant to act as a main base should such strategies be adopted, while its possible development as a secondary base was frustrated in 1949 by the need to divert troops and engineers to the Far East. From Suez, on the other hand, operations could be supported over a wide arc from Iraq to Greece. The base itself could be supplied by two sea routes. Some £500 million had been spent on its development: an alternative site could hardly cost less than £250 million. With 200 square miles of installations and 600,000 tons of stores it resembled an industrial estate rather than a conventional military base. It employed about 75,000 Egyptians, and at its peak in the Second World War it had handled some half a million tons of stores and equipment a month. With such facilities the services hoped that at worst they might hold a line from the Taurus mountains to the Gulf of Aqaba against the Soviet Union.

The service chiefs could also argue that part of Attlee's main condition for a continuing British presence was in fact being fulfilled. True, the United States had yet to commit itself in the Middle East, but in 1946 it had decided to become a Mediterranean naval power, and to support Turkey against Soviet demands for territorial concessions and for military rights at the Straits. The arrival of American warships had been warmly welcomed by the Admiralty.[15] Britain, however, was still the only western power to be giving aid, including about one division of troops, to the Greek government in its struggle against Communists, while it was calculated that it was quite beyond her resources to achieve the desirable modernisation of the armed services in Turkey. The forces of the latter were said to be proportionately weaker than in 1914. To secure American aid for these states would not only relieve the British economy, but would commit the United States to the defence of the eastern Mediterranean. This would add immeasurably to British security in the whole region. The British knew only too well from their experience in the recent war that the logic of events – certainly in the event of a conflict with Russia – would draw the Americans from the Near to the Middle East. The ground had already been prepared in Washington[16] before Britain sent her famous warning of 21 February 1947 that the state of her economy made it impossible for her to give further financial aid to Greece beyond the month of March, or to retain as many as 15,000 troops there. The United States stepped into the breach under the banner of the Truman Doctrine. Some British troops continued to serve in Greece until the end of the civil war in 1950, but the essential British objectives had been secured.

Fears concerning the future of Greece had already led to an unequivocal assertion in October 1945 that Cyprus must remain part of the British Empire. The decision to evacuate Palestine in 1947 prompted the development of some airfields, and additions to the island garrison. The continuing importance of Malta was reflected in the fact that in 1949 the Admiralty was employing 3000 more workmen in its dock-yards than in 1938 and 12,000 were being employed down to the end of the 1950s. Treaties were concluded with Jordan in March 1946 and 1948. These provided for a joint defence board, and enabled the R.A.F. to use the airfields at Amman and Mafraq. Efforts to negotiate a similar treaty with Iraq in 1948 failed owing to local nationalist protests, but the existing treaty of alliance had another nine years to run, and this enabled the air force to use the vital bases of Habbaniyah and Shaibah. From these, in the event of war, it was hoped to strike at cities in southern Russia, and to hamper the advance of any invading force. The R.A.F., at this time, had only the obsolescent Lincoln for long-range bombing operations, and Britain's ability to hold forward bases against Russia was very much in doubt. Nevertheless the British Chiefs of Staff left their American counterparts in no doubt in November 1948 concerning their intended strategy. They were determined to hold the Middle East if possible, and believed it could be done if sufficient reinforcements were despatched in time.[17]

This clarification of British policy concerning the Middle East was reflected elsewhere. In 1948 Francis Williams, who was closely acquainted with the thinking of Attlee and Bevin, published an important explanation of Labour policy entitled *The Triple Challenge*. Williams wrote:

> So long as she remains a world power Britain cannot but be interested in varying degrees in the future of Turkey, Persia, Iraq, Syria, Lebanon, Palestine, Transjordan, the countries of the Arabian Peninsula, Egypt and the Sudan, and even Ethiopia, Eritrea and the Somalilands.[18]

It is clear from this and other sources that British Middle Eastern strategy was seen not only in the context of the defence of oil supplies, but also in the denials to Russia of access to Africa, where the economic development of British colonies was expected to ease the dollar and balance of payments problems of the Sterling Area. Sir Ian Jacob was to write in 1950: 'Britain requires a peaceful, contented, and prosperous Africa and must, if necessary, fight in the Middle East to ensure this requirement.'[19] Command of the same area would also seal off the Indian Ocean from Soviet interference. A variety of motives were combining to dispel such doubts

B

as some Labour leaders may originally have entertained in 1945–7 concerning a continued British presence in the Middle East. Now it seemed essential for both military and economic reasons. The potential strength of Arab nationalism was not yet properly appreciated; the imminence of colonial emancipation in Africa was not yet visible. The loss of India and British economic problems were offset by more pressing considerations. The possibility of disengagement in the Middle East was now felt to be an illusion.

The last great concentration of British armed strength after the war lay in Europe, especially in north-western Germany. That Britain would have to maintain occupation forces there – and in Austria and Venezia Giulia – for some time after the war was not disputed. But as relations with the Soviet Union steadily deteriorated so, even before the Communist coup in Czechoslovakia on 22 February 1948 and the beginning of the Berlin Blockade that summer, the government and its defence advisers were being forced to consider their strategy in the event of an outbreak of war in central Europe. Admittedly this still seemed a remote contingency, but less remote than in 1946 when Montgomery drew his picture of the long-term development of the British army. In a paper of 26 June entitled *The Problem of the Post-War Army*[20] he had thought it desirable to train and equip active peace-time forces so that they would be equal to any miscellaneous conflict by 1951, but gave 1961 as his target date when all active and reserve forces should be ready for a major war. The government and Air Staff would appear to have made a similar calculation when they began a cautious, research-orientated and long-term programme for the re-equipment of the R.A.F. with ultra-modern aircraft, which was not expected to come to fruition until the late 1950s.

Circumstances were steadily to erode this optimistic forecast that no major war need be expected for at least fifteen years. The government, however, was to retreat from its original calculation with the utmost reluctance, and was to do so in a thorough-going fashion only after the outbreak of the Korean War in 1950. But from the first it was necessary to try to divine the type of forces that might ultimately be required – and provided. An assessment of Britain's probable enemies had to be attempted, and differences with the Soviet Union before and after 1945, especially over the future of central Europe, left little doubt in this respect. The British service chiefs were soon busily trying to restore their wartime links with the United States. As we have seen, suspicion of the Soviet Union was a major stimulant to the maintenance of strategic interest in the Middle East, and a similar discussion speedily developed concerning British strategy with respect to Russia and Europe. But here the Chiefs of Staff were less united in their diagnosis than in the Middle East. Montgomery from the outset of his appointment as Chief of the Imperial General Staff in the summer of 1946 argued that Britain must be prepared to maintain a large army whenever needed in central or western Europe. He found Lord Tedder, the Chief of the Air Staff, most unsympathetic, and as late as the early months of 1948 the matter was still being furiously discussed by the service chiefs and the government itself.[21] The traumatic experience of Dunkirk and the fall of France in 1940 were vividly recalled. Would not France and the Low Countries collapse even more quickly another time? Indeed, in 1946–7 they had few forces with which to put up any resistance at all, while France was increasingly torn by political and labour troubles. The novelty of any long-term British commitment to assist in the defence of western Europe must also be stressed. Preparation for a part in European land warfare had been the least likely contingency in British strategic thinking in the later nineteenth century. Only force of circumstances and dire necessity had produced varying degrees of involvement between 1906 and 1920, and again from 1938 to 1945.

Information concerning this debate remains sketchy, but it clearly ranged over most of the fundamental aspects of British defence policy. The debate was coloured by service rivalries – especially the air force against the army; by a continuation of the historic clash between the 'continental' school of strategic thought and the advocates of 'limited liability' or 'peripheral' methods of warfare; and by such questions as the impact of new weapons, and the type and size of armed forces that the nation's economy could afford to support. Discussion was further complicated by uncertainty as to the timing and quality of any military assistance that might be expected from the United States in the defence of Europe. Some consolation could be drawn from the American promise of September 1946 to maintain an occupation force in Germany for as long as the other powers. For the moment Britain was committed to the same policy.

These world-wide responsibilities were costly both in men and resources. Simultaneously it was necessary to carry through the demobilisation of the bulk of those who had fought in the war, replacing them where necessary with newly-conscripted men, all of whom had to be trained and transported. Shipping space was in short supply. Delays and waste were inevitable. The government was torn between the demands of the Treasury and Board of Trade on one side, the service chiefs, Foreign and Colonial Offices on the other. Some hints concerning this controversy emerge from the pages of Hugh Dalton's memoirs.[22] Early in 1947 he, as Chancellor of the Exchequer, and backed by Sir Stafford Cripps at the Board of Trade, was trying to impress his Cabinet colleagues with the growing seriousness of the nation's economic situation. 'What shall it profit Britain', he asked, 'to have even 1,500,000 in the Forces and Supply, and to be spending nearly £1,000 million on them, if we come an economic and financial cropper two years hence?' Two years hence, however, was too remote a date to alarm the Cabinet sufficiently, and Dalton was told that to give up 100,000 men and to spend only £750 million would be 'unilateral disarmament'. As a compromise the defence estimates for 1947 were finally cut by 15 per cent – from £1064 million to £899 million. Dalton was far from satisfied, and there was hostile comment from both Labour and Liberal benches in Parliament. Indeed, Labour dissatisfaction spilled over in April when 76 back-benchers voted against and perhaps as many abstained when the government sought to introduce National Service for eighteen months from 1949. The motion was carried, but the Cabinet, dismayed by this revolt, and contrary to the advice of the Chiefs of Staff, changed its mind and opted for twelve months.[23] Naturally much would depend upon the actual state of events in 1949, but twelve months' National Service would cost the services valuable training time as well as most of the utility of the conscripts in an active role.

Meanwhile the economic crisis was only half a year, not two years distant. Already rising world commodity prices were devouring the American loan faster than expected. The savage winter in the first months of 1947, with the consequent coal crisis, cost Britain exports she could ill afford. And then in the summer sterling was made freely convertible, in accordance with the original terms of the American loan. This was too much. So great was the outflow of gold and dollars that convertibility had to be suspended on 20 August, but with three-quarters of the dollar credits already gone other steps were necessary. A more rigorous review of defence spending had become inevitable. The net cost in foreign exchange of British forces overseas was put at some £225 million in 1946, or more than half the balance of payments deficit for that year. Long-term economic planning had already detected a grave manpower shortage of over half a million – 'the biggest problem' facing the economy according to a government white paper of January 1947. From August 1947 to January 1948 the services were therefore under repeated pressure for economies of all kinds. The decision in September to abandon the costly Palestinian mandate would, of course, release a great deal of manpower in 1948, but in general, so extreme were the economies demanded that the government seemed to be acting on the assumption that the nation would be faced by no serious emergency situations in the near future. This assumption had indeed already been made in connection with the parliamentary crisis over National Service previously quoted.

The War Office was warned in January 1948 that the strength of the army must be reduced to 305,000 by 1950.[24] Although this was about half as many again as the inter-war average, the number of Regulars could well be fewer, while the remainder, made up of twelve-month conscripts, would be of little value for foreign service, and would impose a heavy training burden on the service. As it was, at the end of 1947 there were only 91 active infantry battalions, 50 fewer than in 1939. The latest economies threatened the existence of the last of the armoured divisions. Training and overseas responsibilities delayed the resumption of large-scale manœuvres until 1949. It is true that the Secretary of State for War himself conceded on 23 September 1948 that the best use was not always made of available manpower. The 'tail' of the fighting units had grown alarmingly, the motor transport of a division having doubled since 1939. If increased firepower and more sophisticated equipment provided some justification for the increase, criticism on this point was to recur regularly in the future.[25] The strength of the R.A.F. was also falling away to about 100 squadrons, supported by some 200,000 personnel, compared with 75 squadrons and under 35,000 men in the early 1930s. Even so, sufficient skilled manpower was not forthcoming to enable aircrew to squeeze as many hours out of their aircraft as they would have liked. By the beginning of 1949 less than a quarter of air force personnel had served for more than three years, and only one-tenth, or 20,000, for more than ten years. In the navy, despite the small proportion of National Servicemen, half were recent entries, with a quarter of all personnel engaged in training or being trained. So acute was the shortage of trained manpower in the navy in the autumn of 1947 that only a handful of active ships remained in the Home Fleet. As a further economy, to save oil fuel, the autumn exercises were cancelled. The measure of dislocation being experienced by the services at this time can be gauged from the fact that 60 per cent of those serving in January 1947 had departed fifteen months later. Critics, Labour and Conservative, of the disparity between the limited fighting strength of the armed forces and the large resources assigned to them on paper would have done well to pay a little attention to such problems.

Meanwhile the service chiefs in the winter of 1947–8 were confronted by government demands for a ceiling on defence spending of about £600 million by 1949–50. The Chiefs of Staff thought £825 million a realistic minimum, but in practice they had to settle for less than £700 million in 1948 and plan for further drastic cuts.[26] These economies, following close upon and, up to a point, coinciding both with the problems of demobilisation and occupation forces, still further complicated the task of long-term defence planning.

The Opposition complained of a lack of coherence in defence policy: the government euphemistically referred to years of transition, and to flexibility in the management of the armed services. It is clear from several remarks by A. V. Alexander as Minister of Defence in 1948 that the government wished to give priority to research into and the development of new weapons. The air force, navy and army were ranked in descending order of preference, and great reliance was placed on the existing stocks of arms and equipment. These, it was felt, would serve for some years to come. Overseas commitments, however, distorted this policy, and compelled the maintenance of a larger army than the government desired. Such commitments were indeed to defeat the hope that National Service might be limited to twelve months – a time too short to make worthwhile use of a conscript overseas.

The original rationale behind National Service had been the creation in the 1950s of a readily mobilisable reserve. The army, with Montgomery in the vanguard, were insisting that any future war would be a faster-moving, more sophisticated struggle than that of 1939–45, and that better-trained reserves, with a much higher degree of readiness than the inter-war Territorial Army, would be required. In time it was hoped that British foreign commitments would come into line with regular recruitment, so that the use of conscripted men overseas would cease. This, however, was to prove a pipe-dream as one international emergency succeeded another, while Regular recruiting, especially for the army, continued to fall below expectations.[27]

Attlee justified National Service to Parliament on 12 November 1946 in the following terms. 'The development of modern warfare has made this country more vulnerable. We are now part of the Continent. . . . While in the past we always had a breathing space . . . [now] we must have trained reserves who can take their part right away without waiting for six months' training.' The nation, by and large, accepted conscription as an unfortunate necessity, but some Liberal and Labour critics were supported by military experts such as Liddell Hart and Sir Giffard Martel. They questioned whether effective front-line and reserve forces could be built up by such means. Both favoured an *élite* volunteer army, with much emphasis upon armour. Sir Eric Speed, Permanent Secretary at the War Office in the late 1940s, also doubted the value of conscription. But Liddell Hart's target of a Regular army of a quarter of a million never seemed feasible. The Secretary of State for War was to conclude on 8 March 1955 that experience of the years 1920–39 and the period since 1945 suggested that neither pay nor civilian unemployment had much impact upon recruiting trends, and that 180,000 seemed the maximum number that could be persuaded to opt for the army in the most favourable circumstances.

Admittedly the existence of National Service may have injured Regular recruitment, since without it higher pay and better living conditions would have been possible, and in many ways service life could have been made more attractive. To house a large army, inflated by conscripts, necessitated the retention of much substandard accommodation. As late as 1956 there were troops living in eighteenth-century stables: barracks built before the Crimean War were still in use, as were huts of pre-1914 vintage. The Secretary of State for War conceded on 8 March 1955 that the nation was in danger of having an army of 'slum-dwellers'. Not that the army was alone in this problem. Even a service so steeped in tradition as the navy could not willingly use accommodation that dated from the time of Nelson. National Servicemen also imposed monotonous training duties upon many Regulars, and even when partly trained, added to the instability of service life. Up to 70 per cent of the British forces in Germany were usually composed of conscripts, most of whom came fresh to each annual exercise. Even when the term of National Service stood at two years, fifteen months was usually the longest possible overseas posting. In these circumstances it was difficult to develop highly efficient units; continuity was lacking. Regulars found themselves caught up in the process of frequent postings – also of cross-posting from one unit to another – and a high proportion of their time was spent overseas, with much family separation or dislocation.

The services, and especially the army, had other problems with which to contend in their quest for recruits. Their attractiveness as a profession had fallen by comparison with the inter-war years. Full employment was becoming a feature of the post-war world, with a widening range of attractive openings for the intelligent and enterprising. More mundane disadvantages also existed. Upon completion of an engagement the ex-Regular would find himself at the bottom of council-housing lists; he might have difficulty in securing trade union recognition of any skill he might have acquired. Two-thirds of all married men serving abroad in the early 1950s were separated from their families; those with their families often had to put up with poor living conditions. All the services shared these problems to some extent, so that re-engagement after an initial term of service was becoming much less frequent than before the war. Before 1939 an average of 60 per cent of those in the navy re-engaged after twelve years' service: in the early 1950s the proportion had fallen to 43 per cent. An army warrant officer pointed out in *The Times* of 14 July 1953 that he would receive a better pension as a police constable. Once a man had learned a trade and/or exhausted his sense of adventure there was little to hold him.

The services were also in need of a higher proportion of skilled men, owing to the growing sophistication of military equipment. But skilled men were similarly in short supply in industry, where the financial rewards were better. Not surprisingly, advanced trades in the R.A.F. in 1953 were about 30 per cent below establishment. In general Regular recruitment from 1946 to 1950 was rather erratic, but by the latter date an army of barely 150,000 Regulars was in prospect or less than half the force currently maintained in the light of the world-wide Communist challenge. A conscript was reckoned to be worth between half and two-thirds of a Regular, so that an all-Regular army would have entailed the recruitment of another 100,000 men at least. The R.A.F. was faring rather better, while the navy could almost meet its needs with volunteers. But clearly there was a limit to the number of men who could be drawn to service life, however attractive the conditions, and it was especially difficult to attract those with the scientific and technical qualifications of which the forces stood in increasing need. Before

1957, therefore, no satisfactory alternative to National Service seemed in prospect, and even the intention to limit the term of service to twelve months from 1949 was never implemented. So short a spell would have prevented any overseas postings save to Germany, and without assistance from National Servicemen it would have been quite impossible for British forces to meet all their commitments. According to Shinwell on 1 December 1948 there were still 176,000 troops overseas, nearly as many as the whole army of the early 1930s.

Difficulties were also being encountered in the recruitment of officers, especially in the army.[28] At the root of much of the trouble were changing economic and social conditions. In the past the British upper classes had not only supplied officers in large numbers but had supplied them with extra or alternative sources of income. Twentieth-century methods of taxation were forcing families to weigh the economic advantages of various careers with ever-increasing care. Not only did many professions offer better financial returns than the services, but they did not possess the additional hazard of early retirement for all but the most successful officers. The social status and prestige of officers fell steadily in the twentieth century. Ironically some British officers noted with envy the proportionately higher status and rewards enjoyed by their counterparts in the Soviet Union. The position was further complicated by the growing service need for more technically qualified officers and for higher educational standards in general. But such candidates were always in short supply as industry and the professions increased their own intake of qualified personnel. By the early 1950s the officer corps of the army was 10 per cent below strength, and only half its officers were Regulars. A big effort had already been made to tap new sources for recruits, Emanuel Shinwell claiming from his experience as Secretary of State for War that he was convinced of the sincerity of the War Office's quest for cadets outside the traditional officer-producing classes.[29] But even in the early 1960s it was estimated that three-quarters of the successful applicants came from the top 12 per cent of the population; that efforts to attract more candidates from Northern and Midland grammar schools in particular had been disappointing; and that in general candidates were still coming forward

in insufficient numbers, and with too few of real intellectual
distinction among those who did. This was a disappointing
situation, since many reforms had been introduced in the
intervening years to try to improve the attractiveness of the
army – and the other services – as a profession.

Among the reforms of the 1950s were pay increases which
began to bring remuneration more into line with civilian
professions, but the really decisive breakthrough in service
pay, both for officers and other ranks, did not occur until the
abandonment of National Service after 1957. Attempts were
also made to prolong the career prospects of middle-ranking
officers until the age of fifty or fifty-five. The navy introduced
shorter commissions at sea from 1954 for the benefit of all its
personnel, so that spells of service abroad would be reduced.
But, as we shall see, the problem of recruitment in some form
or other was rarely to be absent after 1945.

One of the most important decisions to be taken by the
Attlee government was that to develop nuclear weapons.[30]
Serious British interest in atomic power dates from 1940 when
the wartime coalition government under Churchill became
convinced that the nation must endeavour to acquire nuclear
arms as soon as possible. In June 1942, however, on grounds
of economy and security against air attack, it had been agreed
that all work on the programme should be concentrated in
the United States. Several efforts were made to safeguard
British access to all information concerning nuclear developments in the United States, but the agreements themselves
were never watertight, while the Americans were steadily
gaining all the advantages that accrued to a monopolist. They
were in a position to decide and dictate, whatever had been
put down on paper. The British were not unprepared for this,
but the possibility of further co-operation with the United
States was too attractive a prospect to be abandoned without
a struggle. The British had a good case – on paper – and a
meeting of Attlee, Truman and Mackenzie King of Canada
in Washington in November 1945 produced yet another
affirmation of allied solidarity. 'We desire that there should
be full and effective co-operation in the field of atomic energy
between the United States, the United Kingdom and Canada.'
This agreement was speedily rendered impotent by joint

pressures within Congress and the American administration itself in favour of complete secrecy in the interest of American security, or pending the negotiation of an international treaty for the control of nuclear energy. The era of Anglo-American co-operation was at an end, symbolised by the McMahon Act of August 1946, which forbade the disclosure of nuclear information to other states. The British had, however, recovered access to about half the uranium production of the Congo and other sources open to the West. The United States had been given control of all such supplies in 1944. The foundations of a British nuclear programme had also been laid before August 1946. American policy, therefore, threatened to do no more than delay the emergence of Britain as a nuclear power, and to add to the cost of the undertaking. Indeed, thoughts of renewed co-operation soon appeared, and a limited release of information on production plants was agreed in the winter of 1947–8.

Nuclear policy in Britain was decided by the Prime Minister and the Defence Committee, with little reference to the Cabinet as a whole. Attlee, as we have seen, followed logically in the steps of his predecessor. He would have innovated only had he stopped the programme. There were many reasons for not doing so. If the power of Russia and the United States now clearly eclipsed that of the United Kingdom, the latter had no rivals in this second rank of influence. She could and did think naturally of herself as a world power, so that as in the past it seemed right and proper that she should possess the most formidable weapons available, especially if they seemed relevant to her needs. Nuclear bombs, indeed, might provide the R.A.F. with that decisive weapon which it had hitherto sought in vain. British vulnerability to nuclear attack made it all the more essential that she have the means to retort in kind. Certainly the government did not exclude the possibility of international control of this frightful force, but in the interval Britain should not rest inactive. The commercial possibilities of nuclear power had also to be considered. At the same time, if contemporary British needs and thinking were pushing remorselessly in this one direction, they were also assisted by the exposed position in which Britain found herself at the end of the war. Attlee himself was later to emphasise his fear in 1946 that the United States might return to isolation, or at least adopt a policy which would leave her position with respect to the defence of Europe in doubt. Meanwhile it was evident that in Europe for many years to come the greatest single force would be the land power of the Soviet Union. The future of Germany was in doubt; the reconstruction of western Europe would take time.

In 1945–6 work started on a research and experimental establishment at Harwell, production reactors at Windscale, and a low-separation diffusion plant at Capenhurst. The Air Staff began plans for a long-range nuclear delivery force in Bomber Command, and were able to issue specifications for a new design of bomber as early as 1 January 1947. The actual decision to make atomic bombs was personally taken by the Cabinet's Defence Sub-committee in the late spring of 1948, and both the Cabinet staff and Parliament were subsequently informed – the latter on 12 May.[31] But for the first few years the programme was pursued at a fairly leisurely pace. Relations with the Soviet Union might deteriorate, but no early collision with that war-ravaged country was anticipated. With Britain's own burden of post-war reconstruction, her nuclear policy could not be given unqualified priority. As the *Economic Survey for 1947* remarked: 'The Central fact . . . is that we have not enough resources to do all we want to do. We have barely enough to do all that we *must* do.' Resources included manpower, of which there was an acute shortage, especially of skilled men, while a survey of British scientists made in 1946 concluded that unless the annual number of new graduates was doubled by 1955, only about two-thirds of the likely openings in that profession would be filled. A slow start to the nuclear programme was therefore not surprising, but there could be no question of the government's ultimate intention. It is, however, interesting to note that, as Emanuel Shinwell, Labour's second Minister of Defence, subsequently told the Commons, the atomic bomb at this time was viewed more as a super-explosive than as a decisive weapon. 'We did not believe that the atomic bomb in itself would prove an effective deterrent.' Certainly this was the view of many defence experts, and British defence needs in general, as illustrated earlier, precluded excessive concentration on a single weapon. Atomic bombs would also be of little value to Britain until new bombers entered squadron service.

The explosion of the first atomic bombs in 1945 had precipitated many dire prophecies concerning the future. For a time imagination ran riot, and many contended that all conventional weapons were obsolete. A Chatham House Study Group in 1946 referred to the possibility of paralysing surprise nuclear attacks being launched by an aggressor – a super-Pearl Harbour that might prove decisive.[32] Many Conservatives sat up in Parliament on 22 November 1945 when they heard Anthony Eden argue that some diminution of national sovereignty was inescapable if the world was to be made safe in the nuclear era. A more hopeful comment was made by the scientist, Sir Henry Tizard, who thought that nuclear weapons might replace the medieval 'Hell' as an incentive to more peaceful conduct. Expert opinion, indeed, was increasingly swinging to the view that atomic bombs, for all their fearful power, would not in fact determine the outcome of wars in the immediate future, and that other weapons would still have a part to play. Not that atomic bombs were belittled. Analysis of the attack on Hiroshima suggested that a similar bomb dropped on a British city would kill 50,000, destroy about 30,000 houses and render up to 350,000 people homeless. The average number of fatalities inflicted by each V-2 was only 15. Francis Noel-Baker, reminiscing on 14 March 1963, said that he had been told by an Air Ministry mission, sent to examine the effect of nuclear attacks on Japan, that 30–120 such weapons would cripple Britain. Certainly, nuclear weapons would alter the character of wars, shortening their length, and placing a premium on national preparedness from the outset. The long, slow Anglo-Saxon mobilisations of the two world wars would no longer be feasible. National Service and a modernised Territorial Army reflected this thinking – at least in theory. Meanwhile the navy's case was stated by the First Lord of the Admiralty on 7 March 1946. Should Britain lose command of the sea an enemy would have no need to blast her into submission with nuclear weapons.

Neither army nor navy therefore felt threatened with obsolescence, and the government gave limited acknowledgement to their claims, even if both services ranked below research and development and the air force in its theoretical list of priorities. The army was allowed to proceed with the development of the advanced Centurion tank, though most other preparations for its re-equipment languished, and great reliance was placed upon existing stocks and patterns of weapons. Some attention, however, was paid to Montgomery's demand for a formidable and speedily mobilisable reserve, and National Service was in part designed to provide a steady flow of trained reserves into a Territorial Army of the 1950s which would be made up of an airborne, six infantry and two armoured divisions. In training, equipment and organisation, these were to approximate as closely as possible to those of the active army, and were intended for early service in an emergency in the front line as well as for home defence. Montgomery himself doubted if active and reserve forces, fit for a major conflict, could be prepared before 1961. Certainly occupation and other miscellaneous responsibilities, coupled with the shortage of Regulars and the treadmill of National Service training, would drain most of the energies of the active army in the late 1940s. On the other hand, immediate necessities maintained the size of the army.

Where the threat of Communist land power was explicit from Germany to Malaya, there was no such clear challenge to the British navy.[33] The Soviet navy had not performed with much distinction in 1941–5; the fleet of the late 1940s constituted no serious surface threat, though it was reasonable to assume that submarine and mine-laying capabilities would steadily increase. British naval operations in some European waters might also encounter serious air attacks. Russia was not expected to become a nuclear power until the 1950s, whilst two American tests against warships at Bikini Atoll in 1946 suggested that warships would stand a good chance of survival at a distance of three-quarters of a mile or more from a nuclear explosion. In November 1948 Lord Tedder agreed with the Admiralty's claim that it would be able to operate aircraft carriers in the Mediterranean, at least at the beginning of a war with the Soviet Union.[34] Naval confidence in the future of the carrier was reflected in the current building programme. At the end of the war work was continued on six fleet carriers and several smaller ships. The carrier had replaced the battleship as the most important unit in the fleet and about a quarter of the navy's strength was devoted to the air arm. But tradition died hard, and five battleships were retained. Churchill protested that more should have been kept in reserve.

The post-war fleet thus had a very conventional appearance. Outside Europe cruisers and frigates continued to show the flag, and occasionally their teeth against guerrillas in Malaya, or in the epic of the *Amethyst* on the Yangtse. The navy continued to prepare for a third Battle of the Atlantic, for the defence of European waters, and to some extent for amphibious operations. To some the thinking of the Admiralty appeared to be rooted too firmly in the period of the Second World War. Sir Percy Gretton thought he detected a polite scepticism among air force officers as they attended inter-service discussions and exercises relating to conventional warfare. Behind the scenes, however, a start was being made to the modernisation of the fleet. Little of this was to bear fruit until the next decade – and in some instances not until the 1960s – but the foundations were laid in the 1940s for drastic improvements to the efficiency of British carrier, submarine and anti-submarine forces, and a start was made to the development of the first surface-to-air missiles. These will be examined in more detail later.[35] The sheer volume of resources at its disposal was to enable the United States navy to modernise its fleet more rapidly and on a broader front, but the Americans were in fact to copy some of the British innovations in the 1950s. Meanwhile American dominance at sea was accepted and welcomed by the British. The American navy was larger than the fleets of the rest of the world combined, and was three times the size of the British. But a contributor to the *Navy League Year Book* of 1947 could write, 'it is neither necessary to take American strength into account in estimating the threats to that [i.e. Britain's] security, nor to view the increase of that strength, whatever level that increase reaches, with anything but welcome'.[36]

The modest modernisation programmes of the army and navy stood in sharp contrast to the more radical hopes of the air force. Lord Tedder, the new Chief of the Air Staff, unfortunately did not extend his memoirs into the post-war period. Nevertheless a few hints of his thinking have appeared.[37] He emerged from the Second World War convinced that Britain could not again afford to expend lives and resources in the prodigal fashion of 1914–18 and 1939–45. 'I am sure we must be far more selective in the allocation of our national effort to military defence. We must pay far more attention to the principle of economy of force.' He wished to escape from 'the slugging matches of the twentieth century', and argued that British defence policy in time of peace should aim at the creation of a 'fully-grown David', not an 'embryo Goliath', so that bankruptcy in either peace or war could be avoided. 'The last war is not modern,' he insisted, 'it is out of date.' Instead of big, fixed garrisons, he dreamed of highly trained, highly mobile forces, with great firepower, which could nip trouble in the bud at all levels of conflict. Much of this grew out of the traditional thinking of the air force, with Lord Trenchard as the obvious inspiration. But Tedder had shown in the recent war that he was not an extreme supporter of strategic bombing, for instance, nor a simple believer in the dominance of air power. Both in the Mediterranean, and later as Eisenhower's deputy in western Europe, he had worked well with generals and admirals. His strategic breadth of view was complemented by great administrative skills, considerable experience in the management of technical questions, and no mean persuasive gifts. He and Montgomery stood temperamentally at opposite poles, as well as on many issues of policy. Although Tedder did not spell out his ideas in public, it is clear that he anticipated much air force and overall defence thinking in the 1950s, when nuclear weapons came into prominence, R.A.F. Transport Command was enlarged, and new amphibious task forces were conceived. All this, however, lay in the future. In the late 1940s the instruments of such a policy did not exist.

The R.A.F. was to retain a Second World War appearance for some time to come.[38] Almost all its front-line strength of 8000 aircraft in 1945 consisted of piston-engined types which had been conceived in the 1930s, but whose design had been successfully 'stretched' during the war. Such were the Spitfire, Mosquito and Lancaster. Apart from the development of jet propulsion, Britain had concentrated upon conventional aircraft technology, arguing that the war would be won before revolutionary weapons could be perfected. Thus even the new jet-fighters, the Meteor and Vampire, had unexciting airframes, and in consequence the full potential of their engines could not be realised. The Germans, in contrast, had been busy probing the problems of supersonic flight, and experimenting with new wing shapes. The British aircraft designer thus faced a host of problems in 1945, most of which he had yet to attack in a serious manner. How soon would supersonic flight become feasible? Which would prove the most effective wing shape in the future? Did the centrifugal or axial-flow jet-engine offer the most promise? It was an exciting, bewildering and expensive prospect. Britain had some grounds for confidence, given her current world lead in jet-engines, and her past success in aircraft design, but at the same time her overall shortage of resources was compounded by the multiplicity of aircraft firms, and by the failure to erect a really effective structure in which all aircraft interests could co-operate. As we shall see, delicate lines of communication, with an accompanying network of understanding and trust, had to be established between the research worker and designer, and the user, purchaser and manufacturer. In the post-war world technical change was to outstrip the evolution of the relationship between Air Ministry, government and the aircraft industry. For reasons of safety and economy the government also imposed an unfortunate, if temporary, ban on manned supersonic experimental flight, and did not authorise the immediate development of a swept-wing fighter. No satisfactory wind tunnel for supersonic research was in use until 1955, research plant being given no priority after the war. The clear decisions to emerge in 1945–7 were the postponement of a major re-equipment programme for the R.A.F. for at least a decade until Britain's economic circumstances had improved and the future of aircraft design had been clarified.

Piston-engined aircraft consequently filled all roles save that of the day-fighter until 1949–51, when jets were introduced to ground-support fighter-bomber, photo-reconnaissance and night-fighting operations. Jet aircraft did not begin to serve in the Mediterranean until 1949, or in the Far East until 1950. Despite Opposition complaints of official secrecy concerning the state of the R.A.F. – Eden remarking in 1948 that occasional flights by fighters over London were Parliament's main source of evidence – there was general satisfaction with the quality if not with the size of Fighter Command. Churchill as late as 16 March 1950 thought that Britain had the best fighters in the world. This was no longer true, though they would have acquitted themselves well against current Soviet bombers. Government defence statements also leave no doubt of their determination to restore the power of Bomber Command, and in theory this task was given priority second only to research for overall defence purposes. In fact Bomber Command possessed no aircraft that could strike at a distant or sophisticated opponent. The Lincoln was merely an improved version of the wartime Lancaster, and no replacement was expected until the mid-1950s. The government argued that to build an interim aircraft with current jet-engines would prove a costly undertaking in proportion to the length of service one might expect from it before it became obsolete.[39] In contrast, the much greater resources of the United States enabled it to build three such interim aircraft of quite impressive performance. Fortunately a new jet-powered British light bomber, the Canberra, was promised for the early 1950s, and was to prove an outstanding success.

From 1948 to 1950, before the Korean War, the government managed to keep the running costs of the services more or less constant, although expenditure on research and production rose by about one-half. This was a useful advance, yet perforce a limited one in relation to the openings presented in weapon development by science and technology at that time. For this clearly was the start of a revolutionary era. Apart from atomic weapons and jet aircraft, there had been the dramatic advance in missile technology by the Germans, with their V-1 and V-2 rockets which had bombarded southeast England with no small success. German development of fast-battery-drive submarines, together with the schnorkel to supply submarines with oxygen while remaining under water, threatened to regain for such craft many or all the advantages that they had enjoyed in the first half of the war. There remained a vast potential to be tapped in many existing instruments of war, especially radar, Asdic (sonar), the firepower of automatic weapons, and armoured vehicles – to mention but a few.

Before the war defence spending on research projects had been counted in thousands: thereafter it was counted in millions. In thirty years, between 1934 and 1963, expenditure soared from £2 million per annum to nearly £250 million. After 1945 it was obvious that the development of nuclear weapons and the new generation of jet aircraft would constitute the heaviest burdens, but technology in the other services was not standing still, and it was also essential to explore the field of rocket projectiles, a much neglected subject in Britain. During the war itself, apart from jet-engines and nuclear energy – which had finally been entrusted to the United States for reasons of economy and security – the British had been content to develop existing weapons to the full rather than seek revolutionary breakthroughs. Efficiently and intelligently as Britain had used her scientists and engineers in the war, they had attempted nothing comparable to the German-built V-2 rockets with a payload of one ton over a range of 150–220 miles. British science and technology were indeed to be assisted by German experts from 1947 when the post-war missile programme was begun in this country. The start was hesitant and parsimonious: the first development contracts were not awarded until 1951, and long-range missiles were neglected as impracticable.

Britain's great problem after 1945 was the allocation of scarce resources to best advantage. Initially she hoped for a breathing-space of a decade or so in international rivalries which would give her both time for economic recovery and some clearer indications of the respective merits and feasibility of the new weapons. There could, however, be no question of the importance of atomic weapons, jet aircraft and radar. She could not ignore developments in submarine warfare, given her dependence on overseas trade, unless one concluded that nuclear weapons would be able to decide a war unaided. The navy pressed for more than an anti-submarine role, and argued that its fleets of the future would require carriers, with strike and defensive air power, and with sophisticated ship-borne anti-aircraft defences. The army, if it were to remain a force designed for operations in Europe, must have new tanks, artillery, and a wide range of supporting weapons, vehicles and equipment. Unless the government chose to impose severe restrictions on the future roles of its armed forces, an expensive proliferation of new weapons was essential. In practice, as we have seen, too few resources were forthcoming in the later 1940s to keep pace with all these service demands, and only the most favourable set of circumstances for many years to come would enable the nation to escape serious embarrassment in a crisis.

The difficulties that arose in the formulation of defence policy in the first of the post-war years highlighted the need for a carefully balanced and integrated administrative structure.[40] The war had demonstrated the need for close service co-operation. Shortage of resources after the war re-emphasised this fact, and in turn necessitated a satisfactory relationship between the defence ministries and the exchequer. Defence policy had also to be related to foreign affairs, colonial policy, and the manpower, industrial and material resources of the country. A Minister for the Co-ordination of Defence had been appointed before the war in 1936, but his powers had been too limited to make much impact. The Chiefs of Staff Committee, instituted in 1923, had been another and more successful innovation in the quest for interservice understanding, though it had often been the scene of compromise rather than of service co-operation. During the war, under Churchill, it had become the supreme instrument for the direction of grand strategy. In this role it had performed well. Clearly it would remain a vital instrument in peace, but equally in time of peace it had to be subordinated to other political entities apart from the august personality of Churchill. Since 1902 the Committee of Imperial Defence, and its many sub-committees, had served as the meeting-point of ministers directly or indirectly interested in defence, and of the professional experts. An advisory, not an executive body, its meetings had proved the starting-point of many important inquiries, of cross-fertilisation between departments, and of new departures in British defence policy. Here, clearly, was the basis for any post-war machinery that was not to represent too radical a break with the past, though some hoped that any new defence committee would be able both to transcend party divisions, and to escape from the influence of the Treasury. Such hopes were of course utopian.

The Attlee government at the end of 1946 decided to institute modernised versions of the Committee of Imperial Defence and the Minister for the Co-ordination of Defence. The new Defence Committee was to consist of the Prime Minister, the new Minister of Defence, the Lord President of the Council, the Foreign Secretary, the Chancellor of the Exchequer, the service ministers, the Ministers of Labour and Supply, the Chiefs of Staff, with other leading and relevant figures summoned according to need. This committee was responsible to the Cabinet for the supervision of defence policy, current strategy, and the co-ordination of departments concerned with war preparation. This last point was vital, since the nuclear era intensified the trends towards closer civil–military relations that had been developing since the 1900s. Deputy chairman of this committee was the new Minister of Defence. Assisted by a small ministry, he was to be responsible for certain joint-service matters, represent the services in the Cabinet, and in general endeavour to promote service co-ordination. It was hoped that once the Cabinet had decided on an overall sum for defence he would be able to achieve a satisfactory distribution 'in broad outline' of that sum between the three armed forces. He was also to chair the Ministerial Production Committee, composed of the service ministers and the Ministers of Supply and Production. The Service Ministers' Committee was evolving from 1946 under his chairmanship.

Meanwhile the Chiefs of Staff would retain their right of appeal to the Cabinet, although they were expected in the main to work with the Minister of Defence. The latter would also play a vital part with the Defence Committee at the top of the elaborate hierarchy of committees and other organisations concerned with research, supply, intelligence and war planning. Experience was to underline the inadequacy of this post-war structure, but according to both Lord Ismay and Geoffrey de Freitas its creators viewed it in no way as definitive, and intended to revise it according to need. The new structure occasioned some respectful attention from the United States, where service friction and administrative problems loomed very large. British parliamentary criticism was unimportant, with Lords Hankey and Chatfield chasing the red-herring of Commonwealth integration. The complaints of Montgomery[41] and Hollis from within the machine itself were more to the point. They warned that service disunity had not been overcome – far from it – and would continue so long as the three Chiefs of Staff thought essentially in terms of their own service, and produced 'wishy-washy' compromises when forced to make overall defence recommendations. Inter-service battles were to include the naval bid for control of Coastal Command, the army–R.A.F. debates of the 1950s on the control of certain ground-to-air missiles, as well as the strategic debates of 1946–9 concerning the defence of Europe. Defence discussions too often consisted of inter-service squabbles and unsystematic compromises over the allocation of funds largely determined by the Cabinet. The latter in its turn made matters worse by abrupt changes of policy which upset long-term service planning, compelling further compromises. Meanwhile Montgomery argued that it was essential for the Minister of Defence to have his own Chief of Staff, who should try to rise above narrow service loyalties. This could not be done by the existing Chiefs of Staff, each of whom was immersed in his own narrow problems and responsibilities. Montgomery also thought A. V. Alexander, Labour's first Minister of Defence, too weak for the post. Certainly Alexander was an administrator rather than a strong leader; not necessarily the best person to work with Montgomery. His successor, Shinwell, was a more formidable character, and had more resources to share out between the services.

Little progress was made in these years to increase service co-ordination, despite the lessons of the war and the lip-service paid to the principle. This can be clearly seen in the lack of interest displayed in combined operations during this period. The work of the School of Combined Operations at Fremington in Devon from 1946 was small in scale and mostly theoretical in character. The Joint Services Staff College at Latimer in Buckinghamshire from 1947 proved much more

vigorous and exciting, and interposed a useful stage between
the separate service staff colleges and the old Imperial Defence
College for senior officers. Unfortunately it catered for only
about 200 officers each year, and there was no similar joint-
service provision for really junior officers. Suez in 1956 was
to reveal how far British inter-service thinking and preparation had languished since 1945. Most officers found it difficult
to transcend their own service outlook, since tradition, habit,
doctrine all weighed heavily upon them, with advancement
depending largely on winning the approval of one's own
service seniors, themselves mostly moulded in this fashion.
McCloughry suggested in 1955 that special agencies should
be introduced to facilitate the promotion of those with inter-
service experience and the right cast of mind.[42]

Another outstanding weakness in post-war administration
was the comparative failure to achieve a satisfactory relationship between the traditional formulators of defence policy,
the senior service officers and administrative civil servants on
the one hand, and the host of new types of expert required
by the armed forces in the nuclear, electronic, jet age.
Good intentions were not lacking, especially with respect to
scientists, many of whom had successfully emerged from the
'back-rooms' during the war to enjoy greater status and
influence.[43] The novelty of radar, especially, had obliged the
services to admit scientists to a detailed knowledge of operational requirements and conditions, and even their tactical
thinking had been influenced by scientific guidance as to
what was feasible. The 'Sunday Soviets' at the Telecom-
munications Research Establishment, Swanage, had produced
close informal co-operation between air marshals, top civil
servants and scientists. Alanbrooke and the first post-war
Chief of the Air Staff, Tedder, were among the enthusiastic
advocates of the closest possible co-operation with scientists.
A war-experienced scientist, Sir Henry Tizard, hoped to see
the complete integration of his profession in defence planning. Following his long and distinguished, if sometimes
controversial, association with the scientific aspects of defence,
Tizard was made the first chairman of the new Defence
Research Policy Committee from October 1946, as well as
scientific adviser to the Defence Committee and the Chiefs

of Staff. Compared with the 1930s the influence of scientists had greatly increased, but theirs was still an advisory role. Tizard was both pleased and frustrated.

Among the weaknesses to develop in the first post-war years was a decline in the overall quality of technical experts assisting the services – compared with the height of the war – while the remaining scientists were unable to maintain their wartime degree of access to operational information.[44] The great aviation expert, Oliver Stewart, was later to conclude that many scientists lacked the political guile needed to advance their case. One of the ablest damaged his cause with 'murderous replies to silly questions'. Aircraft manufacturers, engineers and some accountants were all to experience disappointments in their dealings with civil servants and senior officers. Old traditions and past practices did not readily lend themselves to the idea of management teams in which a variety of professionals of widely differing backgrounds would enjoy a complete or a considerable measure of equality. In particular, the failure to achieve a full measure of understanding and integration between the Air Ministry, the Ministry of Supply and the aircraft industry was to lead to many delays and setbacks in aircraft production in the ensuing decade. The Ministry of Supply[45] was a cumbersome body, whose responsibilities embraced most of the needs of the army and R.A.F., and one-quarter of the navy's needs as well as major civil commitments. These were to be reduced in the early 1950s, so that the Ministry became mainly a fourth department of defence.

Many of the initial calculations made by the Attlee government with respect to defence between 1945 and 1947 thus proved inadequate. In their reform of the administrative machine they had gone neither far nor fast enough. Yet in the light of the satisfaction of most contemporaries and the difficulties experienced after 1957 when further change was attempted, one should not judge them too harshly. They were undoubtedly right to give first priority to research and development. Their retention of National Service was unavoidable given the assumptions of British, foreign and colonial policies, though in this, as in some other aspects of defence policy, the physical return on their investment was disappointing. Certainly the government imposed a great strain on limited British resources, and it could not have done what it did without American financial aid. There were those, especially on the Left wing of the Labour party, who urged that Britain's many world commitments should be reduced, but they were less specific concerning the details of such a retreat. So long as Britain avoided financial disaster and made some progress in her economic recovery, the arguments in favour of the maintenance of the three most expensive commitments – Germany, the eastern Mediterranean – Middle Eastern complex, and Malaya – were very formidable. The fact that the German and Middle Eastern presences were questioned within the government only to be preserved shows that such commitments were not retained merely out of habit or from illusions of grandeur. The situation was also made much more difficult for the government by the unexpected speed with which East–West relations deteriorated into the Cold War, by the rising cost of imports from the United States, by the harsh winter of 1946–7, and by eastern nationalism. Part of the art of politics is, of course, to overcome the unexpected, but the art also embraces the ability to choose the least bad of many bad alternatives. Judged according to that light, and recalling that Attlee and his colleagues had no strong ally before 1948 on which to lean automatically, the government emerges with much credit. Policy might have become progressively a hand-to-mouth affair, but important options had been kept open, which, once greater resouces became available, might prove viable courses of action.

2 The Communist Challenge and Rearmament: 1948-51

By 1948 the pattern of the post-war world was becoming clearer. The Communist coup in Czechoslovakia and the start of the Berlin Blockade, while giving rise to passing fears of immediate trouble, more fundamentally smashed the hopes of many in Britain and western Europe that a *détente* might yet be negotiated with the Soviet Union. Sir Hartley Shawcross, for instance, observed that, though a friend to Russia two years earlier, he now thought Soviet aims and methods akin to those he had prosecuted at Nuremburg. For many others, of course, the events of 1948 merely confirmed earlier fears. Already in August 1947 Bevin had asserted: 'I do not think we can avoid any longer common defence and acceptance of common economic principles if we are to avoid recurring crises.' His proposals for a western alliance antedated the Czech crises, whilst the parliamentary debates of 22-3 January 1948 found party leaders on both sides of the house vying with each other in their ominous descriptions of the Communist threat. At the same time British defence precautions were to advance little beyond the point of paper reassurances and verbal protestations.

The Anglo-French Treaty of Dunkirk of 4 March 1947 had not been followed by any military staff talks, and these were still being described as 'premature' by the Foreign Office in November. Indeed, Bevin had had to protest in the Cabinet the previous month that for British troops to be pulled out of Germany would reduce this country to a third-class power, and would open all western Europe to Soviet influence.[1] Bevin, A. V. Alexander and Montgomery also found themselves engaged in a long, hard fight when, early in 1948, they advocated a firm British commitment to the defence of western Europe, arguing that without such an assurance other western states might become too demoralised

to make any serious efforts for their own defence.[2] Attlee, the
other Chiefs of Staff and the Joint Planners retorted that such
a policy would risk the almost certain destruction of the committed forces in the event of war, or at best must lead to a
second Dunkirk. They preferred to put their trust in air
power to weaken the attacker, and to gain time for an Anglo-
American mobilisation to roll back the attacker, striking this
time perhaps from the line of the Pyrenees or from Britain.
Churchill's leaning towards such an air/sea strategy has
already been noted, while Tedder would qualify his aversion
to a continental policy only in the event of a massive
American commitment to the defence of Europe. But early
in 1948 American forces had fallen to 115,000, and Bevin
found that his inquiries in Washington as to the possibility
of a great Atlantic alliance were premature.

Nevertheless, however strong the military case against a
firm British commitment in Europe, the political and moral
arguments were now becoming stronger. Given the fact that
a direct Soviet attack was usually not thought probable in the
near future, a British presence would do something to revive
confidence in western Europe. American policy was also
evolving hopefully, if slowly, towards a closer involvement
in the affairs of Europe. In May 1948 Montgomery and Bevin
were rewarded by government acceptance in principle of 'the
essential need of fighting a campaign in Western Europe'.
This was, however, no more than a paper agreement, for no
extra troops were sent to the continent at this stage. Meanwhile the fifty-year Brussels pact of mutual collective assistance against any aggressor had been signed on 17 March 1948
with France, Belgium, the Netherlands and Luxemburg.

The British and their allies also knew at this time that they
could look forward to massive American financial aid under
the projected Marshall Aid programme. This was passed by
Congress on 4 April, though some time had to elapse before
this assistance would make much impact. Both the *Economic
Survey for 1948* and the Chancellor of the Exchequer, Sir
Stafford Cripps, emphasised the enormous economic problems that were facing the country. Cripps indeed warned that
without American aid Britain would be unable to maintain
either her present standard of living or her influence in the

world. Consequently neither the Czech crisis nor the start of
the Berlin Blockade in June 1948 immediately reversed the
defence cuts announced from August 1947, and it was not
until the autumn that the downward trend in service manpower was checked. In January 1949 Montgomery's plea for
the despatch of an extra infantry brigade group to Germany
to act as a morale-booster on the continent was only grudgingly
accepted by the Chiefs of Staff, and was then vetoed by the
Cabinet. Not surprisingly the first plans prepared by the
members of the Brussels Pact were mostly concerned with the
problem of an organised retreat – perhaps to the Pyrenees if
not to Britain.[3]

In 1948 it was the evolution of American policy that most
interested London. The latter had hoped that the close wartime alliance, especially as exemplified in the Combined
Chiefs of Staff Committee, would outlive the war. This had
not proved to the taste of Washington at first, until experience
of Soviet post-war policy led to a renewal of Anglo-American
staff contacts from August 1946.[4] The evidence of the
American Secretary of Defence, James Forrestal, suggests that
the importance attached to Montgomery's visit to the United
States in September has been exaggerated. In December 1946
the British and American air forces agreed to exchange officers
to study each other's organisation, equipment and research,
and this relationship undoubtedly facilitated the despatch of
two groups of American B-29s to Britain in July 1948 as part
of the western response to the Berlin crisis. Although Attlee
told the Commons on 6 December 1951 that a nuclear strike
against the Soviet Union by such aircraft from Britain would
have depended upon circumstances, Forrestal in the autumn
of 1948 gained the impression from both Attlee and Cripps
that they saw Britain as the main base for such operations
against Russia, and such operations as the main safeguard
of the West against Russian attack. By the winter of 1951–2
Labour–Conservative negotiations with the United States had
reached the agreement that any American nuclear strikes
against the U.S.S.R. from British bases should be the result of
a joint decision in the light of current circumstances. Meanwhile Tedder was urging the Americans to agree to detailed
planning of a nuclear war in conjunction with the British.

At the same meeting of the Anglo-American defence chiefs in November 1948 the British insisted that direct participation by the United States in a western defence alliance was essential: merely to send equipment would be 'totally inadequate'.[5] Fortunately American opinion was moving in the same direction, while in October 1948 agreement was finally reached concerning Marshall Aid whereby Britain was to receive nearly $1000 million (net) with which to try to bridge her recalcitrant trade gap with the western hemisphere. Good progress was being made at the same time towards the creation of the North Atlantic Treaty Organisation which was to unite Britain and nine western European nations with the United States and Canada in the spring of 1949.

Meanwhile in September 1948 the government decided that the time had come to improve the nation's defences. American aid should soon ease the economic situation. Although the Russian blockade of Berlin was being met by an Anglo-American air-lift, it was impossible as yet to be sure that this would force a Soviet reappraisal of policy in the near future. Outside Europe, too, the prospects were darkening. The Communist insurgents had become so active in Malaya that a state of emergency had to be proclaimed on 17 June. The failure to negotiate new defence treaties with Iraq and Egypt meant that a wary eye had to be kept on that theatre. Certainly the assumptions on which the service cuts of 1947–1948 had been based no longer held good, and on both 29 July and 21 September the Chiefs of Staff addressed direct appeals to the Prime Minister, expressing their 'grave concern' at the state of British defences. Montgomery, indeed, claimed that in all his forty years of service he had never known the army to be so weak in proportion to its commitments.[6]

Herbert Morrison, for the government, admitted to Parliament on 14 September 1948 that all was not well, and that more resources would have to be devoted to defence. Thus 1950 was to find about 7 per cent of the national income devoted to defence – about the same as in 1938.

This new phase in British defence policy was to last from September 1948 until June 1950, when the Korean War created a more critical situation. True, there was at this time no radical departure from existing policies, with their

emphasis on long-term re-equipment, but two major concessions were made to current circumstances. In the first place
it was acknowledged as early as 23 September that the army
was too small to meet all its commitments.[7] The release of
National Servicemen was delayed for three months as an
interim measure, and finally in December 1948 it was conceded that the plan to limit National Service to twelve months
from January 1949 was no longer feasible. Eighteen months
was substituted to make service overseas possible, and so
relieve the hard-pressed Regulars – in the air force as well as
the army. Nevertheless this reversal in the reduction of service
personnel was to be only temporary. An overall strength of
790,000 became the target for April 1949 instead of 716,000
as previously intended, and thereafter the downward trend
was resumed, reaching about 720,000 in the spring of 1950,
with only 680,000 in prospect for 1951. It was claimed that
an inter-service review in 1949 would make great savings in
manpower possible at little or no expense to the fighting
units. Even if achieved on paper, this could still result in a
loss of fighting strength. In the R.A.F., for instance, Transport
Command, having carried about one-sixth of the supplies air-
lifted into Berlin during the Soviet blockade of 1948–9, was
to be reduced from 1950 to release aircrew for combat duty:
those who saw this as a short-sighted step were to be amply
vindicated. Hopes that Regular recruiting would improve,
and thereby strengthen the services, were also disappointed.

The government secondly acknowledged the need for some
re-equipment of the forces from September 1948. Many war
stores were becoming depleted or obsolete. Expenditure on
production rose by nearly one-third to over £200 million in
1949, though the Minister of Defence pointed out on 3 March
that if war should break out in the near future it would be
fought with arms mostly of Second World War design. The
air force and navy were given priority; indeed, production
for the army was cut back again in 1950. Whereas the air
force and navy estimates rose by £50 million and £40 million
respectively between 1948 and 1950, those of the army fell
by £6 million. The most important objective at this time
was the strengthening of the air defences of Britain. Much
emphasis was placed upon the doubling of jet-fighter output

and the number of aircraft in Fighter Command. There was widespread concern at the overall state of the R.A.F., and even the Secretary of State for Air was forced to agree on 20 January 1949 that the 'standards of morale in the R.A.F. are not entirely satisfactory at the moment'. Front-line strength had probably dropped to about one hundred squadrons and less than 1000 aircraft. For the moment no new long-range planes were in prospect for Bomber Command, although the latest Meteors appeared to meet the qualitative needs of air defence. An interim fighter, the Venom, was on order. The radar screen was being modernised, and good results were claimed for the defending forces during an exercise in 1949.[8] Unfortunately there were as yet no jet night-fighters, and an announcement that obsolescent Spitfires, Lancasters and Mosquitos were to be reconditioned was hardly reassuring. The Opposition, meanwhile, bitterly condemned the sale of some jet-fighters to Egypt and Argentina as contrary to the national interest.

The Civil Defence Corps was revived in 1948–9; instructors were trained in the first stage, and the recruitment of ordinary Civil Defence volunteers began at the end of 1949. Some thought was also being given to the use of mobile columns of Regular and Territorial troops to assist in the event of major disasters, and a paper exercise on these lines was conducted at Camberley in May 1949.[9] The Home Office set up a Joint Planning Staff, representing all government departments involved in civil defence.

It will be noted that at this time only the minimum of extra resources were devoted to commitments overseas. Additional expenditure was incurred mainly to improve the security of the homeland against air attack, and to a lesser extent against attack at sea. The major economic crisis of 1949, with the consequent devaluation of the pound in September, forced the government to cast a critical eye over defence spending yet again. Certainly this helped to slow the tempo. Nevertheless the government presented its defence policy in 1950 with an unusual air of confidence, claiming that it was based on a thorough inter-service review conducted in the previous year by the Chiefs of Staff, and which was intended to determine the future of the forces for some time to come. The priorities remained as before, with the army at the bottom, save in so far as actual emergencies – as in Malaya – and other immediate commitments around the world necessitated the retention of more troops than the government would have wished. The modernisation of the army's equipment was being slowed to help meet the cost of the extra soldiers: the pay of other ranks had risen by 75 per cent since 1938, and the number of troops by 80 per cent. Even so the share of the defence estimates devoted to research, development and production rose from 24 per cent in 1948 to 32 per cent in 1950.

Thus neither the Brussels Pact of 1948 nor the establishment of NATO on 4 April 1949 had had any radical effect upon British defence policy. The expressed desire in the autumn of 1948 to bring the Territorial Army up to its intended strength of 150,000 volunteers might be interpreted in part as a move towards the defence of Europe, but it was not a very meaningful one as long as the re-equipment of the army was delayed. These facts had some influence on NATO planning before the Korean War. Strategic bombing would be the responsibility of the United States, as the only western nuclear power, and as the only possessor of modern long-range bombers. The European states, and especially France, were to provide the bulk of the ground forces. Although other allies would contribute also, the security of sea communications would rest mainly with the American and British navies. Britain and France would provide most of the European air defence and tactical air forces.[10] Initially, indeed, until the recovery of the European aircraft industry was complete, continental states were to be heavily dependent on British aircraft designs and aero-engines, and were to look to Britain for guidance in many aspects of air policy. There existed, however, no small dissatisfaction with the British preference for an air-maritime role, and the apparent calculation that a Third World War could only be won by a repetition of the Anglo-American strategies of 1941–5, with great emphasis upon air strikes, the attrition and dispersal of enemy forces, and only then the liberation of conquered territory. Western Europeans doubted the utility of liberating a corpse.

It was estimated that at least twenty-five divisions would be needed to hold the Rhine against an initial Soviet assault,

c

but in 1949–50 less than half that number were at the disposal
of NATO. Appropriately the ceremonial that accompanied
the signature of the alliance in Washington included a spirited
brass-band rendering of the currently popular song, 'I've
got plenty of nothin' '. The presence of only twenty-five of
Russia's estimated 175 divisions in eastern Europe provided
some reassurance as did American nuclear power.[11] Some of
the best western political commentators, such as George
Kennan, believed that the Soviet leaders preferred to advance
along the lines of least resistance, and had no desire to risk
a head-on military collision. Yugoslavia had been excom-
municated by Stalin in 1948, but he had contented himself
with political intrigues against the leadership of the arch-
heretic, Tito. No great sense of urgency in fact existed in the
West. France was preoccupied with domestic problems, while
the war in Indo-China drew some ten of her divisions away
from Europe. Neither Britain nor the United States intended
to station large land forces on the continent: the rearmament
of West Germany was as yet politically unthinkable. The air
of unreality that pervaded so much of western defence policy
was also present at British army manœuvres in Germany in
1949. No division attempted to hold a front of more than
seven and a half miles, although twenty-five miles was the
likely distance in a real emergency. General de Lattre de
Tassigny was said to have remarked that the British forces
were apparently manœuvring on the assumption that they
were engaging an inferior enemy.[12]

On behalf of the British it must, however, be pointed out
that in 1948–9 they were spending on defence one-fifth more
than the rest of the Brussels powers put together. Even the
United States was spending proportionately less of its national
income. The British were further convinced that any war
would be determined by the United States, with British
assistance, and not by any independent quixotic British
gestures in Europe. Only limited American reinforcements
could be sent to the aid of their two divisions in Germany at
short notice. Washington had even declined the bait of an
American as supreme allied commander in Europe. If the
worst came to the worst Britain might well find herself in
the same position as in 1940–4. Dunkirk and the consequent

Battles of Britain and the Atlantic weighed heavily on the minds of British strategists. Special attention was consequently paid to air defence from 1948, while in the longer run the arguments of the Air Staff in favour of nuclear bombs and long-range bombers carried great weight. At the very least such weapons could severely damage enemy submarine bases, airfields and rocket sites, all of which might threaten Britain's survival as in the previous war. The British nuclear pro-gramme was accelerated in 1949, but on grounds of economy a major bid was made in the second half of the year for a second nuclear alliance with the United States.[13] Close Anglo-American co-operation was envisaged, with Britain receiving a stock of atomic bombs for her own use 'in accordance with joint strategic plans'. For a time agreement did not seem impossible. Ultimately, however, it was killed by divided opinions in the United States, fears of complications with other allies, and doubts as to the safety of American secrets in Britain in view of the success of the British scientist, Klaus Fuchs, as a Russian spy. There was a small consolation prize at this time. Early in 1950 some seventy surplus American B-29 heavy bombers were transferred to the R.A.F. Although no longer a modern aircraft, the B-29 (known to the R.A.F. as the Washington) was superior to any British bomber. Pending the arrival of new jet-bombers they would assist in the train-ing of aircrew, providing at least one stepping-stone between the lumbering Lincolns and the stratospheric 600-m.p.h. Valiants. In war, without nuclear weapons, they were too few in number to make much impact.

Meanwhile Britain was taking a circumscribed view of her responsibilities in the Far East. After some hesitation the garrison in Hong Kong had been strengthened in view of the Communist victory in China, while on 13 April 1949 Attlee had assured the population of Malaya that Britain was deter-mined to smash the insurgents in that country. But, as an ex-commander-in-chief of the Far Eastern fleet, Admiral Sir Denis Boyd, explained to the Royal United Service Institu-tion on 16 November 1949, British forces in the region were sufficient only to combat internal subversion, and to 'show the flag'.[14] He personally complained of a lack of official interest in the Far East, and of the lack of co-ordination between the three services. Australia and New Zealand also hoped for greater British interest, and were anxious to devise an equivalent of NATO in the Pacific. With the United States as yet showing no interest in such a body, their anxiety for closer defence ties with Britain is understandable. Sir Robert Menzies, the Australian Prime Minister, complained in 1950 that the fine Commonwealth brotherhood was in danger of becoming a lawyer's exercise. Australia, however, had yet to introduce compulsory service, and her defence expenditure remained modest.

The British were not wholly inactive. A Far Eastern regional defence organisation had some appeal, especially if India could be included.[15] When the latter remained invincibly neutral, some negotiations proceeded with Australia and New Zealand, and the same year saw the emergence of a vague entity known as ANZAM. This was to co-ordinate defence planning in the Commonwealth from Malaya to New Zealand, but, as the Chief of the Imperial General Staff was to re-emphasise on 27 February 1963 during a visit to Canberra, its purpose was essentially consultative. It is difficult to see what more could have been done – certainly by Britain. The immediate threat to the Commonwealth, in any case, took the form of subversion, and no direct attack was to be anticipated. Should it ultimately materialise from Communist China, the outcome would be dependent upon American policy. When North Korea invaded South Korea on 25 June 1950, the British decision to support the United States against the North was mainly prompted by the belief that a failure to resist Communist aggression anywhere in the world would encourage further Soviet moves, and that support of the United States in the Far East was needed to guarantee American involvement in the defence of Europe. A Soviet invasion of western Europe no longer seemed so unlikely or distant a possibility. Memories of the 1930s flooded back: Attlee, with the support of most of his countrymen, described the North Korean action as 'naked aggression', and authorised British naval forces to assist those of the United States in Korean waters. The first air strikes were launched from a British carrier on 1 July.

The rapid advance of the North Korean forces soon made

it clear that only ground reinforcements could save the South. The United States possessed no large reserves of readily mobilisable soldiers and appealed to its allies. The British army in January 1950 was nearly 382,000 strong. More than 150,000 of these were already overseas, while a very high proportion of the 215,000 or so in the United Kingdom were in training establishments, or otherwise unprepared for battle. Two battalions were scraped together with some difficulty, and did not reach Pusan, in South Korea, until the end of August. Although the British contribution to the United Nations forces was to rank second only to that of the United States, it was still a small effort in comparison. In the three years of fighting British casualties totalled just over 4000 compared with more than 140,000 suffered by the United States.

The first British troops in Korea found themselves holding a front of more than ten miles with only 2000 men, and were almost immediately engaged in a desperate defence against the Naktong offensive in the first week of September.[16] The arrival of an Australian battalion led to the formation of the 27th Commonwealth Brigade, which was active both in the advance beyond and retreat behind the 38th parallel in the topsy-turvy campaign of September–December 1950. British naval forces helped to cover General MacArthur's brilliant Inchon landing which outflanked and almost annihilated the North Korean forces in September. But MacArthur's subsequent advance to the River Yalu and the border of Manchuria showed an alarming disregard of political and military realities. According to Bevin's statement to the Commons on 14 December the British Chiefs of Staff doubted the wisdom of this strategy, and would have preferred a halt further south, where the Korean 'waist-line' ended. Whether this would have reassured the Chinese sufficiently to have prevented their massive intervention in November it is impossible to say. The Chinese do appear to have hinted at a possible compromise with a 'rump' Communist state north of the 'waist-line'.[17]

The great Chinese offensives at the end of 1950 were finally checked after the South Korean capital, Seoul, had once again been lost. Hard fighting in the New Year carried the allies back to the 38th parallel, and roughly to the former boundary between North and South Korea. But the end was not yet in sight. Chinese counter-attacks included a furious assault on the 29th British Infantry Brigade as it bestrode a main route to Seoul on the Imjin river north of Uijongbu. Six thousand men held a 12,000-yard front against three Chinese divisions. This attack, begun on 22 April 1951, included a furious three-day battle with the 1st Battalion, the Gloucester Regiment, which was almost destroyed after a most desperate resistance. This stand of the 'Glorious Gloucesters' was described by an American commander, General Van Fleet, as 'the most out-standing example of unit bravery in modern warfare'. The brigade as a whole suffered more than a thousand casualties, but its stand helped to save the left flank of the allies, and made an orderly retreat possible. The Chinese were finally turned back five miles from Seoul. Thereafter the fighting quickly settled down into a stalemate roughly along the parallel, though a 'quiet day' in the lines of the Common-wealth division in July 1952 could still include the exchange of 2000 of its own shells for 500 from the enemy. Always it remained a savage, depressing conflict, one of the most demoralising of wars.

Meanwhile R.A.F. Sunderlands were assisting with patrol work, and British pilots flew operationally in American air-craft. The other main British contribution was made by the navy, which was given operational control on the west coast of Korea. Light fleet carriers, including one from Australia, were operated in turn with outstanding efficiency.[18] More than 25,000 sorties were flown against the enemy, and only twenty-two aircrew were lost in action although the navy had no jet-fighters to throw against the remarkable Russian-built Mig-15s. In general the excellent training of British pilots enabled them to offset the superior aircraft of the enemy. British ground forces similarly emerged with great credit, and were warmly praised by their allies, notably by the experienced American generals, Mark Clark and Matthew Ridgway. The tactical doctrines of the infantry were proved sound in practice; British infantrymen had not forgotten the art of marching – a vital asset in so rugged a terrain – nor did they display undue dependence on heavy equipment and vehicles. They proved less road-bound than the Americans. Plenty of initiative was shown by junior officers and other ranks in what, for nearly a year, was a very fluid war. It took time, however, to overcome some of the shortages of equipment. Winter clothing arrived late in 1950, and some of the vehicles proved unsatisfactory. Finally, although no British jet-fighter aircraft were engaged, the performance of the Russian Migs and the American Sabres rudely dispelled the complacency so recently shown in Britain. Swept wings gave the Mig-15 a handsome margin of speed over the British Venom, although the engine of the latter was of similar power. The Mig-15 in its turn was outclassed as a weapon by the radar-ranging gunsight of the American Sabre.

Stalemate in Korea and the armistice of 1953 could contribute only indirectly to the security of Europe. In the months immediately before the outbreak of that war both American and NATO planning had been taking account of the Soviet atomic test in August 1949, with the implication that the credibility of the American nuclear deterrent would be much diminished or eliminated – perhaps by 1954. But it was the crisis in the Far East that stirred western states to strengthen their conventional forces in Europe in practice. Western Europe seemed alarmingly exposed in June 1950. Montgomery commented from NATO headquarters: 'As things stand today and in the foreseeable future, there would be scenes of appalling and indescribable confusion . . . if we were ever attacked by the Russians.'[19] General Eisenhower, following his appointment as Supreme Allied Commander in Europe later in the year, thought that no more than a 'token resistance' could have been offered: the dozen or so divisions that existed were not properly deployed, while the necessary pipelines, communications network, dumps and other installations had yet to be constructed. The two British divisions in Germany, for instance, were under strength, and were supplied from Hamburg along an autobahn a bare ten minutes' drive from Soviet forces near Lübeck. The armoured division was deployed behind its own base, with the infantry division behind again. The allied position in the air was no better. There were few airfields from which jets could operate, and there were fewer than 1000 planes. The Russians were believed to have 6000 in East Germany alone, and nearly 20,000 in all. Only the American Sabre could match the speed of the Mig-15, a point of particular concern to the new Chief of the Air Staff, Sir John Slessor.[20]

Paul Reynaud, the veteran French statesman, feared that the Russians would reach the English Channel before the United States could mobilise. NATO planners believed that atomic bombs would make a second Normandy-type landing impossible, or at least highly unlikely, any amphibious armada proving an ideal target. One might add that even before the Soviet acquisition of nuclear weapons such a landing could only succeed after Russian ground strength had been virtually crippled by allied air power. There would be no eastern ally, as in June 1944, to draw off one hundred and sixty-five of the enemy's three hundred divisions. In 1950, with perhaps only one hundred atomic bombs, the nuclear power of the United States gave the West no guarantee of victory even in favourable circumstances. The faith of the American Strategic Air Command in the atomic bomb, given enough of them, was questioned by many. In Britain a three-service symposium in the *Royal United Service Institution Journal* in 1950,[21] which discussed the future of war in each of the elements, was certainly sceptical. Dr O. H. Wansborough Jones, scientific adviser to the Army Council, claimed that 'Military thought has settled down very steadily into the rational belief that, terrible as it is, it [the atomic bomb] may not after all be all-powerful.'[22] Tizard and P. M. S. Blackett,[23] a distinguished mathematician well versed in defence problems, agreed.

General Eisenhower, in his report to Senate Committees on 1 February 1951 concerning western defence, seemed averse to the use of nuclear weapons, save in the last resort. With twelve American divisions in Europe to stiffen the local forces, he believed that any Soviet attack could be sufficiently delayed for a full-scale mobilisation in the United States to take place. The Chief of the Imperial General Staff, Sir William Slim, forecast in Hanover on 23 September 1951 that British troops fighting a war in Europe must expect to encounter heavy artillery and great armoured masses, which they should meet with elaborate anti-tank defences, and a powerful counter-bombardment. A fighting retreat, gaining time for both Western mobilisation and American nuclear strikes, was the implicit strategy.

Western strategists could turn for inspiration to the brilliant fighting retreat conducted by German forces on the eastern front during the Second World War. As the line shortened the Russians had advanced with growing difficulty, even when the odds were heavily in their favour. Western experts believed that although the Russians could probably double their reported current strength of one hundred and seventy-five divisions in the event of mobilisation, their weaknesses in communications, technical services, logistics, as well as the low standard of education – and therefore the lack of initiative that should result – of the mass of their troops, should make their advance slow and ponderous. Some comfort could also be drawn from the belief that Russia was weak in long-range bombers, in anti-aircraft weapons, and at sea. True, Russia was credited with three hundred and fifty submarines, but these were scattered around the Eurasian land mass, with no ready access to western sea-routes at the beginning of a war, though with their long-range capabilities shrouded in mystery. Unfortunately NATO as it existed in the summer of 1950 was in no condition to exploit any such weaknesses.

NATO planners agreed in 1950 that a massive increase in the conventional forces of the West must be attempted. As we have seen, the ability of the American deterrent to deter the Soviet Union in the long run was believed to be in doubt. It was essential to hold as much of western Europe as possible in the event of war in the interest of the Europeans themselves, and because a second Normandy might prove impossible. Serious preparations on these lines would, it was hoped, acquire a momentum of their own. If Europeans could be offered the hope of an effective land defence – the so-called 'forward strategy' – their morale would improve, and their readiness to contribute more to their own defence should increase. But to prepare on these lines would entail an Anglo-American departure from their past tendency to view their contribution to NATO largely in air and naval terms, and it would also necessitate the rearmament of West Germany. Some radically new thinking would be required in Britain.

The first British moves, announced on 26 July, were decidedly modest.[24] Britain was already spending a higher proportion of her national income on defence (some 7 per cent) than any other member of NATO. An extra £100 million was to be spent in 1950–1 to remove the most obvious deficiencies in the nation's armoury, but much larger sums would be required to place the forces 'in a condition of readiness'. The British government was plainly awaiting a lead from the United States before committing itself to a longer-term programme. An American appeal of 26 July for details of any such programme was apparently accompanied by an intimation of assistance should it lead Britain into further balance of payments difficulties. There was no formal pledge, but the government certainly included this expectation of aid in its calculations when it tried to estimate the scale of rearmament that might be attempted without jeopardising the post-war economic recovery. To have insisted on a guarantee of American aid might have been wiser economically, but would have weakened the political impact of the British programme, which was intended to demonstrate to sceptics in the United States that Europe could be defended, and that some Europeans at least were prepared to help themselves. Britain's NATO commitments were to ensure American involvement. Economic risks should be run in the hope of greater strategic gains. President Truman, in any case, was asking Congress for $4 billion in military aid for America's allies, while the British economy seemed to be making sufficient progress in 1950 for Marshall Aid to be dispensed with at the end of the year. Attlee later recalled that his advisers thought that no 'unbearable strain' would be imposed on the economy if American aid was forthcoming, and providing the necessary imports could be purchased in the right quantities and at the right prices. It was in this mood that the government informed Washington on 4 August that it expected to spend £3400 million on defence over the next three years. This was later increased to £3600 million, and the full details of the programme were spelled out to Parliament on 12–14 September.

Averaged over the three years, 1951–4, this represented an increase of about 50 per cent compared with spending in

1950–1. Yet there were hints that the United States found this rise disappointing – they had hoped for £6000 million –[25] while *Le Monde* of 13 September commented unfavourably on the limited expansion of British ground forces in Europe. Opinion in *The Times* was divided: a political leader on 4 August questioned the adequacy of the programme, whereas the City page on 8 August foresaw great, if not insuperable, economic problems. Experts in *The Economist* were also sceptical. The government itself claimed that this was the maximum that could be attempted without resort to a war economy, direction of labour, and the construction of new arms factories. Even so the services would require an extra 327,000 persons in supply or the forces themselves – a figure soon to be further increased – at a time when labour was scarce. Some loss of foreign earnings was expected, as the industry most affected by rearmament, engineering, had the most buoyant export record. A balance of payments deficit was not expected, though there would be a drop in home consumption. Nevertheless the programme would be dependent upon American aid, the availability of certain imports – including some foreign machine tools and strategic goods. By the end of 1950 even this bold policy seemed inadequate, hopes of an early peace in Korea now giving way to the possibility of defeat as Chinese forces swept south, while suspicion of Russian intentions in Europe also mounted.

On 29 January 1951 it was announced that rearmament over the next three years would entail an expenditure of £4700 million, or nearly double the level of spending envisaged in 1950 before the Korean conflict. This expansion was authorised at a time when there was no immediate prospect of American aid, but when the Sterling Area's reserves were increasing rapidly. Once again the government professed great optimism concerning the impact on the balance of payments, domestic consumption and new investment. There would be losses, but these should prove tolerable. The Prime Minister explained to the Commons on 29 January:

> We intend to carry out this production programme to the limit of the forces under our control. The completion of the programme in full and in time is dependent upon

an adequate supply of materials, components and machine tools. In particular, our plans for expanding capacity depend entirely upon the early provision of machine tools, many of which can only be obtained from abroad. . . .

. . . In meeting this situation the Government have one clear aim before them; to see that we carry as much of the load as possible ourselves, now, and refrain from mortgaging the future by running into debt abroad or reducing the investment on which our industrial efficiency depends.

. . . If we carry it in the way I have suggested, we shall not destroy the recovery which we have made in the last few years, nor shall we imperil the future strength of our economy.

Indeed, there seems to have been an element of window-dressing in government policy, with the amount of rearmament being determined by circumstances. Certainly the programme remained behind schedule in 1951. At the same time full credit must be given to Attlee and his colleagues for achieving as much as they did given the doubts and dissensions within their own party.[26]

The *Economic Survey for 1951* expected the cost of imports to rise by about £1000 million, but if overseas earnings reached the expected total of £3200 million, there would be a gap in the nation's balance of payments of no more than £150 million, most of which would have been spent on extra strategic stocks, and so would represent no real loss at all. Unfortunately imports were to exceed the estimate by about £150 million, in part owing to rising world prices, and in part owing to increased consumption in Britain. Overseas earnings fell nearly £250 million below expectations, largely on account of the Anglo-Iranian oil crisis. This situation was made far worse by the fact that other members of the Sterling Area also ran deficits in their balance of payments, so that in the second half of 1951 alone the nation's gold and dollar reserves fell by some £600 million. Bad luck, excessive optimism and excessive demand had all helped to create this situation. The coincidence of a world boom and the Korean War had been too much. Nor had Cassandras been wanting. Three ministers, including Aneurin Bevan, had resigned from the government in April. Their motives were complex – if not confused – but among their objections had been the scale of the latest rearmament programme. In July there had appeared the 'Bevanite' pamphlet, *One Way Only*, which argued that £100 million, not £400 million extra per year, was the maximum that the British economy and society could afford. The Conservative party spoke vaguely of less government spending, reduced consumption, and more economic freedom as its solution to the current economic situation, which Oliver Lyttelton on 26 July bluntly described as dangerous. An immediate drop in personal and government expenditure was essential. He affirmed, 'to rearm on a sufficient scale to be safe, export on a sufficient scale to be solvent, consume on a sufficient scale to be comfortable, and to enjoy and maintain social services on a sufficient scale to be secure upon the present scale of working hours and productivity is beyond us'. The government, however, continued to act as though marginal economies would suffice, and as if the economy were broadly equal to all these demands. Only in the autumn did it become clear that the pessimists were right.

The government's position was a difficult one, possessing as it did a tiny majority in the House of Commons, and with the nation itself unwilling to accept yet another spell of austerity after a generation of slump, war and post-war reconstruction. Its bid for 'defence without tears' was a failure. The year 1951 was one of rapidly rising prices and of industrial unrest. The Trades Union Congress supported rearmament, but the unions would not forgo wage claims yet again so soon after their response to the self-denying appeals of Cripps. Nor could a free labour market supply half a million hands for defence without wage increases when only about half that number were unemployed. Worse, productivity actually fell in 1951–2: industrial production stagnated, or, as in the case of the steel industry, fell. Shortage of scrap was mainly responsible for the latter, and in 1952 one million tons of steel had to be imported from the United States. The government, while it recoiled from the imposition of a war economy, reintroduced many raw material and price controls, and prepared to requisition factories and warehouses if necessary. Nevertheless the nation's consumption of goods was far too high in 1951 in view of the added defence burden and escalating prices of many imports. Restraint in consumption was the only practicable answer to high-priced imports. In the case of scarce and costly raw materials needed for stock-piling, one could only grin and bear it. The establishment of the International Materials Conference in 1951, in collabora-tion with the United States and France, achieved little. It lacked the powers and opportunity to repeat the success of the Anglo-American wartime Combined Raw Material Board in the control and purchase of scarce commodities. British emergency measures included the resumption of tungsten ore mining in Devon.

The election of October 1951 returned Churchill and the Conservatives to power. The new government at least pos-sessed plenty of self-confidence, in contrast to its predecessor in its declining months, though the economic prospect re-mained grim – some thought desperate – for several months. It cut both imports and defence spending. Rather higher priority was given to the supply of raw materials to export industries, and fortunately the terms of trade began to move in favour of Britain in 1952. Stalemate in Korea eased the world demand for raw materials, while other members of the Sterling Area began to move out of 'the red'. Yet it was not until the second half of 1952 that the reserves began to recover. There was good news, too, from the United States, £121 million being promised on 29 January under the Mutual Security Act. This grant was said to be essential to prevent a cut of £250 million in British defence spending. Washington further argued that Britain deserved this bonus since her arms production exceeded that of all her European NATO partners combined, and since she alone – apart from the United States – was rearming according to her capacity. Vulnerable as the British economy had proved in 1951, it still occupied a unique place in western Europe, a fact which partly accounts for the excessive demands placed upon it. Britain's industrial production represented one-third of the total produced in non-Communist Europe; 40 per cent if only the European members of NATO are counted. Her produc-tion was two and a half times that of France, 50 per cent more than that of West Germany. An American pamphlet published in August 1951[27] reported that Britain alone of the western European states had the resources which entitled her to be treated as an independent military power. In 1952–3, after the pace of Britain's rearmament had been slowed, she was still contributing more than 40 per cent to the total defence spending of the European members of NATO, even if this figure was dwarfed tenfold by that of the United States, and much of it was expended on her extra-European role.

It was planned in 1951 that more than half of the three-year defence programme would be spent on construction and production for defence, research and development. By 1954 the production of certain crucial weapons, such as aircraft and tanks, should have quadrupled. The arms industry as a whole would be employing over one million workers, or only about a quarter of a million less than in 1939. Ten per cent of the nation's industrial production would be devoted to arms compared with $2\frac{1}{2}$ per cent in 1950. No less than 20 per cent of the engineering industry would be so engaged – compared with 80 per cent at the height of the war. These aims were too ambitious, the rate of expansion in 1951 – before the deliberate deceleration under Churchill – being slowed by labour and raw material shortages, and to a lesser extent by the late arrival of machine tools.[28]

Some 35,000 machine tools were ordered in 1951, just over half of them abroad, but even so it was expected that civilian deliveries in Britain would have to be cut by about one-third. The machine-tool industry responded rather slowly to this challenge, in part through lack of skilled labour, but in part through its own conservatism and lack of flexibility. It was also losing labour to higher-paid boom industries, such as motor vehicles. In desperation some aircraft firms made their own tools. A 20 per cent increase in home production was achieved over the next five years, but machine-tool delays were mainly responsible for the non-completion of two tank factories until 1953. Aircraft firms in general suffered from the lack of skilled labour, and the difficulty of attracting workers to an industry that already had a reputation for instability (it had been paying off employees early in 1950). Housing was not always available locally, and there were complaints of lack of co-operation by the Ministry of Housing.

Areas where defence industries were suddenly expanded were reckoned to need an extra 10,000 houses in 1951. Some witnesses before the Select Committee on Estimates early in 1951 thought the overall labour problem so difficult that they feared direction of labour would be needed to fulfil the aircraft production target. For rearmament in general greater use of women was urged, together with the up-grading of semi-skilled labour and the introduction of more retraining schemes. Service departments reported that their scientific and technical staffs were up to a quarter below strength, although universities were awarding twice as many science and engineering degrees as in 1945. Some production was being lost through the call-up for National Service of skilled workers who had just completed their apprenticeships. Only with the Conservative decision to slacken the rearmament drive, and the fall in civilian demand for labour in 1952, did the situation improve, so that by 1953 surplus capacity was appearing even in the engineering industry. A bright spot was provided by the manufacturers of electronics, who contrived to quintuple production between 1950 and 1954, and to increase exports by 50 per cent despite rearmament.[29] Nor was there a shortage of factory space for arms manufacture, since many war-built factories had been retained. The Royal Ordnance Factories had not been run down to the low level of 1936, the real starting-point of the previous rearmament drive.

In other respects, however, rearmament was a more difficult, more costly and complex task than in the late 1930s. Weapon technology had advanced a great deal since then, and demanded new and more elaborate manufacturing techniques. New machining techniques might speed the production of some tank parts, gun barrels and breeches, but gun-mountings took longer with their more intricate electrical and hydraulic fittings. Radar, predictors and similar equipment had become much more sophisticated. The radio-electrical equipment of a bomber of the mid-1950s was to weigh about sixty times as much as that of its pre-war counterpart. Airframe manufacture was being revolutionised by the introduction of giant forging presses and skin milling (the machining away of the unwanted parts of a piece of metal) in place of rivets and sheet-metal. The revolutionary jet-engines required special lathes to bore large-diameter rings; turbine-blades had to be produced in large numbers – not an easy task. Indeed, the introduction of the more efficient, though less robust, axial-flow jet-engine in place of the Whittle centrifugal compressor type, was increasing the strain on skilled manpower and machine tools. The average jet-engine required at least three times as many man-hours and three times the number of machine tools as a piston-engine. It also required new materials such as nickel, which was in short supply, and if possible titanium, a great weight-saver, but of which a mere twenty-five tons was being produced a year in Britain in 1953. The United States produced 20,000 tons. I.C.I. was to build a giant new plant to fill this void. Great new quantitative and qualitative demands were thus being imposed upon industry by all services, especially the R.A.F.[30]

Costs were rising, too, compared with 1945. By 1951 a rifle cost nearly £12 compared with £7 11s 3d at the end of the war. A Bren gun's price had risen from £35 to £65, and when the cost of more sophisticated new equipment was taken into account as well the rise was still more dramatic. Thus the equipment of an armoured division stood at £50 million compared with £18 million in 1938. New fighter aircraft averaged over £16,000 compared with less than £10,000 in 1945. New bombers cost £77,600 as opposed to £16,000 for a comparable aircraft, and this was but the start of a sharply rising trend. The first of the projected V-bombers was expected to cost at least eight times as much as the Lincoln. More than 40,000 special jigs and tools would be required to start the production of only one of the V-bomber types, and Julian Amery was graphically to compare the procurement of such an aircraft with its predecessors to 'the difference between the seven-day creation of the Book of Genesis and the evolution of the "Origin of the Species" '.

These problems were compounded by other circumstances. Disappointment and criticism were to mount steadily in the early 1950s concerning the state of the RAF. Where the complaint had formerly been one of lack of numbers, now it centred more on the lack of quality.[31] Until the second half of the decade Britain was to be outclassed by the United

States and the Soviet Union in several types of aircraft; was indeed to be dependent upon the United States for some types of front-line aircraft, and all this despite Britain's recent lead in the design of jet-engines. A major difficulty arose from the decisions of the later 1940s, that, given the probability of a generation of peace and the actuality of the nation's economic problems, the overall re-equipment of the R.A.F. should be postponed until the later 1950s. Apart from the Venom and the Canberra – and perhaps the SA-4 – the plan was to leap-frog from the first jet-warplanes to the advanced models of a decade hence. This was a gamble militarily and technically, the latter all the more so since airframe and high-speed research was not being pushed forward with great vigour before 1950. Soviet capabilities were grossly underestimated, the Mig-15 confounding all British expectations. The only comparable British aircraft had not left the drawing-board. Fortunately the only known Soviet long-range bombers were the TU-4 and -72 developments of the American B-29, Soviet expertise in strategic bombing was an unknown quantity, and had certainly been singularly undeveloped down to 1945. Nevertheless a government spokesman on 1 August 1951 thought it necessary to warn the country that the present Soviet capability constituted a graver threat to the country than anything possessed by Germany in 1939–45. He implied that if only a few Soviet bombers broke through the air defences, armed with nuclear weapons, they would be able to inflict disproportionate damage. Furthermore, even if Soviet jet-aircraft were confined to central Europe, the R.A.F. would still be at a disadvantage.

Three decisions were taken by the government in 1950. The first was to order in large numbers such fighters as could speedily be produced – Meteors, Vampires and later Venoms – despite their near or partial obsolescence. The Chief of the Air Staff argued that they were better than nothing, would help to train aircrews, and would provide first-hand experience for the elaborate ground components of air defence.[32] Secondly the government sought to procure some American Sabre fighters, the only Western aircraft with a performance comparable to that of the dreaded Migs. Only in 1952 was it arranged as part of the Mutual Defence Assistance Programme that Canada and the United States should supply Britain with about four hundred of these aircraft. Thirdly, two British aircraft were ordered off the drawing-board in the hope that they could be scrambled into production in the not-too-distant future. Such were the origins of the belatedly valuable Hunter and the ill-fated Swift. The Hunter did not enter service until 1955–6, a disappointing rate of progress. The difficulty of blending a new airframe, a new engine, and a new cannon of extraordinary power was grossly under-estimated. The Swift was intended as an insurance policy, in case the Hunter disappointed or was delayed, but there were sceptics from early days as to the feasibility of turning a slender research aircraft into a usable warplane.[33] Hasty improvisation could not make up for the years lost after 1945.

Not that the government had been totally inactive. According to some, there had been too much activity, with an unnecessary proliferation of projects. Both Conservative and Labour were responsible for this confusion. Certainly many were necessary research projects, indispensable to designers as they strove to find ideal aerodynamic shapes for supersonic or near-supersonic aircraft, with a variety of roles in mind. But there was also unnecessary proliferation, a point conceded by a Minister of Defence on 28 February 1956 when he agreed that limited resources had been spread too thinly over too many projects. Attempts were made to justify the production of three V-bombers in the 1950s by emphasising that the last two represented an important advance on the first, and that these were duplicated in case ambitious experiments in wing design should fail in one case or the other. But Sir Arthur Vere Harvey, deputy chairman of Handley Page, the makers of the crescent-winged Victor, told Parliament on 5 March 1956 that until recently this aircraft had been starved of funds, with inevitable delays in the work. Earlier, in January 1955, Petter, the designer of the Canberra, had argued that 'On the industrial side our gravest fault has been over-commitment.' Sir Roy Fedden, another air expert, thought that British air policy suffered from 'delusions of grandeur'. Too many ambitious aircraft projects had been attempted.[34] Yet the temptation to insure was strong: also to preserve aircraft manufacturing capacity.

The existence of sixteen aircraft companies (plus seven subsidiaries) encouraged this proliferation of projects, with consequent dilution of resources and personnel. It was surely not wholly accidental that Rolls-Royce, who produced about half of the nation's aero-engines, should have emerged with so much credit during these years. Aero-space success was dependent upon more than a few imaginative designers; it required capital, business know-how, and professional excellence throughout a company. These Rolls-Royce certainly possessed in greater measure than the average British firm. It was estimated that the American air industry employed at least four times the proportion of qualified staff compared with Britain. American production engineers, in particular, often had degrees, whereas their British counterparts had usually started as floor-apprentices. The latter's practical competence, according to some experts, was not sufficiently backed by scientific and technological understanding: a close and profitable partnership with the scientifically or technologically trained expert could not so easily be established. Even more elementary, thought Richard Stokes, was the fact that the average American firm had 50,000 employees against an average in Britain of only 15,000. He thought each V-bomber required the former scale of manufacturer.

These were serious weaknesses, but the critics had not yet done. They pointed to the panicky government decisions to start the Hunter and Swift, the attempt to proceed in too large design steps, the over-ambitious specifications, which, for instance, in the case of the Javelin all-weather fighter's avionics caused so many delays that by the time the aircraft entered service in 1956 it was too slow to do all that was intended of it. Reginald Maudling as Minister of Supply on 29 February 1956 agreed with many critics that there had been a governmental failure to relate specifications sufficiently to industrial possibilities; that too many modifications had been permitted after the completion of the original design; and that in general too much had been attempted. The need for closer consultation between industry and government was conceded. Meanwhile cases were cited in which the government had either been too parsimonious or had gone to the other extreme and had given the manufacturers no incentive to watch costs. Amateurism and unrealism had been widespread, but especially in government circles, with the Ministry of Supply as perhaps the most favoured scapegoat. The late 1950s produced many promises to do better, but still left the way open for the TSR-2 with its over-ambitious specifications and the totally ineffective efforts at cost-control.

Given so many competing claims, Transport Command could not but remain a Cinderella branch of the R.A.F. in these years, though the first gesture towards its re-equipment was made in 1951. Coastal Command was dependent in part on American aircraft, while the only really modern aircraft at the disposal of Bomber Command in the early 1950s was the highly successful light bomber, the Canberra. A number of four-jet Valiants were ordered, but a government spokes-man admitted on 1 August 1951 that 'for the present' the United States would undertake 'almost the whole' of allied strategic bombing. The major re-equipment of Bomber Com-mand with medium bombers was not authorised until after the Conservatives had taken office.

Fighter Command's best aircraft remained American Sabres until the Hunter's many teething-troubles were cured. On the other hand, the service certainly expanded numeri-cally. It was claimed early in 1951 that Britain had more fighters than in 1939: more than 1000 planes were being pro-duced each year. The original plans for the winter of 1950–1 had been even more ambitious, until they were reduced by the Churchill government as it grappled with the Korean economic crisis. A fourfold intended increase in production fell away to one of 225 per cent over the years 1950–5. According to Selwyn Lloyd on 3 March 1955, the Attlee government had left an 'astonishing' number of aircraft on order for which no proper financial or industrial provision had been made. Arthur Henderson pointed out on 2 March 1955 that the 1951 air plan had aimed at a front-line strength of between 3000 and 4000 aircraft. This was not to be achieved, operational strength probably averaging only about half this figure. The original programme, as we have already seen, had not been very selective. It was left to the Conserva-tives in the winter of 1951–2, with one anxious eye on the

balance of payments and the other more hopefully cast towards the partial easing in the international situation, to
cancel many obsolescent aircraft, and accord super-priorities
to the more advanced Swifts, Hunters and Valiants. Yet at
least three years were to elapse before such aircraft began to
appear in the front line.

Nevertheless the R.A.F. and Britain's aircraft industry had
a key role to play in the air defence of NATO, second only to
that of the United States, and far ahead of any European
state. Indeed, the British air force possessed more aircraft than
her European allies combined. It had been agreed that she
should provide about one-third of the 4000 aircraft planned
for the air defence of western Europe. At the same time
Britain was exporting aircraft, equipment, designs, technical
knowledge and expertise in aircraft operation to these
countries. Nine countries, including the United States, were
building nine British aero-engines under licence. Similarly
several types of British aircraft were being built abroad,
notably the Canberra in – of all countries – the United States.
Apart from 485 built for British use, more than 600 were
built or sold abroad. Exported and foreign-built Hunters
totalled 900 against 1135 for home use. British influence over
European air forces was reflected in the use of English swear-
words by Dutch pilots – overheard in one exercise. British
air power was thus a conglomeration of strength and weakness: a subject of much debate and criticism, but also a source
of some legitimate pride. In general the aircraft that entered
service in the later 1950s were first-class, but unfortunately
Britain was to make too little progress towards the solution of
some of the basic weaknesses already noted, and it was France
and the United States who were to produce the military aircraft of the next generation that attracted foreign buyers
rather than Britain.

Less dramatic and controversial was the speed-up in the
re-equipment of the navy.[35] Much of this took the form of
modernisation rather than new construction, and although
the proportion of shipyard labour devoted to naval work rose
from 2 per cent to 11 per cent between 1948 and 1951, much
of this was concentrated on small craft in the lesser yards.
The big shipyards found themselves short, not of capacity,

but of steel, and mercantile launchings fell away disappointingly in 1952. Some metals and electronic equipment remained in short supply at first, while Lord Teynham told the Lords on 18 July 1951 that the Royal Corps of Naval Constructors was under-staffed, a shortage that was to continue. Ship design was becoming increasingly complex, a point dramatically illustrated by the fact that the *Hampshire* class (designed in the late 1950s) were to require eight times as much effort as the *Didos*, of roughly the same displacement, conceived a generation earlier. Already in 1951 a destroyer cost as much to built as a pre-war cruiser: the cost of a carrier's radio and radar equipment had increased fifteen times, and it was soon clear that this was but the start of an inflationary spiral. Improved steam propulsion units had to be fitted to the latest ships to close the lead opened up by the United States navy in this department during the war. Not that inventive imagination was wholly lacking in Britain. Steam catapults, angled decks and improved landing aids were pioneered in the British navy, and were speedily imitated by the Americans. The modernisation of British carriers proceeded sedately, and jet aircraft were not operated regularly from their decks until 1952. The latest British naval aircraft had a very limited performance, and there was a heavy dependence upon American machines for some years to come. Naval helicopters served with distinction in Malaya in 1953, but only came into general use at sea a year later. At least the old title, Fleet Air Arm, was revived in 1953, displacing the prosaic post-war substitute of Naval Aviation.

Both the submarine and anti-submarine forces required modernisation, with improved speed and electronic equipment. The conversion of thirty-three Second World War destroyers into fast frigates was begun in 1949 to help combat the advantages derived by hostile submarines from fast-battery drive and the schnorkel. Semi-automated anti-submarine mortars improved the firepower of these frigates. One of the first to be converted, H.M.S. *Rocket*, visited the United States in 1952, and was widely praised. In general the Soviet submarine threat, both in numbers and quality, was being viewed with growing apprehension by NATO experts. On paper the enemy appeared stronger and the allies weaker than during the second Battle of the Atlantic. The Under-Secretary of State for Air, on 18 March 1952, thought that the current aircraft of Coastal Command were 'likely to be less effective than . . . in the last war'. NATO planning for a third Battle of the Atlantic proceeded, great emphasis being placed upon convoys, air and sea escorts, with an allied authority to pool and make the most effective use of allied shipping. This last-war flavour was questioned by some experts, who argued that even if the great concentrations of shipping themselves escaped nuclear attack, and were success-fully fought across the Atlantic, there was no guarantee that sufficient European ports would remain open, following nuclear attacks, to receive them. Lord Cunningham of Hynd-hope, the most distinguished of Britain's living admirals, pointed out in 1951 that it might be necessary to unload ships over the beaches. The practicability of this on a large scale was doubtful. Nevertheless Britain, with her NATO partners, continued to make some preparations for an anti-submarine campaign, inadequate or excessive as these might seem accord-ing to the lights of the critics. Certainly much of the moth-balled fleet would have been too slow to put up much of a defence against the latest submarines, even had they been given the chance. The Reserve Fleet as a whole was spring-cleaned from 1951, when more manpower and new preserva-tive techniques such as 'Kooncoting' and 'dehumidifying' became available.[36] Many ships were transferred to commer-cial ports for civil maintenance, while a host of shipyards began the construction of a large coastal and inshore mine-sweeping force, many of which then joined the Reserve. With the advantage of hindsight it is clear that this programme was excessive.

Although the army had been given the lowest priority after 1945, it nevertheless enjoyed the distinction in 1950 of possessing a first-class tank that was ready to start produc-tion.[37] The success of the Centurion was achieved against the odds of small official design establishments and private industry's doubts concerning the profitability of tank manu-facture. Over the next decade or so some 2500 Centurions were to be exported – sales that were worth more than £100 million. Although helped by the weakness of foreign competition in this period, the Centurion has fought in various campaigns under many flags, and repeatedly proved its worth. The British Army used about 1500 Centurions. Unfortunately it was less well placed with respect to most of the remainder of its equipment in the early 1950s. Much of the rearmament programme had to consist of repeats of Second World War designs for want of new developments. No automatic rifle was in prospect; much of the artillery required modernisation, while in motor transport some chassis designs were running two or three years behind engine design. Indeed, the War Office was sharply criticised for undue perfectionism in its specifications, and the production of up-to-date vehicles could not start until 1952.

The defence plans of 1950–1 envisaged a large expansion of service manpower.[38] National Service was extended to two years, and pay increases were granted to Regulars in the hope that recruiting figures would once again move upwards. The three-year short-service engagement certainly proved a popular alternative to National Service. Overall it proved possible to raise the number of service personnel to 809,000 by April 1951 and to about 870,000 in 1953. Male Regulars numbered rather more than half a million, but the complaint was still to be heard that there were too few re-engagements. In fact, by 1952, service manpower was no less than 80,000 below expectations, while, as we shall see, Britain's overseas commitments were heavier than anticipated. The navy was little affected by the expansion, the air force taking about half and the army a little less than half of the extra personnel. It was hoped that divisional strength could be increased from just over six to about ten or eleven, of which three, and later four, were to be stationed in Europe. The Egyptian crisis eliminated most of the intended reserve of two divisions in Britain, while the only other possible reinforcement for the British Army of the Rhine (B.A.O.R.), the Territorial Army, could not be prepared for active service in less than several months. By 1954 it was hoped that the Territorials, with the Supplementary Reserve of technically qualified men, would number more than 400,000, organised in twelve divisions for home and European service, and also manning the anti-aircraft and coastal batteries for home defence. The Z Reserve of some

$2\frac{3}{4}$ million war-veterans would fill any gaps in these ranks. But the Territorials as a whole could never be brought up to the level of efficiency and readiness deemed necessary for a European war, while their first major post-war exercise did not take place until the summer of 1953. Indeed, one of Churchill's first acts after he had returned to office in October 1951 was to reactivate part of the Home Guard – a part-time, lightly-armed defence force – so dismayed was he by the state of Britain's defences with all the active divisions out of the country in the winter of 1951–2.[39] There was more than a touch of melodrama in this, and it shows the ambivalence in Churchill's thinking as he looked both backward and forward in his defence policy. But it also helps to highlight the shortage of trained combatants.

This, then, was the rearmament programme that Britain unsuccessfully embarked upon in 1950–1. In 1952 the United States was to acknowledge that Britain was in danger of over-straining herself, but in the excitement of 1950–1 the belief had been strong that even more should be attempted. Sir John Slessor, for one, had found himself resisting quite un-realistic demands from the American Secretary for Air for a much bigger effort. In Europe, and especially in France, there was disappointment that so few British divisions would be available. The French Minister of Defence in the middle of 1950 had said: 'There should be no question of having a French infantry, a British navy, and an American air force.' Slessor became very conscious of French fears that strategic bombing would become the main role of the R.A.F., and promised that if necessary Bomber Command would be employed against the communications of an advancing Soviet army.[40] The Conservative party in Opposition thought that Britain should maintain six or eight divisions in Germany, but once in office could do no better than four on a long-term basis, and even that number soon proved illusory. Overall it was generally agreed in Britain that her defence forces should not be of a highly specialised or limited kind. Britain must aspire to a strategic bomber force, as well as air defence and tactical air forces. She must have carriers and large warships as well as anti-submarine and minesweeping flotillas. She must have a general-purpose army which could fight anywhere in the world, and not simply in Europe. Such wide-ranging capabilities were expensive, and not easily borne by post-war Britain. But, if Britain was to remain a world power, they had to be preserved. From October 1951 the Churchill ministry set out to try to provide for British security at a lower cost than Labour had deemed unavoidable in 1950–1.

3 The Start of the British Nuclear Era: 1952-5

Politics are full of ironies, but there can be few better examples than that of 1951-2, when Winston Churchill found himself engaged in the reduction of a defence programme devised by a Labour government. For the first few months he served as his own Minister of Defence, a decision that caused some of his leading colleagues a little uneasiness. Harold Macmillan was later to remark that it 'was not really possible for him at his age to undertake this dual role'. Early in 1952 he appointed Field-Marshal Alexander in his stead, but he continued to take a very active interest in the formulation of defence policy until his retirement in 1955. Macmillan, who served briefly under Churchill as Minister of Defence, found his interest and interference something of an embarrassment, but gave the Premier full marks for the way in which he conducted the first Conservative defence review in the winter of 1951-2 immediately on his return to office. His energy and decisiveness then were quite remarkable.[1] In general, however, Churchill seems to have been very much at the mercy of events, political and financial, as well as military. The most radical thinking on defence matters came from the services themselves, especially the Chief of the Air Staff, Sir John Slessor, from the scientists associated with defence, and from ministers such as Duncan Sandys and briefly Macmillan. Churchill and all his advisers were also under constant pressure from the Treasury. Some financial experts thought that something like national bankruptcy was impending in the winter of 1951-2.[2] Domestic political considerations further discouraged heavy defence spending. The Conservatives won the October 1951 election by the narrowest of margins: they were determined to prove their commitment to full employment, the welfare state and the release of the nation's productive energies. They had also promised to build 300,000 houses a year.

Nevertheless, although the new government was to slow down rearmament from its first months in office, it also permitted itself an early gesture of apparent vigour. Churchill expressed his concern at the despatch of almost all the fighting strength of the army overseas. With Liddell Hart he feared a sudden descent by Russian paratroops upon the virtually defenceless south-east of England.[3] A great effort was made to organise combat units among the quarter of a million troops in depots at home, and the Home Guard was reactivated east of a line from Flamborough Head to Selsey, with cadre forces elsewhere. Civilian enthusiasm for this part-time force was disappointing, and in the first year only 25,000 volunteers were forthcoming out of an intended strength of 125,000. The idea of a sudden Soviet paratroop attack appears somewhat far-fetched in any case. The Soviet defence planners were more likely to be aiming at the paralysis of British industrial strength and ports by bombing attacks – both conventional and nuclear – with their own versions of the American B-29 aircraft.

Meanwhile the government's review of the nation's defences had brought economies as early as 6 December 1951, and many more were to follow in 1952. Churchill himself insisted on 30 July 1952 that the original rearmament plans were 'utterly beyond our economic capacity to bear'. Privately the Treasury could see but 'a continuing mountain range' of economic difficulties; some asked whether the nation could ever escape from such problems without dropping the reserve currency role of sterling.[4] As far as defence was concerned the year 1951 had proved that the economy could not bear the current burden without a larger drop than $2\frac{1}{2}$ per cent in personal consumption. Exports and domestic fixed capital formulation were also suffering, together with the national stockpile of imported raw materials. Even the most drastic government action against living standards and the welfare state might not have sustained the 1950–1 rearmament programme. A vast expansion of the engineering and metal industries, for instance, would have been essential. As it was, even after the services' share of their production had been cut back from an intended 20 per cent to 15 per cent in 1952, exports and new plant for civilian factories still suffered. These industries were contributing a growing proportion of Britain's exports – about 40 per cent of the total in the early 1950s – but where was the skilled manpower to meet all these needs simultaneously? Several economists, such as Professors R. S. Edwards and F. W. Paish, and politicians, such as Richard Crossman and John Strachey, blamed rearmament in part for Britain's slow rate of economic growth in 1951–3 compared, for instance, with West Germany. These criticisms were to be heard even after the Conservative cut-backs in defence from December 1951, cut-backs which first spread the 1951 programme over four instead of three years, and which slowed it down even further from 1953. Thus expenditure on defence production averaged only £600 million in 1952–3 and 1953–4 compared with a projected £800 million.[5] Manpower engaged in such work was reduced from 900,000 in 1952 to 850,000 in 1953, though this still represented an increase of nearly 400,000 compared with 1950.

Economies in service manpower were still harder to find. Strachey, though haunted by the fear that Britain would over-strain herself like Austria-Hungary in 1914, doubted whether any early savings in British strength overseas would prove possible outside the Canal Zone. In Europe a NATO Council meeting in Lisbon in February 1952 had set an overall target of ninety-six divisions and 9000 aircraft for two years hence.[6] Britain was to contribute eighteen divisions by D-day plus thirty. It was difficult to see how Britain could contribute more than sixteen at the very most, many of which would be Territorial divisions, requiring a minimum of three months' training to fit them for the front line. NATO was to admit the unreality of its plans in due course and place more emphasis upon quality. The four divisions in B.A.O.R., however, remained an indispensable element in NATO, consti-tuting nearly one-third of its immediately effective strength on land. Britain was expected to contribute a similar pro-portion of the 4000 aircraft intended for the defence of western Europe, but she was, not surprisingly, below her promised target in 1952.[7] The government, however, decided quite properly that the danger of a Soviet attack had receded sufficiently for the emphasis in aircraft production to be shifted from current obsolescent types to more advanced models. Super-priorities included several aircraft types, Centurion tanks and guided weapons. About one-sixth of the programme was soon thus classified, though with no remarkable consequences.[8]

Opposition pleas for a review of the length of National Service were not very helpful. To have cut the period by six months would have meant the loss of 100,000 men for much of the period of their highest utility to the services.[9] Despite the Korean stalemate and the diminishing tension in Europe by 1952, the calls upon the army in particular were tending to increase. Thus the equivalent of five divisions was committed to various parts of Europe, and as many more were soon deployed over the Middle and Far East. In particular, the worsening situation in Egypt was demanding reinforcements, while the Mau Mau movement forced the proclamation of an emergency in Kenya from October 1952. One of the two battalions released from Austria had to be sent there. No reduction in service manpower was possible until 1953 – and then only by some 20,000 men – so that defence overall continued to absorb nearly 10 per cent of the nation's labour force in one way or another.

Anglo-Egyptian negotiations over their future defence relationship had been resumed in 1950, with the Egyptians insisting upon a total British withdrawal. Sir William Slim, the Chief of the Imperial General Staff, despite a reputation for tactful persuasiveness, failed to convince Cairo in June–July 1950 that from ten to fifteen Soviet divisions could reach Egypt within four months of the start of a war. The Egyptians doubted the reality of such a threat, especially if the British removed themselves from the Canal Zone, and consequently any motive for a Soviet attack. The British, in turn, doubted the capacity of the Egyptians to defend themselves unaided – they had fought badly in the recent war with Israel. They also questioned Egyptian trustworthiness once the last troops had departed.

Beyond that was the British belief in the value of the base itself, with its admirable location and invaluable equipment.[10]

As Shinwell in expansive mood was later to recall before the
Commons on 9 March 1960:

> When I was at the Ministry of Defence, and we were dis-
> cussing the possibility of abandoning the Canal Zone, I
> was told that its abandonment would be the greatest
> disaster that had ever occurred in this country, and we must
> remain in the Canal Zone. When suggestions were made
> that we might proceed to Libya to construct a cantonment,
> or go down to McKinnon Road in Kenya, we were told by
> high-ranking officers that this was of no value at all, and that
> it was military nonsense.

In the middle of 1951 the Egyptians suggested the Gaza Strip
as an alternative site for the base: the British equally vainly
offered to evacuate Suez in return for a close defence relationship which might be extended to include the United States,
France and Turkey. This last offer was made in the middle
of October, and coincided with the Egyptian decision to
denounce unilaterally the Anglo-Egyptian treaty of 1936.
Attacks on British persons and property in Egypt followed.

The Egyptians had been much encouraged by events in
Iran, where the Anglo-Iranian Oil Company had been
nationalised on 20 March 1951. Anglo-Iranian differences had
arisen over the implementation of nationalisation, and
British naval forces had moved into Persian waters in June
when British lives were believed to be in danger. Herbert
Morrison, the Foreign Secretary, would have liked to send
troops to protect the Abadan oil refinery, but neither they nor
transport were readily available. Attlee was averse to force,
arguing that quick, decisive action was impossible, and that
any attempt would prove morally and politically disastrous.[11]
Deadlock was reached in the negotiations in September,
though circumstances in the long run were to favour Britain
despite her military inactivity. Dr Mossadegh, the Iranian
nationalist leader, was an ill-starred figure, with less of the
understanding of the modern world that was to be displayed
by the future Egyptian leader, Gamal Abdel Nasser, for
instance. The Soviet Union made no significant move; the
international boycott of Iranian oil proved effective; and
though the United States was slow to share Britain's view of

Mossadegh, in time it was to assist in his overthrow and the creation of an oil consortium.

All this took time, and no solution was reached until 1954. Conservatives believed that a stronger line would have deterred others from stepping up their demands against Britain, but no government, given the nation's current military responsibilities, could lightly have adopted a more positive policy. It was widely agreed that the return of only a small Conservative majority in October 1951 owed much to the public's fear of an adventurous foreign policy, while, as to the forces available, Churchill told the Commons on 6 December 1951: 'Practically all our Regular formations have been sent to the army in Europe or are engaged in distant theatres.' The general situation in the Middle East also made it inadvisable to act unless one was sure of quick success. One good ally, King Abdullah of Jordan, had been assassinated in July, and there was no certainty that his successor would be able to make good his assurances of continuing friendship. Another ally, Nuri es-Said, the most powerful figure in Iraq, warned London in the autumn of 1951 that it would soon be necessary to revise the Anglo-Iraqi treaty of 1930 in view of nationalist criticism. Meanwhile the situation was rapidly deteriorating in Egypt, with a growing number of violent anti-British incidents in the winter of 1951–2. Serious riots broke out in Cairo on 25–6 January, while the security of the Suez base was becoming a major problem. Ultimately three divisions, or about 75,000 troops, were to be concentrated there, in uncomfortable conditions, and to no purpose if the chief task of the forces in Suez was to be the defence of their own base.

So unpromising a situation necessitated a new approach. Alternatives to Suez had once again to be considered. Gaza was finally rejected at the end of 1952,[12] and suggestions of Haifa, in Israel, also proved a non-runner. According to General Marshall-Cornwall, the Israelis offered Haifa to the British as a base for ninety-nine years in 1950. He personally passed on the offer to the War Office, and it was then properly turned down by the Foreign Office as too dangerous for Anglo-Arab relations.[13] The idea, however, was by no means dead. On 29 July 1954, for instance, both Attlee and Colonel

D

Wigg insisted to the Commons that Haifa would prove a better base than Cyprus. But official thinking was moving on different lines. The overthrow of the Egyptian monarchy in July 1952 gave rise to hopes that a strong military régime, which was less at the mercy of factional politics, might adopt a more co-operative policy. Variants of the Middle Eastern defence pact of 1951 were put forward, though with diminishing conviction. Total evacuation remained the Egyptian price, though a limited bilateral defence agreement might prove possible. Political and strategic developments in the early 1950s were beginning to make a compromise on these lines seem acceptable to a growing number of influential figures in Whitehall. The debate, however, was by no means over.[14]

About forty Conservative M.P.s remained obdurate to the last; Churchill was reluctant, and sought more favourable terms, while among the military Lieutenant-General W. G. Lindsell[15] and Sir George Erskine,[16] the British commander in Suez, pleaded for the retention of the base. Erskine continued to insist that Suez was needed to develop operations on the southern flank of NATO, but the indispensability of Suez in this context was challenged by others, and notably by the Chief of the Air Staff, Sir John Slessor. Shortly after his retirement he argued, in *The Times* of 30 September 1953, that the inclusion of Turkey in NATO had transformed the situation. The British had originally hoped in the summer of 1951 that Turkey could be fitted into a Middle Eastern defence agreement rather than into NATO itself. They had been defeated on this point, and it could now be argued that Turkey herself would make a rapid Soviet advance to Suez less likely. British air power might operate from Turkish bases in an emergency. New thinking was also being encouraged in 1952–3 by the dawn of the thermo-nuclear era. Reservations might have been possible concerning atomic weapons as decisive weapons in themselves, but the hydrogen-bomb was so devastating that there could be no question of a Soviet conquest of western Europe which might then be rolled back by an amphibious Anglo-American strategy, in which Suez might play an important initial part. Suez, in any case, could be paralysed by the new weapons, while the latter would prevent the large-scale movement of troops once a major war had started. The needs of global war consequently no longer justified a massive base at Suez.

One might, of course, still envisage situations in which Britain might be assisted by such a base, but did it make strategic sense to try and hold it at vast cost against Egyptian hostility? Not only were large numbers of troops tied up in its defence, but the base could function efficiently only with a local labour force of about 35,000. These points were forcefully put by, among others, the defence correspondent of the *Daily Telegraph*,[17] while the judges of an important service essay competition awarded the Trench Gascoigne Prize to a candidate who argued on the same lines.[18] An American diplomat recalled a conference in London in 1952 'when the question of evacuating the Suez base was discussed between British and American diplomats, and where a paper by the Imperial Chiefs of Staff was tabled which stated as its premise that the maintenance of a military base in hostile territory is in the long run impossible'.[19]

A running battle with the Egyptians could not fail to harm Anglo-Arab relations in general, and while it continued there could be no question of building up a much-desired strategic reserve in Britain. Smaller, cheaper bases would suffice to protect Britain's Middle Eastern interests in limited or small wars. A twenty-year defence agreement was concluded with Libya in July 1953. Hopes of a satisfactory treaty relationship with Iraq and Jordan persisted. There was also Cyprus, where Britain was sovereign, but at least one service expert was dismayed by the easy optimism displayed by Her Majesty's ministers in 1954. He recalled listening to one debate in which it was asserted that Cyprus 'had a friendly population and no internal security problem, and many other advantages. I was Director of Operations in the Admiralty at the time. As I sat there I could hardly believe my ears. There was no mention of the arms which the Greeks were then running into Cyprus, and not a word about naval port facilities in Cyprus.'[20]

Such were some of the arguments that began to prevail in Whitehall in 1952–4 to warrant a British withdrawal from Suez. Such a possibility had at least been implicit in the strategic thinking of the Air Staff for some years: both the Minister of Defence and the Secretary of State for War began to argue on these lines, so much so that Churchill was heard to complain that all the soldiers had turned against him. It was agreed, however, that the manner of withdrawal must not be allowed to damage British prestige in the world, or the Cabinet's position with its own party. A limited defence agreement with Egypt might also have its uses. The treaty of 19 October 1954 therefore laid down that all British servicemen should leave within twenty months, but that from 1956 until 1963 British civilians should help to maintain the base, which could be reoccupied in the event of an attack upon an Arab state or upon Turkey. On the face of it the treaty was a sensible compromise, and it had the special attraction of releasing for other duties or for demobilisation some two and one-third divisions.

Another loose end, following the collapse of the plans for a Middle Eastern defence agreement that would embrace the United States, France, Turkey, Egypt and the British Commonwealth, had been the future of the British Mediterranean fleet. This could not be completely dovetailed into NATO, given the fact that its responsibilities ranged beyond the security of southern Europe. Liaison and planning links were employed at first, but these were inadequate. With Turkey and Greece in NATO from 1952, and no Middle Eastern defence pact in prospect, it was finally agreed in December that an Allied Mediterranean Command, within NATO, should be set up. The commander-in-chief of the British Mediterranean fleet should control this force from Malta. But complications still persisted, since the American Sixth Fleet was not included in this command, and the Mediterranean members of the alliance retained control of their ships in coastal waters. Only with difficulty was it finally agreed that coastal waters should not extend for more than three miles, and six subordinate commands had to be set up, each to be controlled by the locally dominant naval power. Its value in war looked doubtful, and it did not promote Britain's Middle Eastern interests. The United States continued to avoid commitments outside NATO, though limited support for Britain both in Egypt and Iran in 1954, and the existence of American air bases in North Africa and Saudi-Arabia, provided some reassurance.

Further East it was the British who found themselves left on the sidelines. In September 1951 the Pacific Security Treaty known as ANZUS was concluded between the United States, Australia and New Zealand.[21] Britain was excluded and continued to be excluded despite her efforts to gain admission. She was, however, involved in talks with the United States and France concerning the Communist threat to Indo-China, which she agreed was serious, but which, when the great crisis developed in 1954 and the French position in Indo-China seemed in jeopardy, she believed could best be controlled with a political compromise. Eden's contribution to the provisional division of Vietnam was not appreciated in Washington, but Britain found a place in the rather nebulous South-East Asian Collective Defence Treaty (SEATO) which was set up in September 1954.[22] In the early 1950's, with about 10,000 troops committed to the war in Korea, and with the Malayan emergency but slowly responding to military treatment, Britain was in no position to do more in the Far East. Hong Kong and Singapore had to be garrisoned, and the equivalent of between two and three divisions was scattered over the region. Naval and air strength had similarly to be maintained, and both helped in the struggle in Malaya. British forces also formed part of the Commonwealth Strategic Reserve based on Malaya and Singapore from 1955, but it is noteworthy that Australian participation was dependent on American assurance of support should serious fighting develop.

By 1951–2 British troops in Malaya[23] numbered about 25,000 with a further 10,000 Gurkhas. Total security forces equalled about 300,000 in 1953. Even so, progress against guerrillas, who never numbered more than 8000, was painfully slow. It was much more than a military operation. Indeed, General Templer, as he departed from Britain early in 1952 to become High Commissioner in Malaya, declared that the political, economic and social policies would be decisive: 'The military problem is nothing.'[24] More precisely it might be said that the military problem of the guerrillas themselves seemed, in the short run, insoluble, given their ability to disappear into the deepest jungle. The immediate aim had to be the provision of adequate security for the other struggle to win the people's 'hearts and minds' with political, social and economic reforms. If one could insulate the mass of the population from the guerrillas, and isolate the latter from their sources of food and intelligence, real progress would be possible. Lieutenant-General Sir Harold Briggs, Director of Operations in Malaya, produced the so-called Briggs Plan in 1950 whereby 423,000 Chinese 'squatters' were moved to 410 'New Villages' where, heavily guarded, they could no longer voluntarily or involuntarily aid the guerrillas. The latter were also harassed by offensive patrols, with air and at times naval support. The guerrillas themselves decided in 1951–2 to revise their tactics and operate in smaller and more elusive groups, stepping up their political activities at the same time. They could never, however, attract sufficient local support, and were especially handicapped by the racial barrier between themselves and the Malays who formed a majority of the population. It is true that Templer himself expressed some doubt in 1953 as to whether a military solution was feasible in the light of current conditions, while the situation seemed to deteriorate momentarily in 1954. Nevertheless at least one-third of the population remained in 'white' or guerrilla-free areas.

In retrospect 1951–2 could be seen as the turning-point in the campaign. Victory had been denied the terrorists; demoralisation had been averted, and as the 'white' areas inched forward so the reforms began to make their impact. An independent, western-orientated Malaya became possible. As the security patrols probed deeper into the jungle, the isolation of the guerrillas increased. The first truce overtures were made by the Communists in 1955, and by 1957 their numbers had fallen to around 2000. Nevertheless the magnitude of the security forces' task is well illustrated by a War Office statement in 1955, wherein it was reported that an average of 1000 patrol hours were needed to capture a 'terrorist' and no less than 1600 hours to achieve a 'kill'. Ambushes, dependent upon good intelligence, were rather more rewarding, with a success for every 350 hours spent in wait. Air support included helicopters, first introduced in 1950, and regularly used from 1953. These proved invaluable, increasing troop mobility, making deep penetration into jungle possible, and improving the soldiers' morale, particularly since they could speedily remove the wounded to medical care. A naval squadron alone carried 10,000 troops and 300 casualties in 1953 and the first months of 1954.[25] The navy also operated along the coast, further restricting guerrilla mobility and supplies. Finally the army moved into central Malaya and the northern border state of Kedah to try to deny the guerrillas a last refuge. Medical and technical aid helped to win over the local primitive tribesmen, and throughout Malaya the soldiers did much to win the confidence of the population. Malaya became independent on 31 August 1957, but five British and six Gurkha battalions were still needed to help maintain internal security. The emergency was officially ended on 31 July 1960 when some 80 per cent of the country was declared 'white'.

A crisis had developed in another British territory in 1952. This was the terrorist movement, Mau Mau, in Kenya, which had begun to inflict so many casualties on Kikuyu tribesmen and European settlers that a state of emergency was proclaimed on 20 October. One African and two British brigades were soon committed to this struggle, two British battalions fortunately being released from garrison duty in Eritrea in 1952–3. By August 1954 about 35,000 troops and local forces, exclusive of police, were involved. As in Malaya, a great effort was made to isolate the guerrillas from possible supporters, and by August 1954 46,000 tribesmen had been detained as suspects. Twenty-eight thousand alone were removed from Nairobi in Operation Anvil in April. Protected villages were set up, and the guerrillas harried in their hide-outs by offensive patrols. Air supply and bombing assisted in these operations, and by 1955 specially trained police teams were taking over the main offensive role. By the end of 1955 more than 10,000 terrorists had been killed, and a further 4500 had been wounded or captured, and it was possible to recall 2500 British and 1000 African troops. British troops were finally withdrawn from these duties in 1958, though the state of emergency continued until 1960. But again, as in Malaya, judicious political, economic and social reforms were essential.

The commander-in-chief in East Africa, Sir George Erskine, was insistent on this point, despite difficulties with some of the local white population.[26] Kenya was launched on the road to independence, which was finally granted in 1963.

A short-lived and minor diversion of forces to British Guiana occurred in October 1953, when the constitution was suspended through fears that a 'Communist-dominated' state was in the making. More serious was the mounting discontent in Cyprus which came to a head as the situation was easing in Kenya and Malaya.[27] The joint headquarters of the army and R.A.F. in the Middle East had been transferred to Nicosia from Suez in December 1954, and it was intended to expand service facilities there in general at an expected cost of some £40 to £50 million. No full-scale substitute for Suez was envisaged, but rather an administrative centre for the Middle East with, in normal circumstances, about 7500 troops to intervene in small-scale or limited war emergencies. Air force plans were rather more ambitious, since Cyprus was not only a useful stepping-stone to the East, but was a valuable air base in the context of the defence of both the Middle and Near East. Eden declared in 1956: 'No Cyprus, no certain facilities to protect our supply of oil. No oil, unemployment and hunger in Britain. It is as simple as that.'

Unfortunately it was not as simple as that. This growing British strategic interest in Cyprus dismayed Greek Cypriots, who correctly feared that this would destroy their hopes of union with Greece (*Enosis*). The British were adamant, or as Lord Avon subsequently explained: 'It was not then thought enough to lease certain sites on the island from some future administration on whose policies we could not depend.'[28] There was some fear of Communist activity on the island, but more important was the British desire to be able to use Cyprus as a base in defence of Middle Eastern interests. It was far from certain that a Greek or Cypriot government would permit a base on their territory to be used for such a purpose, ready as they more probably would be to approve operations on behalf of NATO. Field-Marshal Lord Harding, who served successfully as C.I.G.S. (1952–5) and Governor of Cyprus (1955–7), explained in 1958[29] that he had urged the retention of British sovereignty on the ground that the island might be needed as a base for sizeable land forces – for use in the Middle East or with NATO – and, to make this feasible, assured British control of all key installations and services on the island was essential. He said he abandoned this view only when the development of the H-bomb threatened to make a long war and large troop concentrations impracticable. A smaller base would not necessitate the control of the whole island. Such were the calculations of British strategists, despite the general unsuitability of the island as a base, with its poor harbour facilities and its limited resources. It was rash, too, to believe that Cypriots could be denied what Afro-Asians and Arabs were increasingly demanding elsewhere in the world, and with growing success. But anything less than a sovereign base was believed to be too precarious, and with the retreat from Suez there was no other point that would equally serve British interests in the Near and Middle East.

The British, having dug their toes in, encountered growing opposition, and in November 1955 yet another state of emergency was proclaimed. Fourteen major army units were soon devoting most of their energy to the maintenance of order, but here, unlike Kenya and Malaya, they could look for little constructive political assistance, at least for the time being, since Britain could discover no formula that would reconcile the interests of herself, the Greek and Turkish Cypriots, not to mention Greece and Turkey. Her one slight consolation was that by the mid-1950s the world-wide demand for troops was past its peak. The situation, as we have seen, was easing in Malaya and Kenya: political settlements in Europe were making it possible to remove British garrisons from Austria and Venezia Giulia, and British forces were soon to leave Korea. From 1954 it was again possible to begin the creation of a strategic reserve in Britain, while the seven extra battalions that had been reconstituted as an emergency measure in 1952 were disbanded in 1955. Yet there were still some 200,000 troops overseas, not least because of the British promise in 1954 to maintain four divisions in Europe on a long-term basis – ostensibly one of the most precise military commitments ever made by Britain in peacetime.

This commitment had resulted from the collapse of the European Defence Community in the summer of 1954, an

ambitious attempt to secure some measure of rearmament
in West Germany without reviving the danger of German
militarism and aggression. It had been recognised in 1950
that West German assistance would be required if even a
modest number of divisions were to be raised for the defence
of Europe against a massive Soviet attack. American atomic
power might be able to paralyse the Soviet Union, but much
of western Europe would probably have been overrun by
superior Russian forces in the meantime. It was anticipated
that when the American nuclear monopoly came to an end,
and the United States itself was open to attack with atomic
weapons – probably by the mid 1950s – additional conventional forces would be essential for the credibility of the
West's defence posture. Washington, after the outbreak of
the Korean War, had insisted on German rearmament, and
Britain began to move in the same direction. The French,
dismayed by this prospect, put forward the Pleven Plan for
a European army in October 1950, whereby each member
should contribute its forces in the smallest possible units,
so that the maximum international integration should take
place. By such means it was hoped to prevent the emergence
of another Wehrmacht. Much argument followed over the
details, but in November 1951 tentative agreement was
reached that a European army of $1\frac{1}{4}$ million should be set
up, composed of forty-three national groups, each about
30,000 strong. France would contribute fourteen, Germany
and Italy twelve each, and the Benelux states the remaining
five. To the great dismay of the French it had proved
impossible to bring British forces into this army. In this
respect the Conservative party in office were as unco-operative
as Labour, despite general expressions of sympathy for the
idea of a European army, and other federal developments,
while they had been in opposition. Again and again, down
to the summer of 1954, the French returned to the subject,
requesting, for instance, an Anglo-American guarantee that
they would commit roughly their current ground strength
to Europe for the next twenty years. But no formula could
be discovered that would satisfy the French that they would
be safeguarded against a remilitarised Germany in all circumstances. The British vainly offered to second officers to the

European Defence Community, to participate in joint training and exercises, to place an armoured division within one
of the army corps of E.D.C. and to co-operate in air defence
in a similar manner. Eden told the Commons on 14 April
1954: 'These arrangements are designed to last as long as
they are desired by the Supreme Allied Commander.' But
always the policy was one of association, not of full-scale commitment. And the French understandably objected. There
were, of course, other reasons for the French Assembly's
refusal to join the Community of 30 August 1954, but the
British were left in no doubt as to the need for a major gesture
on their part to revive confidence in and the coherence of the
western alliance.

Whitehall hummed with ideas and discussions, especially
in view of the reaction of the United States. It was not
impossible, though hardly likely, that European ties with
Washington would be loosened as a result of this display of
European factionalism. Two things were needed – a political
formula that would be acceptable to France and West
Germany, and a more positive military commitment.[30] The
former was to be found in the Brussels Treaty of 1948, which
had no supra-national overtones, but which was sufficiently
precise to reassure the French. Eden was also delighted to
find at the end of September that the Chiefs of Staff had no
objection to more precise military obligations in Europe now
that responsibilities outside Europe seemed to be lessening
– or gave some promise of doing so. The service chiefs had
great hopes that nuclear weapons would act as deterrents to
further Korean-type wars, and that a strengthened Transport
Command could lead to smaller overseas garrisons. In normal
circumstances European commitments should not prove too
embarrassing. These were the two keys with which Eden set
out to unlock the door to the rearmament of West Germany
which had been slammed by the collapse of E.D.C. The Paris
Agreements of 23 October 1954 followed. West Germany and
Italy were both to be admitted to the Brussels Treaty, or the
Western European Union as it was now to be called. The
former was to contribute twelve divisions and a tactical air
force to NATO, though her rearmament was to be closely
supervised and controlled by the other powers. NATO was

described as 'applicable' for an 'indefinite' period, while Britain gave the following additional guarantee to reassure France.

> The United Kingdom will continue to maintain on the mainland of Europe, including Germany, the effective strength of the United Kingdom forces now assigned to the Supreme Allied Commander in Europe, four divisions and a tactical air force, or whatever the Supreme Allied Commander regards as equivalent fighting capacity. The United Kingdom undertakes not to withdraw those forces against the wishes of the majority of the Brussels Treaty Powers, who should take their decision in the knowledge of the views of the Supreme Allied Commander in Europe.
>
> This undertaking would be subject to the understanding that an acute oversea emergency might oblige Her Majesty's Government to omit this procedure.
>
> If the maintenance of United Kingdom forces on the mainland of Europe throws at any time too heavy a strain on the external finances of the United Kingdom, the United Kingdom will invite the North Atlantic Council to review the financial conditions on which the formations are maintained.

President Eisenhower thought the October agreements one of the 'greatest diplomatic achievements of our time', but Churchill in private remarked that materially they altered nothing, and that their value was essentially moral.[31] Certainly, in practice, it was not long before Britain was seeking permission to reduce her forces in Europe, and in effect she had done no more than underline her current intentions. There was a general readiness in NATO to pick up the pieces following the E.D.C. fiasco, and the agreements were dominated by the British desire to be of Europe but not in it. In so far as Britain gave anything, the escape clauses were sufficiently generous to leave her a way out when needed. For the moment, however, paper promises and strategic necessity tied four divisions to Europe, while the build-up of the second tactical air force was to continue. As in Africa and Asia, circumstances were leaving the government with little room for manœuvre, and were compelling it to maintain service manpower at roughly the levels planned in 1950–1. If naval and air personnel began to dip from 1953, no real drop occurred in the army until 1955.

When Churchill resigned the premiership in April 1955 there were still more than 823,000 with the active forces, a decrease of less than 50,000 from the manpower peak two years earlier. But if his government had been at the mercy of events in the short run, it had nevertheless given much thought to the creation of a more economical and formidable defence establishment in the long term. In many respects, of course, they were merely carrying further the tentative first steps taken by their predecessors, whose policy had been swamped by the Korean War crisis. Clearly Labour had hoped to manage with a smaller army, with much reduced overseas garrisons, and had made some progress towards the re-equipment of the R.A.F. The nuclear programme was well advanced in 1951, though that in guided missiles had hardly started. The coherence of their policy, moreover, had been wrecked by economic crises, and the unexpectedly rapid deterioration in the international scene. The Conservatives, from 1951, were also under economic constraint, which naturally encouraged radical new thinking, and they were assisted by a gradual relaxation of tension with the Soviet Union. The early 1950s similarly witnessed a great clarification of the technological future of war, with the emergence of the H-bomb, the growing practicability of guided missiles, and Britain's own practical breakthrough into the nuclear era. Firmer decisions were thus both possible and, indeed, essential.

Much of the new Conservative thinking arose from direct experience of office. This is very clear from their belated recognition that four divisions were the maximum that Britain could maintain in Germany in normal circumstances. Churchill's anxiety to protect Britain against a sudden assault by paratroopers had a decidedly retrospective look about it. His views on an American admiral in the Atlantic, his reluctance to abandon the Suez base in 1954, put him out of step with his advisers. Macmillan as Minister of Defence grew restless under his chairmanship of the Defence Committee – a saddening experience.[32] Churchill's response to nuclear weapons was ambivalent; he recognised their importance, but much of his military thinking seemed to remain in the pre-nuclear era. Among politicians Macmillan was perhaps the first leading figure who wished to carry the apparent logic of nuclear weapons to the extreme conclusion that defence policy should be essentially a question of nuclear deterrence.[33]

On his return to office in October 1951 Churchill found that more progress had been made towards the completion of a British atomic bomb than he had expected. In opposition he had long insisted that American nuclear power was the main western guarantee against Soviet aggression, and a visit to the United States in January 1952 opened his eyes still wider as to the tremendous power at the disposal of the Strategic Air Command, and its even greater potential in the future. He was also becoming convinced that the Cold War was more likely to take the form of a long competition between East and West than to lead to an early global war, and that therefore Britain must think in terms once again of a long-term defence policy that was within her capacity to sustain. Such calculations justified first a slowing down in the 1951 defence programme, and later a reduction in expenditure on arms that would be needed in the event of war in the next few years in favour of those that would serve in the later 1950s or the next decade. Churchill was thus predisposed to listen sympathetically – if not wholeheartedly – to the radical suggestions that were emanating from the Chiefs of Staff in 1952.

Sir John Slessor, Chief of the Air Staff, has been described as the chief motive force behind these ideas,[34] but it is worthy of note that Slessor himself had favoured the policy of 1950–1 to expand the R.A.F. and equip it with such aircraft as were available, even if they were obsolescent. His thinking in 1952 also appears to be a logical development of the ideas of Lord Tedder, to judge from the hints he dropped in the later 1940s as to how he believed British defence policy should evolve. One can go further and say that it develops naturally from Trenchard's conception of the R.A.F. and British strategy in the 1920s. Slessor himself, while Chief of the Air Staff, occasionally discussed air policy with Trenchard at Brooks's

Club in London – a natural thing to do with one whom he regarded as the 'Nelson of the R.A.F.'.

The Chiefs of Staff paper argued that a global war would probably result in a massive nuclear exchange. This would be immensely destructive, but it might still be followed by a 'broken-backed' phase. The first conclusion to be drawn from this terrible prospect was the importance of preventing war in the first place, and this could best be done by the maintenance of overwhelming air power which an aggressor knew would be immediately unleashed against it in the event of war. Powerful as was the nuclear capability of the Strategic Air Command, a British strategic bomber force would strengthen the western deterrent, and would ensure that enemy air and submarine bases that might particularly threaten Britain would be destroyed. Their elimination would also improve Britain's position should a 'broken-backed' war follow. A strategic, nuclear bomber force was also needed to preserve Britain's position as a great power in the world. The V-bombers were, according to Slessor, the natural successors of the battle-fleets of Nelson and Jellicoe. In Europe the Chiefs of Staff believed it impossible to raise the large ground forces demanded by NATO, and looked to the development of tactical nuclear weapons to economise in manpower, perhaps making possible a reduction in the current strength of B.A.O.R. to a mere 50,000. Nuclear warfare, in any case, seemed likely to make nonsense of the current reserve policy, when, with the best will in the world, Britain's Territorial divisions were unlikely to be fit for battle in under three months. The future of the Territorial Army seemed to lie in home and civil defence. Outside Europe, though current commitments would have to be met, the Chiefs of Staff looked forward to great reductions in due course, and in particular to a more economical substitute for Suez. Much of this document, however, was evidently looking far into the future, a consideration which, with the apparent blurring of many of the details, enabled the Chiefs of Staff to reach agreement among themselves.

Certainly the next few years witnessed only a partial implementation of its implications: circumstances, as well as service conservatism, fought against it.[35] Thus the period saw

Britain formally bind herself to the commitment of four
divisions to NATO, while ministers felt obliged to make
repeated public confession of their belief in the need for not
inconsiderable conventional forces for the security of western
Europe. It is interesting to contrast the parliamentary statements by both Churchill and Macmillan on 1–2 March 1955
on the need for conventional forces to frustrate any Soviet
attempt at a piecemeal advance with Macmillan's private
belief that Britain could not afford both conventional and
nuclear strength. Both the air force and, later, the army must
have nuclear weapons, and must be prepared to use them in
a crisis, whatever the implications. It was, however, premature
to admit this publicly. There might be consternation at home
at so stark a picture of the future, as well as repercussions
among Britain's allies. Such a policy 'politically . . . is full of
danger, at home and abroad, and may lead to a fresh out-
burst of defeatism or neutralism'.[36]

Not all Macmillan's colleagues in government were disposed to so radical a view, and a successor at the Ministry
of Defence, Sir Walter Monckton, would have liked to reduce the British emphasis upon nuclear weapons in 1956.[37]
Macmillan's reluctance to take this ministry in the first place
may even have been swayed by the belief that he would be
unable to give nuclear weapons the prominence he wished.
Certainly he complained in September 1954 that the whole
defence programme had been fixed for the next three years,
and it is clear that this programme was one of uneasy compromise between nuclear and conventional arms.[38] Churchill,
it would seem, was loath to adopt so revolutionary an
approach, and indeed so late as 5 March 1953 was talking
about the importance of being able to expand arms production in time of war. More relevantly, conventional British
forces were badly needed to reassure Britain's American,
French and German partners in NATO. The United States
must feel that Britain was pulling her weight in NATO,
France needed a British presence to offset the revival of
Germany, and Germany needed British arms to help sustain
the fiction that a forward defence would prove possible against
a Soviet attack.

Thus, early in 1955, the government, while admitting the

impossibility of defence against thermo-nuclear attack, also stressed the complementary character of nuclear and other arms. It further warned that the creation of a nuclear stalemate in Europe might result in the intensification of the Cold War in other parts of the world. Indeed, the government's approach to defence prompted John Strachey to complain that British strategy was no more than an unhappy compromise. Too little was being spent on nuclear weapons for them to be effective: they were being merely added to scaled-down conventional forces. The country was 'trying to be strong everywhere and succeeding in being weak everywhere'. Nevertheless many critics believed that they had discovered an Achilles' heel in, for instance, the government's reluctance to reduce the navy's quarter share of the defence estimates. Certainly Churchill's last ministry was a period of uneasy, but usually necessary, compromise in defence policy. Criticism from Opposition benches was easier than practical implementation.

Meanwhile the general introduction of British nuclear weapons remained fairly slow.[39] The first British atomic bomb had exploded over the Monte Bello Islands on 3 October 1952, thrusting 'a ragged letter Z, a grey and grotesque mass' into the sky. It was widely acclaimed as an impressive technical achievement, and in the United States there was talk of amending the McMahon Act to make possible Anglo-American exchanges of nuclear information. Churchill spoke optimistically of this possibility to Parliament on 23 October, and indeed the 1954 revision of the American Atomic Energy Act did much to meet his expectations. But already the United States and the Soviet Union had entered the thermo-nuclear era two years before the first of the British V-bombers began to enter service equipped with kiloton bombs in 1955. Britain would appear to have decided to become a thermo-nuclear contender in 1952, and was to carry out her first successful test in May 1957. Only then could the Anglo-American nuclear partnership be completed, by which time Soviet missile progress was already heralding the start of yet another stage in the arms race. One striking feature of this period had been the unanimity of both front benches in Parliament concerning the wisdom of this quest for a British deterrent. Its utility was believed to extend to the Middle East, where, from bases in Cyprus and Iraq, it could be used to smash any Soviet attempt at invasion from southern Russia. Small atomic bombs could now be carried by Canberras, a useful diversification of Britain's nuclear air power.

The spectrum of nuclear power was being further extended by the American development of tactical nuclear weapons. The first arrived in Europe in October 1953, though as yet for American use only.[40] The British had begun training in anticipation of their arrival early in the same year, and at press conferences on 13 August 1953 and 4 August 1954 the Chief of the Imperial General Staff, Sir John Harding, explained some of the implications of their introduction. His predecessor, Sir William Slim, had already begun to draw on his experience of the war in the Far East,[41] suggesting a parallel between the qualities needed in jungle-warfare – toughness, self-reliance, personal initiative – and those required in the confused fighting that might result in the nuclear era. Above all, army formations must be able to disperse and concentrate more quickly than in the past if they were to avoid destruction themselves, and be able to exploit the effects of nuclear attacks on an enemy. This in turn would necessitate a revolution in logistics, with more attention being given to supply from the air and with cross-country vehicles. Troop formations themselves would become smaller, and would have to attain a higher degree of self-reliance and initiative. Exercises in the mid-1950s underlined the cumbersome character of current armoured divisions, with their 6000 vehicles, and interest grew in the formation of highly mobile armoured regiments, which could be reinforced with additional armour, infantry, artillery and engineers according to circumstances. Efforts were also being made to make infantry units more flexible, with the ability to separate into smaller self-contained units, while at the same time developing greater firepower in proportion to their size. In the second half of the decade the infantry brigade group and the armoured brigade were to emerge as the basic fighting units, each about one-third the size of the old divisions, and each able to operate independently with its own armour, infantry and artillery, or in conjunction as divisional formations.[42]

The process of re-equipment, reorganisation and rethinking, however, was a slow one, and less radical than many would have liked. Two leading members of the Camberley Staff College complained in 1967 that there had been little advance in British tactical concepts since 1944,[43] while there was contemporaneous French comment to the effect that the British were simply dovetailing tactical nuclear weapons into their currently rather inflexible defensive tactics.[44] The 'tail' of B.A.O.R. also remained disturbingly large. Certainly too little equipment was forthcoming to improve British mobility across country until the 1960s.[45] Much of the existing armament was of Second World War vintage, and as late as 1959 only half the British army was equipped with the new automatic F.N. rifle. Many vehicles were old; the artillery was not so well equipped as it would have liked, the design of new guns was temporarily halted in expectation of the battlefield nuclear era, yet the first tactical nuclear weapons did not become operational until 1959; there was a trickle of new scout-cars, armoured personnel carriers, anti-tank guns, rocket-launchers, radio and radiac equipment, and new Bailey bridges. The production of ammunition increased fivefold between 1950 and 1955, while by 1953 the Tank Corps had been fully provided with the new Centurions, a formidable acquisition as wars between Israel and Egypt, and India and Pakistan, were later to demonstrate. Yet overall B.A.O.R. remained very much a Second World War force down to 1959.

From 1953 the British were no longer alone in their mounting emphasis upon the nuclear deterrent. The new Republican administration in the United States was anxious to reduce the danger of Communist aggression at less cost to itself than had been the case in Truman's last years. Increased prominence was soon being given to nuclear weapons and to the concept of 'massive retaliation' in the hope that further Koreas would be prevented. In practice, however, considerable attention was still given to American conventional forces, while initial expectations that tactical nuclear weapons would save manpower were soon followed by further controversy. Detailed NATO studies in the mid-1950s finally led to the conclusion that thirty active divisions were needed for the defence of the Central Front, but that there could be a big reduction in the reserves envisaged in the 1952 force goals. The emphasis on nuclear weapons was now unmistakable, with both General Gruenther, the supreme allied commander, and his deputy, Montgomery, insisting in 1954 that NATO would use them at the outset of a major war even if the attacker did not. Gruenther added on 15 March 1955 that though no specific plans had yet been made, their use in a smaller conflict could not be ruled out.

Even so NATO continued its paper quest for thirty or so active divisions, and reacted critically to all British suggestions that the force goals of the alliance should accord with the military strength likely to be available rather than with some ideal target. Sir Basil Embry, commander of allied air forces, Central Europe, 1953–5, recalled in his memoirs the reluctance with which French and American senior officers in particular adapted themselves to nuclear weapons. Their thinking, in his opinion, remained rooted in the experiences of the Second World War, with nuclear weapons as no more than super-explosives. The British army was more nuclear-minded, but in general he believed that NATO, through its want of centralised authority and because of its failure to grapple seriously with the nuclear challenge, was inhibiting airmen who wished to concentrate on nuclear warfare based on command of the air. Rather inconsistently Embry still felt that air defence had a future, as indeed it did, but only when NATO began to move over to a strategy of flexible response in the next decade.[46] Nevertheless Embry's account provides an interesting glimpse of the uncertainties and divisions that pervaded NATO at this time, and of the disputes that occurred between the extreme radicals and conservatives in matters of strategy.

A debate was also developing in Britain as the degree of reliance or emphasis that should be placed on nuclear weapons. On 2 March 1955 Bevan and sixty-one other Labour M.P.s refused to support an Opposition amendment on defence policy because it failed to dissociate the party explicitly from the government's apparent readiness to use nuclear weapons – even if they were not used first by an opponent. Other Labour spokesmen sought a more precise statement from the government as to the circumstances in which they would use nuclear weapons, arguing that too much was being left uncertain by the official assurance that they were obviously not usable in response to a small incident. Government spokesmen in 1955 and 1956, however, continued to insist that it was vital to leave an opponent in the dark as to the precise point at which nuclear weapons would be introduced lest he should be encouraged to take advantage of the opportunities left open for purely conventional conflict. Another line of argument in the mid-1950s, that was pioneered in Britain notably by Rear-Admiral Sir Anthony Buzzard, was that of 'graduated deterrence'.[47] Its champions argued that the all-or-nothing character of 'massive retaliation' – a strategy of suicide in the thermo-nuclear era – was lacking in credibility save in the most serious of crises. Tactical nuclear weapons should therefore be used in limited war to enable the West to offset Soviet superiority in conventional forces without having to resort to total nuclear war. This strategy was attacked by others, such as Sir John Slessor, as dangerous since it might also encourage Soviet 'nibbling' tactics. Professor Blackett argued that tactical nuclear weapons were too destructive in any case to be used as battlefield weapons, and it was reported that Exercise 'Carte Blanche', held in West Germany and north-eastern France in June 1955, in which over three hundred atomic bombs were 'used', had resulted in more than 5 million civilian 'dead and wounded' in a few days. So great had been the damage that it had been necessary to interfere with the 'natural' course of the battle in order to prolong the exercise over the intended time. The British Chiefs of Staff in the spring of 1955 questioned American efforts to distinguish between tactical and strategic nuclear weapons, while Eden and Macmillan agreed that if such a distinction were possible it was most undesirable, and would weaken the effect of the deterrent.[48] Monckton, on 28 February 1956, thought 'graduated deterrence' a dubious policy, especially as the Soviet Union did not include it in its published thinking. In fact the Soviets at this time seemed to be moving towards a strategy in which medium-range nuclear weapons were designed to smash up western defences, and open the way for a rapid advance of mobile air-supported ground forces. Russia showed no interest in the possibility of devising rules for limited nuclear warfare.

British thinking concerning nuclear warfare, as reflected in successive Defence White Papers in the mid-1950s, brought a steady erosion in the expected roles of B.A.O.R. Thus on 1 December 1954 Churchill likened NATO to an alarm system. It should deploy sufficient forces to compel the Russians to make massive reinforcements to their troops in eastern Europe before they might venture upon a major attack. Eden, soon after he had succeeded to the premiership, was to go further, and argue in a private letter to President Eisenhower that the 'primary military function' of NATO 'seems now to be to deal with any local infiltration, to prevent external intimidation and to enable aggression to be identified as such'.[49] By 1956 Britain's army and tactical air forces were being prepared – on paper at least – for 'cold' and 'limited' wars in the main. The 'deterrent' was coming into its own. The desire to reduce the cost of defence policy was a further inducement. The process was also being furthered by good progress against 'terrorists' in both Kenya and Malaya. The ambivalence that had been so prominent in defence policy during the second Churchill ministry was coming to an end.

4 Retrenchment and Suez: 1955–6

The paramount considerations guiding British defence policy in 1955 were the desire to create an effective nuclear capability, the belief that in Europe the Soviet threat might be lessening but that elsewhere – and especially in the Middle East – it might increase, and the conviction that the current defence programme was still beyond the nation's resources. Fortunately only Cyprus was demanding more manpower, and if the NATO commitment remained constant, elsewhere from Austria to Korea reductions were taking place. Technologically the arrival of the thermo-nuclear era promised some savings in the future, if only because preparation for a long war had become superfluous. On the other hand, with air warfare about to move into the supersonic age, and perhaps soon into that of the missile, technological development could add enormous burdens to defence spending.

The May 1955 election was won comfortably by the Conservatives under their new leader, Anthony Eden. With this behind them it was time to grapple with the rapidly deteriorating economic situation. Defence, while not the sole cause, was certainly an impediment to satisfactory economic growth and a healthy balance of payments, and unless further cuts were soon made it would become an even heavier burden. Duncan Sandys had pointed this out in April 1954,[1] and fifteen months later the Minister of Defence, Selwyn Lloyd, spelt out the danger in detail.[2] Despite the cuts made in the 1951 programme, current policies would cause defence spending to rise from £1527 million in 1955, a ceiling set by the Chancellor of the Exchequer for that year, to nearly £2000 million in 1959. Eden agreed that this would be intolerable. By the summer of 1955 the economy was badly overheated. Unemployment was at its lowest since 1945, a balance of payments deficit of about £100 million was threatened, gold and dollar reserves were falling rapidly and there was inflation at home. Defence purchases, which had more than tripled since 1950, were undoubtedly injuring engineering exports, and were also slowing the re-equipment of British industry. About one-quarter of the product of the electronics industry was being bought by the government, a fivefold increase since 1950, although the industry had also managed to expand its exports by more than half. There were about 372,000 service personnel deployed outside the United Kingdom at an annual cost of £150 million, while with the beginning of German rearmament Britain must expect to bear a growing proportion of the Deutsche Mark costs of her forces in Germany. The latter had borne all such costs (about £70 million) hitherto. American and Canadian defence aid, with offshore purchases, would also end soon. In the period 1951–8 this aid and expenditure reached about £565 million. For this, and other reasons, it was essential to secure a large balance of payments surplus in the near future, check inflation at home, and ensure a reasonable rate of economic growth. Resources, especially engineering and manpower, had to be released from defence to aid civilian industry. Industrialists were complaining that National Service was adversely affecting the training of skilled men. A Combined Staff paper, composed in the summer of 1956, was to conclude that Britain had been bearing too heavy a defence burden since 1945, and that this had contributed to the recurrent economic crises. It believed that priority should be given to stabilisation of the economy. The British public took the same view, a Gallup Poll of October 1955 showing that more (32 per cent) favoured defence cuts than any other form of economy. Both *The Economist* and the *Guardian* questioned the assumption of the Defence White Paper of February 1956 that Britain must remain a world power, while Labour speakers repeatedly argued that Britain could not afford both nuclear and balanced conventional forces. The Chancellor of the Exchequer, according to Sir Walter Monckton, was seeking a £300 million cut, though only 'a pale reflection' of this proved possible. Monckton personally would have liked to economise on nuclear spending, but felt unable to do so for want of American co-operation. As it was he found himself involved in some sharp exchanges with Eden and Macmillan over defence costs.[3]

The efforts to cut defence spending in the twelve months or so before the beginning of the Suez crisis can be treated as an entity. Eden attached much importance to the apparent quiescence of the Soviet Union towards Europe,[4] and to the defence cuts – especially in personnel – announced in Moscow in the winter of 1955–6. True, it was also modernising its forces, and showing greater reliance on nuclear weapons. But aggression against the West seemed unlikely, and could only be met in any case by western nuclear power. NATO ground forces would be needed only to handle minor military incidents, and to hold a line long enough for western nuclear power to paralyse the Soviet Union. Furthermore, thermo-nuclear weapons, carried in high-flying jet aircraft and perhaps later in rockets, would prove so destructive in Russian hands that no successful air defence could be envisaged. Preparations for a long struggle to maintain Britain's sea supplies in a third Battle of the Atlantic seemed equally irrelevant. Further economies in British forces might be found in the threat of nuclear power to deter lesser conflicts outside Europe, and so make possible a reduction in conventional forces in those regions. New aircraft in R.A.F. Transport Command should similarly increase the mobility of the Strategic Reserve based normally in the United Kingdom, and so make reductions to overseas garrisons possible. With the first V-bombers entering squadron service in 1955, and with all the extra-European emergencies, save that in Cyprus, seemingly taking turns for the better, the time had arrived to translate the theorising which had begun in 1952 into practice.

A government review of defence policy in the summer of 1955 led to Eden's announcement to the Conservative Party Conference in Bournemouth on 8 October that over the next two and a half years service personnel would fall from 800,000 to 700,000. The call-up of young men for National Service was to be temporarily slowed down, while conscription itself was no longer needed to build up large reserves in anticipation of a global war. Reserves would be primarily for home defence, and the training commitments of most National

Service reservists would be reduced. Eden, privately, was anxious to abolish conscription, but could as yet see no prospect that the nation's commitments would be so reduced as to permit this.[5] An inquiry in 1954 into Regular army recruitment since 1920 had brought the interesting, though discouraging, revelation that, irrespective of pay and other conditions, 180,000 remained the average size of army that could be maintained by volunteer entry alone.[6] The War Office thought 320,000 troops minimal. Further planning in 1956, however, envisaged a gradual reduction to about 445,000 for all service personnel by 1961. This would entail the increased employment of civilians in many administrative and 'tail' duties. Smaller, better-equipped, more mobile and flexible forces were the objective: the end of National Service was evidently only a matter of time. The War Office hoped that more volunteers would be attracted by the prospect of more home service, once the two-divisional Strategic Reserve was in operation. Pay increases worth £67 million in 1956 were intended to stimulate long-service recruitment for all the forces.

Even the R.A.F., the service whose power the government was most anxious to increase, suffered some economies in 1955–6. As expectations arose concerning the performance of the later V-bombers – the Vulcan and Victor – and the new P-1 supersonic fighter, so it was decided to cancel some Valiants and Hunters. Aircraft production in general, which had risen about two and a quarter times since 1950, was expected to fall. Bomber Command would be the least affected, though the introduction of H-bombs in due course would make fewer aircraft necessary. The expectation of a short war and the impossibility of defending the United Kingdom against thermo-nuclear attack – even if confined to bombers – meant that many fewer fighters would be required. Although early-warning radar systems were being continually improved, and Britain agreed to join NATO in a co-ordinated air defence structure, the British air defence aim was increasingly centred upon ensuring the survival of sufficient of the V-bomber force long enough for a devastating strike to be launched against the Soviet Union. By 1956, too, it was hoped that British surface-to-air missiles would soon be sufficiently effective to replace many fighters, while the efficiency of the fighters themselves would be improved by deliveries of Fire-flash air-to-air missiles. Of all British missiles the latter alone had reached the full production stage, though some other production orders were concluded in 1956 for service trials. Indeed, in 1957 the government was to feel that sufficient progress had been made with ground-to-air missiles to justify the cancellation of a Mach 3 successor to the P-1 fighter that was still under development. Similarly, since 1954 Anti-Aircraft Command had been running down in the expectation that the R.A.F. would ultimately take over all aspects of the air defence of Britain with missiles. In 1955 it was agreed that anti-aircraft guns should be provided only for the field army and for port or key installations which might be subjected to other than high-level attack.

Some British missile projects were in fact cancelled in 1955–6, and American substitutes such as the Corporal ground-to-ground rocket, with nuclear warhead, adopted instead. On the other hand, it was announced in 1955 that Britain had made a start on the development of her own ballistic long-range missile, the ill-fated Blue Streak, which was expected to be completed within ten years at a cost of £600 million. Licensing arrangements with the United States were said to have lopped five years and £400 million off the original estimates for this weapon. Rolls-Royce had secured access to details of a large liquid-fuelled rocket engine that was being developed by North American Aviation for the American Atlas missile, and there was also a licensing agreement for British production of an advanced American inertial guidance system using gyroscopes. This American assistance was vital, as Britain had made little progress in this costly new field of military technology before the 1950s. About thirty-five German rocket experts were employed in Britain from 1946, and plans for the Woomera rocket range in Australia date from the same year. Serious research did not begin until 1947, and even then Selwyn Lloyd could claim on 2 March 1955 that spending on missiles had increased one hundredfold since 1949. The first two development contracts had been awarded in 1949, but costs and development times had been grossly underestimated. The utility of most of the first

generation of British rockets was seriously diminished by
their long gestation periods.[7] Thus the navy's Seaslug was
initiated in 1947 at an expected cost of £1·5 million, did not
begin sea trials until 1956, and finally became operational in
the 1960s at a cost of £70 million. Aircraft performance had
greatly improved in the interval.

Yet the missile programmes were often surrounded by a
heady optimism, such as Duncan Sandys's claims in 1952 that
missiles were within 'measurable distance' of the production
stage, and in 1953 that rockets were being developed that
could destroy any atom-bomber. Britain's difficulties were
greatly enhanced by the fact that many of the engineering and
scientific skills required for missile development were new to
her, especially the need to miniaturise electrical equipment,
and for so much exceptionally high-precision work. Printed
circuits, accelerometers and gyros were much in demand, and
many of the latter had at first to be purchased from the
United States. Without her assistance in the 1950s British
missile programmes would have been even more costly and
even more delayed. Even in 1956 the British were not yet
ready to commit themselves wholeheartedly to missiles, and
spoke vaguely about using both fighters and rockets for the
air defence of the United Kingdom for some time to come,
the balance between the two being dependent on circumstances. A start had, however, been made in 1955 to the design
of a new class of very large destroyers that were to mount the
Seaslug, and the following year a guided-missile group was
added to the navy's gunnery centre, H.M.S. *Excellent*.

Another major decision of 1955–6 was to review the future
of the Reserves. Apart from World War veterans, auxiliary
and reserve forces stood at about 650,000 by 1954. For the
fast-moving and mainly nuclear war of the future it was
expected that only highly-trained Reservists would be needed
for service outside Britain. Two only of the twelve Territorial
divisions were now earmarked for service with NATO, and
reductions were also started to the naval and air force reserves
in view of the intended cuts to the Reserve Fleet and to the
front-line strength of the R.A.F., especially Fighter and
Coastal Commands. The Home Guard was reduced to small
cadres that would provide the basis for expansion in an

emergency, but in general it was now the government's aim
to rely as far as possible on better-equipped and better-trained
reserve forces that should be manned as far as possible by
enthusiastic volunteers. It was clearly felt that many of the
National Service Reservists were becoming superfluous, but
that some were still required in the absence of sufficient
volunteer support. Furthermore, many of these Reservists
were being seen less in the context of their former service
skills or roles than as possibly useful supplements to Civil
Defence in the event of nuclear attacks on Britain.

Civil Defence had been thrown into confusion in Britain
once the full power of the H-bomb became widely known in
the summer of 1954.[8] It had, it was claimed, a force equal to
'five hundred Hiroshimas'. Even in the kiloton era the difficulties confronting Civil Defence had seemed enormous. An
exercise in south-west London in 1952 suggested that one
bomb would have caused a ring of fire, three-quarters of a
mile across, which would have left 40,000 houses totally
destroyed or seriously damaged, and another 160,000 damaged
to a lesser degree. With some preliminary warning it was
believed that casualties might have been kept to about 20,000.
Yet each V-2 had killed only an average of 15 persons!
Recruitment in the atomic years had been disappointing,
under half the intended establishment having been reached
by 1952. War-weariness and doubts concerning the utility of
Civil Defence were blamed. It was found that Birmingham,
by January 1951, had attracted barely 2000 volunteers, 80
per cent of whom had served before 1945. The Select Committee on Estimates criticised Civil Defence administration
as extravagant and inefficient, though the Civil Defence Staff
College at Sunningdale, which was modelled on Camberley,
was said to have impressed a visiting American team in 1951
who were studying British methods.[9] Tizard had also spoken
well of the initial scientific and technical work.[10] Organisa-
tionally, however, little progress had been made, since no
proper national administration hierarchy existed, and despite
Home Office and Scottish Office supervision, local authorities
did as little or as much as they pleased. On the other hand,
eleven food convoys had been formed and stationed at
strategic points, while the first experimental Civil Defence

mobile column of servicemen was formed in January 1953. Two hundred of these were planned to reinforce the civil arm in an emergency.

It was against this background that news of the H-bomb exploded in 1954. Coventry City Council promptly disbanded its force on the ground that no defence was possible, a dramatic gesture which it subsequently reversed in July 1955. The Defence White Paper of 1955 admitted that the country faced a problem of enormous magnitude; all the implications could not yet be grasped, especially the threat from radio-active fall-out. The Bikini H-bomb test of March 1954 had spread severe radio-activity over 7000 square miles, scattering some 200 miles down-wind. Where the 20-kiloton bomb at Hiroshima had destroyed four square miles, a 5-megaton bomb would smash nearly 150 square miles. No city could survive, and a dozen such explosions would paralyse Britain. Civil Defence preparations were nevertheless speeded-up from 1955, with special attention being paid to the creation of a Mobile Defence Corps of 33 battalions (by 1959), whose personnel would be drawn from army and air force National Service Reservists, or about 20,000 in all. The commander-in-chief, United Kingdom, was to prepare plans for these forces, which were to be stationed far from obvious targets for their own safety. From 1953 eleven Civil Defence regions, each linked to a 'Central War Room', were being set up. Regional Commissioners were created to take over in case the central government should be destroyed, and Sub-Regional Controllers were added later in thickly-populated areas. They were to be assisted by scientific advisers and the Royal Observer Corps, but co-ordination with local authorities apparently remained poor.

In 1956 the government announced that it would be too expensive to bring shelter and evacuation programmes up to date, since nearly 12 million people would have to be moved, or two and a half times the Second World War figure. Work was started on emergency ports and their equipment; the Post Office began to establish an ultra-high-frequency network to provide communications in an emergency. Extra oil and food were stockpiled; emergency public services, warning and advice systems were prepared, and orders given for fall-out measuring equipment and similar items. The purchase of gas-masks was discontinued at the same time, this form of attack being considered unlikely with the advent of the H-bomb. One hundred million pounds was spent in 1955–7 alone, but government expectations that a publicity campaign would steadily win public support proved disappointing. Apathy and fatalism were spiced with sceptical or derisive comment. Yet for the government to have done nothing would have been criminal negligence; as negligent, for instance, as making no life-saving preparations for the crash of an air-liner. One could not wholly rule out a crisis in which only a few weapons were used. By 1959, apart from the Mobile Defence Columns, Civil Defence volunteers (with the Auxiliary Fire Service and the Special Constabulary) numbered about 600,000. Given the circumstances this was not too bad a result.

Meanwhile thermo-nuclear weapons were obscuring the future of the oldest as well as the newest of Britain's defence forces. Despite the broad generalisations accompanying the Defence White Papers and Navy Estimates of the mid-1950s it was more difficult to define the future roles of the navy than of either of the other two services. Although the R.A.F. could now claim primacy – in 1955 it displaced the army as the most expensive of the services – there could be no doubt of the value of British troops in Europe. Even in a thermo-nuclear holocaust NATO would require some divisions to hold back the Soviet ground forces while the powers hesitated on the brink between suicide or compromise. Troops were needed to control incidents too small to justify nuclear exchanges; they were needed to deter the Soviets from attempting small incursions which they felt would not precipitate nuclear warfare; and they were needed both to help maintain British influence in the deliberations of NATO and to convince European and American allies of Britain's loyalty to the alliance. Similarly outside Europe troops were needed for a wide variety of operations from internal police duties to holding a front in a limited war.

But the navy had always been at the peak of its influence in long wars of attrition, in which the struggle for control of sea communications had been vital to this country, or to the

enemy, or to both. Its importance had similarly hinged upon
the vulnerability of an enemy to blockade or sea-borne attack.
None of these conditions seemed likely to operate to any
extent in a war with the Soviet Union. Time and opportunity
alike would be lacking. Certainly there would be some movement of allied forces and supplies at sea that would require
protection, but the period when this would be feasible or
necessary was uncertain. The Admiralty had made much of
the possibility of a period of 'broken-backed' warfare following the great nuclear exchanges, but reference to this had
been progressively diluted in the Defence White Papers after
1954. Another naval train of thought was outlined by the
Parliamentary and Financial Secretary to the Admiralty on
3 March 1955 when, to justify the maintenance of a strong
offensive carrier force, he cited the expectation of SACEUR
that NATO's airfields would be prime Soviet targets in any
war. Critics of naval spending, especially from the Labour
benches, remained vocal, and the new First Sea Lord, Lord
Louis Mountbatten, agreed on his appointment in April 1955
that the service was in 'a dangerously bloated condition', both
in ships and shore establishments. Many of the ships in
Reserve would not be needed and could not be prepared in
time to use in a nuclear war. Thus began a steady weeding-
out of ships, which more than halved the strength of the
Reserve Fleet in less than a decade.

But it proved less easy to agree on the type of ships that
would be required in the future. Many Britons had been
startled to learn in March 1953 that the Soviet Union had
displaced Britain as the possessor of the world's second navy.[11]
Though Khrushchev, during his visit to London in 1956, was
to debunk the large Russian surface fleet that had been in-
augurated under Stalin, and though NATO possessed an
abundance of warships to contain it, the Admiralty could not
readily abandon its memories of the *Bismarck* and *Tirpitz* in
the Second World War. It also aspired to use its new and
expensive carriers for nuclear air strikes in support of NATO,
and was in fact permitted to order aircraft for such a role.
Only later was it decided that British carriers were too small
to undertake such a task effectively. A long-term building
programme of new destroyers and frigates was also being

undertaken to provide the navy with ships with a wide range of anti-aircraft and anti-submarine capabilities. Three partially-built cruisers were also being completed as an interim step, and hideously expensive they proved to be. Almost their only claim to fame in their original guise lay in the use of the *Tiger* as the meeting-place of the British and Rhodesian prime ministers for their abortive conference in 1966 following the illegal proclamation of its independence by Rhodesia. New submarines were ordered, while a start had been made in 1954 to the study of nuclear propulsion, the same year as the United States launched its first nuclear submarine, the *Nautilus*. A general-purpose fleet thus remained the objective of the Admiralty in the mid-1950s, and though new ships were to join the fleet at a snail's pace, the Admiralty managed to limit cuts in the estimates to only £10 million between 1952 and 1956 compared with the £75 million suffered by the army. In the absence of any very clear view of the future, naval policy was one of all-round, and consequently fairly limited, insurance.

Vice-Admiral Sir Percy Gretton feels that at this time many officers were upholding this policy for the navy more from 'instinct' than with a sense of 'sound logic', though time was in fact to vindicate their claims as it had in the past.[12] Two lines of argument which fitted in increasingly with the maintenance of a largish navy were indeed being developed in the mid-1950s. On the other hand there were those who were already questioning whether war, if it should break out with the Soviet Union, would necessarily take the form of an all-out nuclear exchange, and whether it was not desirable to make preparations to try to fight a limited war in Europe in the hope that saner counsels would prevail in time to prevent escalation to disaster. In the second place, not all were convinced that a second Korean War was impossible, and in that type of conflict the navy had undoubtedly proved its worth with its carriers, its patrolling ships and its support of amphibious operations. The contribution of the navy in limited wars or in support of miscellaneous operations was given considerable prominence in the 1955 Defence White Paper. It was possible to dovetail this naval role into the Strategic Reserve which was being revived from 1954, and to

E

see it as a complement to the improved Transport Command which was also in process of creation. More flexible and mobile, and therefore perhaps more economical extra-European forces were the aim, and though an ambitious jet transport plane, the Vickers-1000, was cancelled at the end of 1955, orders for Britannias and Comets soon followed as not inconsiderable substitutes. But as Suez was to demonstrate in the second half of 1956, this three-service concept was far from realisation, and it required this experience to instil a real sense of urgency and purpose into the defence staffs. Interestingly Sir Walter Monckton as Minister of Defence early in 1956 had decided against the maintenance of a large force of assault craft, because he expected American co-operation in all amphibious operations.[13]

British extra-European strategic thinking was indeed still trying to free itself from traditional concepts and from hasty improvisation under the pressure of events. The great necklace of bases, linked by sea and air, was almost as extensive as ever despite the retreat from Suez in the first half of 1956. Simonstown had been transferred to South Africa by an agreement of 4 July 1955, but Britain and her allies would still be free to use it and other facilities even in a war in which South Africa remained neutral. In 1955–6 Australia and New Zealand agreed with Britain to establish a Commonwealth Strategic Reserve in Malaya and Singapore. This was to include joint planning and other defence bodies. Britain was especially interested in the establishment and security of air bases. It is significant, however, that Australia only agreed to participate after an assurance of American support in case of need, while the 1957 Australian defence programme was to emphasise the difficulty and danger of relying upon Britain for arms in the event of a global war, and to underline the value of the utmost standardisation with American weapons. Australia was rapidly following the lead of Canada, who, as one writer bluntly put it in 1953, 'is in NATO because the United States is in it, not because the United Kingdom is in it'.[14] If some measure of Commonwealth co-operation was possible, much of it was taking place within the broader framework of the global policies of the United States.

There remained one great strategic centre of the world

where Britain was still the key power. This was the Middle
East. The southern half of this zone was still largely isolated
from modern politics. With the settlement of the Iranian oil
crisis in 1954, British forces in the Persian Gulf could return
to their normal duties. Some account had to be taken of the
Buraimi oasis dispute between Saudi-Arabia and the British-
protected Sultan of Muscat and Oman in 1952-5, the British
affording the latter some aid in the recovery of the oasis in
October 1955. The British-officered Oman Scouts had been
formed in 1951 to assist the local British political agent.
Meanwhile Aden, with the neighbouring protectorate, remained a useful stepping-stone to the East, but it was not yet
a major base, and its protection was entrusted to the R.A.F.
Frontier incidents with Yemen and trouble with dissident
tribesmen within the Protectorate were on the increase from
1955. Such problems, even so, were not beyond the competence of the local levies, reinforced by a few British aircraft
and troops, while the Foreign Office remained convinced that
a strong show of force would solve such problems.[15]

Further north it was a different story. Turkey formed part
of NATO, but due east from Kurdistan ran the exposed
frontier of Iran – exposed, that is, save for geographical
obstacles – with a mere 150 miles separating the Russian and
Iraqi frontiers. Another 400 miles or so would take the Soviets
to the head of the Persian Gulf, or to the Mediterranean,
leaving the Turks outflanked. The British treaty with Iraq
was due to expire in 1957; hopes of a Middle Eastern Defence
Organisation with the United States, France, Turkey and
perhaps some members of the Commonwealth had vanished
with the Egyptian refusal to join; and though some American
support was to be expected in the event of a Middle Eastern
crisis, the British government felt it could not simply wait on
events. In any case, a tempting new prospect was opening
before it, with Turkey, Iraq and Iran drawing together,
apparently with the blessing of the United States. This so-
called 'Northern Tier' of states would not only provide a useful military instrument for the security of the region, but it
was also seen as a means whereby Britain might safely
evacuate her bases in Iraq, with the hope of using them in an
emergency, without at the same time giving ultra-nationalist

critics of the Iraqi government an excuse to start an outcry.
Britain could pose as an equal partner in a Middle Eastern
alliance. An international company had solved the Abadan
crisis; an international alliance had failed to win the
Egyptians in 1951, but it might now succeed with the Iraqis.
On 4 April 1955 Britain joined the so-called Baghdad Pact;
Pakistan and Iran followed before the end of the year.

On the face of it this was a wise move. The Iraqi air bases
would facilitate military flights to the East from Cyprus. They
would also enable the R.A.F. to strike at any Soviet forces
that attempted to invade Iran. The Minister of Defence,
Harold Macmillan, told the Commons on 2 March 1955 that
'the power of interdiction upon invading columns by nuclear
weapons gives a new aspect altogether to strategy, both in the
Middle East and in the Far East'. The narrow mountain
defiles of north-western Iran, the railheads and ports on the
Caspian were all seen as excellent targets for British squadrons, and should any Soviet forces survive this gauntlet it was
hoped that sufficient British and local forces could be
assembled to smash them as they broke out on to the plains.
Iraq possessed three divisions and four air squadrons, whose
efficiency could be increased with British assistance. A British
armoured division was scattered between Cyprus, Libya and
Jordan, and this might be concentrated in Iraq. Libya and
Jordan also possessed workshops, supply dumps and further
air bases which could support such an operation, though there
was some regret at the poverty of the local roads and rail
system.[16] Liddell Hart, however, was to cast a sceptical eye
over this planning, and was to question the ability of the
British and Arabs to assemble sufficient strength against a
Soviet push. He agreed that the use of nuclear weapons
against any enemy columns in mountain passes would prove
devastating, but what if the Soviets used their air power to
leapfrog such a danger? The Anglo-American thermo-nuclear
threat to Mother Russia herself seemed to him the crucial
instrument for the defence of the Middle East and its precious
oil.[17]

As it happened the Baghdad Pact was to bring political
rather than military disappointment. President Nasser of
Egypt bitterly criticised it, claiming that it reawakened Arab

fears of Western Imperialism, and that it divided the Arabs themselves. Political analysts, such as Walter Laqueur, have gone further and have argued that the Baghdad Pact acted as much as a stimulant to Soviet involvement in the Middle East as a deterrent. A majority of the Arab press, even in Iraq, was hostile.[18] Arab nationalists and Eastern Communists came together in the autumn of 1955 when the Czech–Egyptian arms deal was concluded, while Jordan speedily became a focus of Anglo-Egyptian rivalry. The strategic importance of Jordan to Britain has already been noted, so that the desire to include her in the Baghdad Pact was almost irresistible. Negotiations in December 1955 led to such internal stresses within Jordan that they had to be dropped. Pro-Nasser forces continued to threaten the stability of the kingdom – so much so that British forces were ready to intervene in January 1956.[19] The temptation to blame Nasser for all anti-British moves was steadily growing in this country, and according to Anthony Nutting it was the dismissal of Glubb Pasha, the British commander of the Arab Legion in Jordan, on 1 March 1956 that sealed Eden's hostility towards the Egyptian leader.[20] Nasser himself was not reluctant to play the part assigned to him – the American diplomat, Robert McClintock, thought him absolutely anti-British back in 1952[21] – and he proclaimed the need to expel the British from all their strategic strong-points in the Arab world. Only then would Arabs be free. Although Nasser was as much a symbol, a mouthpiece, as he was an activist, there developed in the minds of Eden – and some of his colleagues – a dangerous tendency to believe that all Britain's Middle Eastern troubles would be resolved if this dangerous man could be removed. This personalisation of politics owed much to earlier experience of Hitler and Mussolini, but it also reached back to the nineteenth century, and the comparative success achieved by the removal of strong men such as Arabi Pasha of Egypt and the Khalifa in the Sudan in 1898. This unsophisticated, over-simplified view of Middle Eastern politics was to lead to disaster. The general lack of sensitivity in Britain to new movements in the Arab world is, however, well exemplified by the House of Commons response to the announcement that Britain was joining the Baghdad Pact.

It was mainly criticised on the ground that it might endanger Israel![22]

Egyptian nationalisation of the Suez Canal on 26 July 1956 evoked great indignation in Britain. If the passion of many cooled on further reflection, for others in key positions the conviction persisted that inaction could reduce Britain to 'a second Netherlands', that Egyptian closure of the Canal might gravely injure the British economy, and that submission would mean a return to the mistakes of the 1930s. Plans were immediately prepared in the Foreign Office for the overthrow of Nasser, though not for the creation of an alternative régime.[23] The Chiefs of Staff began planning the seizure of the Suez Canal on 27 July, and 'precautionary measures' of a military nature were announced on the 30th. About 20,000 reservists were called up early in August, but neither the plans nor the means existed for an immediate attack on Egypt or the Canal. British defence preparations and planning were directed towards speedy mobilisation for war with the Soviet Union in Europe, and even here intentions outran performance in many respects. Much emphasis had been placed on the Strategic Reserve, and its versatility and mobility since 1954, but the carrying capacity of Transport Command had been little improved since 1950. One of the few positive steps had been the announcement early in 1956 that part of the Strategic Reserve was to consist of an independent infantry brigade which was to be given special training for Malayan and Kenyan-type emergencies. This, it was hoped, would save some two or three months' training of reinforcements after they had reached their destination. But preparations of this sort were clearly irrelevant at this stage of the present crisis.

The Chiefs of Staff's comparison of the active and reserve forces immediately to hand for use against Egypt with the forces at the disposal of the Egyptians persuaded them that a minimum of six weeks of preparation was indispensable. To have maintained forces for immediate use against a state such as Egypt would have been expensive and would have diverted resources from the deterrent, NATO, and Britain's Commonwealth responsibilities.[24] In the past Britain had relied on a combination of military improvisation reinforced by her prestige and reputation in the world to meet the challenge of a state such as Egypt. Time was rarely vital, and Britain had leisurely assembled forces with which to chastise her secondary foes from the Chinese to the Ashanti. Since 1945 the Abadan oil crisis had been smoothed over without the use of force, while incidents with Argentina and Guatemala in 1948 had been swept under the carpet with small shows of strength. But now Britain faced a more serious nationalist challenge in a greatly changed international environment. Her own power was dwarfed by two giants, one of which wished to exploit her embarrassment while the other refused to associate with a policy which contained so many echoes of an imperial past. Since 1945, too, self-conscious, anti-imperialist states had sprung up in Asia, whose sympathy would mostly lie with Egypt. Meanwhile Egypt herself was led by a politician who was fully conscious of these new currents, who himself represented the aspirations of a grow-ing number of Arabs, and who was equipping his armed forces with modern weapons from the Communist bloc. The real defenders of Egypt lay outside her, in the United States especially and in the world at large. But Egyptian arms first forced the British to delay, and prepare in some strength, and secondly persuaded them to undertake a methodical campaign which would give Egypt's friends yet more time in which to come to her rescue.[25]

It was estimated that Egypt possessed about 270 aircraft, of which about half were modern Soviet Mig-15s and Ilyushin-28s. Against these the British had immediately to hand in the Middle East and Cyprus no more than two squadrons of Canberras and the aircraft of one carrier, the performance of the latter being much inferior to that of the Mig-15s. The Egyptian army of about 100,000 was scattered over four main areas, the main concentration being in Sinai against Israel. Much of its equipment was modern, including semi-automatic rifles from Czechoslovakia, whereas British infantrymen would be using Second World War rifles during the landing in November. The main ground threat, however, appeared to come from more than 100 modern Soviet tanks, which the British were unable to counter save with tanks of their own since they possessed no air-portable anti-tank guns to shield airborne forces. In Cyprus the British had twelve battalions of troops who were mostly engaged in anti-terrorist activities; British forces could not be directly launched against the Egyptians from Libya and Jordan for political reasons, and there were only two tank landing ships and ten landing craft with which to stage a sea-borne assault. There were no pilots available who had been trained to fly in troops for an air assault. There were thus insufficient forces with which to attempt a *coup de main*, whatever one's view of the efficiency of the Egyptian army and air force. French sympathy and support for Britain from the start of the crisis were not backed by adequate armed strength, so that the Anglo-French staffs could do no more from 5 August than sit down and prepare for an attack towards the end of September.

It has been argued that any chance of success the attack may have had was wrecked by the slow-moving tactics that were employed, mainly at the behest of the British. To spread the operation over a week gave world opinion too much time in which to crystallise, and to deny Britain and France the fruits of their belated military success. This, as we shall see, is an over-simplification, and it is open to doubt whether any operation, however speedy, could have permanently secured its objective. Nevertheless it is worth inquiring why it took the form it did. Military caution and political tortuousness complemented each other on the British side, provoking much French exasperation and impatience in the process. The political aim to overthrow President Nasser was clear enough, but the problem of a successor had not been resolved. All that could be done was to try to soften the blow as far as possible for the mass of Egyptians by keeping civilian damage and casualties to a minimum in the hope that a viable puppet régime would soon be accepted. This also made it impossible for Britain to collaborate openly with the Israelis, who were to become involved in this operation from September. Such open co-operation would also endanger British relations with the Arab world in general. For political reasons, therefore, the main fleet should not leave Malta until after the start of the Israeli–Egyptian war, and this meant that no sea-borne landing could take place for another six days. The absence of adequate harbours in Cyprus left the allies no option but to use Malta. Acceptance of this six-day gap, however, gave the diplomats ample time in which to move against Britain and France. Indeed, the Israeli–Egyptian war was really over before the landings could take place.

Nevertheless, the British planners do not appear to have been disturbed by these political considerations. They believed that the six-day interval could profitably be used to soften up Egyptian resistance by means of allied air power from Cyprus, and from carriers. Some apparently hoped the aero-psychological attack would suffice, as if the Egyptians were mere Arab tribesmen, susceptible to air-policing by the R.A.F. It was not until 3–4 November – the Israeli–Egyptian war began on 29 October – that the French were able to persuade their ally to agree to a paratroop landing twenty-four hours ahead of the assault from the sea, which was planned for 6 November. Repeatedly, to the French, British planning appeared too cautious and methodical; too much conditioned by memories of Normandy and the skill of Rommel and Rundstedt. Doubtless the British in their turn thought back to the disastrous results of French *élan* in 1914, the spring of 1917, and more recently at Dien Bien Phu in 1954. In any case they, and not the French, could claim to be experts in combined operations and amphibious war, despite the defeats associated with Norway, Dieppe and Dakar. But if the British service chiefs were well content with the six-day pause, they found their task grievously complicated by the hesitations, vacillations and contortions of the politicians. D-Day was changed more than once; the site for the landing was changed from Alexandria to Port Said in September, and the supreme allied commander, General Sir Charles Keightley, was finally given ten hours rather than the expected ten days' warning that he was to begin operations. Political guidance as to the future, once Nasser had been overthrown, was also lacking, though Lord Montgomery surely exaggerated when he claimed in 1962 that 'In my judgement, it was the uncertainty about the political object of our leaders which bedevilled the Suez operation from the beginning.' In truth there were plenty of political–and military–certainties that contributed to the disaster.

British forces finally assembled for this operation totalled 45,000 men, 300 aircraft and about 100 warships. The French provided a further 35,000 men, 200 planes and 30 warships. On the British side only the fighter bombers and warships were collected with any ease. Transport aircraft were in short supply, much chartering from civil airlines being necessary, while those used in direct support of the military operations were not ideally suited to their tasks. Only nineteen tank landing ships could be assembled, seven of them chartered from commercial firms,[26] which limited the tank force to 93 Centurions. Many deficiencies were discovered in the organisation of the Army Reserves. At times the collection and transport of military equipment were reminiscent of the opening phases of most of Britain's earlier wars, and revived memories of the Crimea, Gallipoli, or Norway in 1940. Some Reserve units found themselves overworked or frustrated at every turn, while others were threatened with boredom and loss of morale. In many ways the French were better equipped, both materially and mentally. There was a Second World War look about much British equipment, while even the helicopters which did yeoman work landing Commandos and removing casualties were undertaking roles for which they were not designed. They were also flying from carriers which had not been specially fitted for such tasks.

British involvement in Franco-Israeli planning for war with Egypt, at least from the middle of October, need no longer be doubted. But for Britain the Israeli attack was to serve as an excuse for Anglo-French intervention; not as a means whereby the defeat of Egypt could be hastened. The Israeli attack on 29 October was therefore followed by the Anglo-French ultimatum on the 30th, and allied air attacks began on Egyptian airfields on the evening of the 31st. By 2 November the Egyptian air force had ceased to exist as a fighting unit, but in the interval forty-seven ships had been sunk in the Suez Canal. Much Egyptian, Arab and world opinion was rallying to the support of Nasser. Every British step forward was increasing the indignation of President Eisenhower. There were strikes and riots as far afield as Kuwait and Bahrein: Syria closed the oil pipeline to the Mediterranean. Meanwhile allied military successes continued to mount. Paratroops landed on 5 November, 600 British troops seizing Gamil airfield without much difficulty, and on the following morning the main allied forces streamed ashore from the great Anglo-French armada. Organised resistance soon ended in Port Said, but at 6 p.m. the same day the British Prime Minister announced his readiness to accept a cease-fire at midnight. American financial pressure was almost certainly the main cause of this decision, since Washington refused to agree to give aid to the faltering pound sterling from the International Monetary Fund until a cease-fire had been agreed. A desperate dash by a column of British troops carried them to El Cap, four miles short of Qantara, or nearly one-third of the way along the Canal, before the cease-fire came into effect. Thereafter the Anglo-French forces could do no more than hold the Port Said beach-head until the United Nations Emergency Force took over. There were still 13,500 British troops in Egypt at the beginning of December, and the evacuation was not completed until the 22nd.

The operation cost twenty-two British lives, ninety-six wounded, and eight aircraft. The economic cost, including the overall damage to the economy, is uncertain. A Labour party estimate put the figure as high as £300 million. Certainly the gold and dollar reserves fell by £100 million in November 1956, while the government put the military cost alone at about £35 million. More than $2000 million were needed from various sources before the balance of payments crisis was brought under control. Ironically a prophetic document was said to have been composed by the Joint Planners which forecast with considerable accuracy the roles of both the United States and the United Nations. But Eden and some of his closest colleagues seemed blind to any such warnings, and to those from Washington. Their policy was not based on a cool and detached appraisal of the facts. They were blinded by their fear and dislike of Nasser; they were haunted by the days of their prime – the 1930s – and what they had and had not done in the years of appeasement. Rightly they saw that British influence in the Middle East was threatened, and wrongly believed there was a solution. They wanted prestige and power for their country that were not obtainable. They were living, too, in the days before the buyers' market in oil had developed, and before the construction of the super-tankers that would eliminate the 50 per

cent increase in cost entailed by the use of the Cape route
from the Persian Gulf to Europe.[27] But it was the supposed
threat from Nasser to Britain's overall position in the Middle
East, rather than the specific questions of the Canal or oil,
that mainly motivated them. And here there was no simple
solution. Nasser might conceivably have been removed, but
where was the successor that would willingly have met
Britain's wishes? Britain had been seeking this elusive figure
since 1882. Even had it been possible to seize the Canal this
would at best have restored a situation akin to that of 1951-2,
with a large British – and French – garrison tied to the thank-
less task of guarding 100 miles of canal against terrorist,
guerrilla attacks and perhaps regular attacks. Israel's problems on one side of the Canal from 1967 are worth noting.
Meanwhile, what would have been the state of Britain's relations with the rest of the Arab world? The problems crowd
remorselessly in even if one somehow circumvents the intervention of the United States and the United Nations. Britain
may, in her own eyes, have slain monsters in the nineteenth
century, but she could not prevail against their hydra-headed
successors in the twentieth unless she chose her ground carefully. Not only had she failed at Suez, but the removal of
troops from Cyprus had strengthened the anti-British EOKA
movement there.

If the decisive reasons for Britain's failure at Suez were
economic and political, nevertheless some attempt was made
to learn from the military mistakes and weaknesses. The inadequacy of much of the equipment had been only too
obvious. Transport Command required more long-range aircraft, especially since neutralist sentiment was growing
among Arabs and newly independent states. Overflying with
military aircraft was likely to become more and more restric-
ted. For the operations themselves tactical transport aircraft
which could use small and primitive airfields, had larger and
better load characteristics, and which possessed a superior all-
round performance were badly needed. Military equipment
needed both to be modernised and made air-portable as far
as possible. A new generation of assault ships was required,
backed by ships specifically equipped to operate helicopters
and Marine Commandos. The Strategic Reserve and the

ordinary Reserves alike required drastic overhaul. More thought, energy and resources were needed to bring the art and material of combined operations abreast of the times. But it was also essential to undertake a thorough-going appraisal of world conditions in general, so that some conception might exist of the circumstances in which extra-European operations of this kind might be feasible and useful.[28]

A review of British air routes to the East had already been made necessary by the agreement of July 1956 with Ceylon that Britain should give up her naval and air bases in that country. Some further use of facilities would be permitted, but these could not be the basis for British planning for an emergency. India, on an annual basis, was permitting a limited number of military flights to and from Singapore via Dum Dum, but this too was not enough. With the delivery of the longer-range Britannia to Transport Command it would be possible to by-pass the Indian sub-continent, using island stepping-stones to the East. There was already an Australian air base on the Cocos Islands, and work began in 1957 on an airfield on the island of Gan which lay about 400 miles south-west of Ceylon. Should neutralism make the Middle Eastern air route unusable, Gan and Cocos could easily be linked to the central African alternatives. Yet independent states would be found there too in the near future! If tiny island bases could not give rise to the political complications that had developed in Suez and Cyprus, or which some feared might make Singapore untenable, they were not and could not be bases of the traditional type – only staging-posts.

In 1957 yet another strong-point was to be lost. The Anglo-Jordanian treaty of friendship ended in March and all British troops were withdrawn. The British were also to be disappointed by their defence agreement with the newly independent state of Malaya, which, in October 1957, insisted that the leased bases could be used only in the event of a direct attack on British or Malayan territory. Nuclear weapons were forbidden, but at least the treaty had a paper life of thirty years. The precariousness of the whole edifice of bases was further demonstrated in 1958 when the Iraqi revolution deprived the R.A.F. of Habbaniyah and Shaibah. Meanwhile the truce of March 1957 with EOKA in Cyprus had come to an end in September, and no settlement was yet in prospect on that unhappy island.

It was therefore possible that the political foundations of a new strategy would be eroded as rapidly as it was built up. There was the further problem of re-equipping the forces on the lines necessary to provide them with sufficient mobility, firepower and flexibility. The government, as we have seen, was determined to keep defence costs steady, while from the Labour ranks there came a stream of varied criticism of government policy. Shinwell insisted on 29 February 1956 that Britain could not afford to maintain a deterrent and forces for colonial and limited wars. He advocated conventional cuts, including aircraft and carriers. Others agreed that the government was trying to do too much, only to be weak everywhere. This was true – indeed it was a truism of which the government itself was only too conscious. What it wanted to know – and here the Opposition could only talk vaguely of reduced commitments – was how to implement it. Labour in office from 1964 was to produce no magic solution, and was to be as much the victim of circumstances as its predecessor. In theory Britain might have extinguished her extra-European commitments after Suez, had she been content to put her trust in commercial methods alone to secure her oil supplies, abandon many treaty obligations and risk the instability that might envelop former protégés. In theory she might have abandoned her nuclear pretensions, but, with the V-bombers entering service and the first hydrogen-bomb test approaching, this seemed hardly rational. She might have seriously reduced her NATO commitments, as critics such as the *Manchester Guardian* and some Labour M.P.s desired, but this made the least sense of all. Apart from her interest in the security of Europe, this would have jeopardised her influence with the United States as well as with her European allies. With no real solution in prospect, the government, with Harold Macmillan as Prime Minister in place of the ailing Eden, turned to the well-tried expedient of cuts across the whole spectrum of defence. A new Minister of Defence was appointed in the forceful person of Duncan Sandys, and the seventh review of defence policy was undertaken since the end of the war, less than eleven and a half years ago.

5 The Impact of Duncan Sandys: 1957–62

Duncan Sandys took up his appointment on 13 January 1957 having been specifically instructed to secure 'a substantial reduction in expenditure and manpower' in the armed forces, and having been granted much more formidable powers than any previous Minister of Defence. Eleven weeks of furious activity followed during which many toes were trodden on, both in the service ministries and in NATO. But the final outcome, the 1957 Defence White Paper, published on 4 April, was less revolutionary than many believed it to be at the time. As one informed observer, Sir John Slessor, commented soon afterwards: 'The White Paper introduces no basic revolution in policy, but merely rationalises and . . . explains in admirably intelligible form tendencies which have long been obvious and policies most of which successive British Governments have accepted and urged upon their Allies for some years.' It reached back to the Chiefs of Staff paper in 1952, and beyond that to the thinking of the Air Staff in the later 1940s. Above all it spelt out two well-established principles in British defence policy – the need for economy, and the need to prevent war on a global scale since thermo-nuclear weapons meant that there could be no victors in such a conflict. The novelties lay with the decisions to look to missiles as the main instruments of British air power in the future, to reduce the strength of British ground and air forces with NATO and to end National Service. Even here Sandys's predecessors had been moving towards the same conclusions. The existing policies of smaller reserves, smaller overseas garrisons and more reliance on mobile forces for extra-European responsibilities were intensified.

A stronger Ministry of Defence had long been necessary, partly because so many aspects of modern warfare required an inter-service approach, and in part because service rivalry

pure and simple, without any department that could attempt
an overall appreciation, was hardly the best way to share out
limited resources. Montgomery had been lamenting the weakness of the Ministry of Defence since 1948, and in 1954–5 he
was suggesting that the service ministers should be demoted
to under-secretaries, while the Minister of Defence should
have his own Chief of Staff to act as special adviser over and
above the service chiefs.[1] Macmillan's short spell as Minister
of Defence convinced him that the office possessed responsibility without power, and as Prime Minister he promptly set
out to rectify the deficiency.[2] He was not, however, to be
really satisfied until the radical reforms of 1963–4 had been
implemented.

Towards the end of 1955 the Eden government appointed
a chairman to the Chiefs of Staff Committee, but according to
Duncan Sandys on 28 July 1958 this officer remained 'more or
less isolated with no actual authority and very little influence'.
Parliamentary debates on 28 February–1 March 1956 brought
the charge from Richard Stokes that the Minister of Defence
'has insufficient staff to enable him to take top decisions over
Departmental Ministries and Chiefs of Staff', a point backed
up by Shinwell from personal experience during the Korean
War when he said that he had had to revise the services' rearmament programme by 'rule of thumb'. Although an active
Minister might exploit inter-service disagreements, and
energetically seek advice from many quarters, the rapid turnover in Conservative Ministers of Defence in 1954–7 greatly
lessened such possibilities.[3]

Macmillan, as Prime Minister, believed that a strong
Ministry of Defence was desirable in itself, if real cuts were
to be achieved in defence spending. The Suez operation perhaps opened more minds to the need for change, though the
radical notions of the new minister, Duncan Sandys, also confirmed the opposition of the advocates of the *status quo*.
Sandys was given increased powers from the moment of his
appointment, but some eighteen months of experiment and
discussion – or controversy – were allowed to take place before
the new structure was finally formalised. This settlement was
awaited with considerable apprehension in many quarters,
but the facts proved rather less revolutionary than the

rumours. Even so, the Minister of Defence could now intervene in the affairs of the service ministries as of right – previously it had been dependent upon their consent – though
the latter retained their right to appeal to the Cabinet. The
control of any function common to two or more services could
also pass under his control in the interest of economy and
efficiency, and overall about one-third of defence expenditure
now fell under his direct supervision. Subject to the approval
of the Cabinet and the Defence Committee, the Minister of
Defence was to decide 'all major matters of defence policy
affecting the size, shape, organization and disposition of the
Armed Forces and their weapons and war-like equipment and
supply (including defence research and development)'. He
was similarly 'ministerially responsible to the Prime Minister
for the execution of military operations approved by the
Cabinet or the Defence Committee'. The service ministers
remained responsible for the efficiency and administration of
their own forces.

The Chairman of the Chiefs of Staff Committee was now
elevated to the status of Chief of the Defence Staff, though not
as a supreme military overlord – only the most senior of the
Minister of Defence's advisers. He was to issue all operational
orders, and assume responsibility over the Joint Planning
Staff, but his power and influence were circumscribed in
many ways. The Service Ministers' Committee was replaced
by a Defence Board, chaired by the Minister of Defence,
and on which sat the Chiefs of Staff, the service ministers, the
Minister of Supply (who had been subordinated in some
matters to the Ministry of Defence since June 1955, and who
was to be replaced by the Minister of Aviation from October
1959), the Chief Scientist in the defence organisation and the
Permanent Secretary to the Ministry of Defence. The cen-
tralising tendency was also to be reflected by the appointment,
in the near future, of local supreme commanders for the
various forces stationed in Aden, Singapore and Cyprus. But
in the longer run further doubts were soon developing as to
the adequacy of the powers of the Minister of Defence to over-
ride service rivalries and parochialism. Some sceptics took the
view that institutional change, however radical, would never
succeed without a change of heart in favour of co-operation

within the services themselves. Fortunately the next Chief of the Defence Staff, Lord Mountbatten, had had great wartime experience of inter-service operations. His considerable natural talents were reinforced by royal connections and by not a little political experience. He was thus unusually well placed to pursue novel and unorthodox policies, and his all-round ability and usefulness is clearly demonstrated by his key appointments under three such dissimilar personalities as Churchill, Attlee and Macmillan.

There were other less dramatic but useful reforms. An attempt was made in 1958 to produce a five-year defence plan, complete with detailed financial forecasts. The Plowden Report of 1961[4] on the control of public expenditure concluded that this had yet to result in 'the formation of a definite and approved five-year programme', but it hoped that this would not be long delayed. When the idea of the long-term programme was combined with the growing interest of the early 1960s in new methods to measure and control public expenditure, a situation was being created in which departments could be released from some of the former minute Treasury supervision and control over their spending, and might experience greater stability in the amount of money at their disposal. National economic difficulties were to wreck many of these hopes in the mid-1960s, but the efforts of these years to devise sounder and stabler methods for the financing of defence were to impress many, not only in Britain but in the United States. In some aspects of financial administration, Britain was said in 1958 to be four years ahead of the United States, and was to remain so until the McNamara era in the Pentagon. The abolition of the much-criticised Ministry of Supply was warmly welcomed in 1959, both the army and air force having suffered from its dispersal of interest and its lack of expertise in many items of military equipment. The R.A.F., however, was required to work with the new Ministry of Aviation in the development and supply of new aircraft, and once more the partnership did not prove a happy one.[5]

The Defence White Paper of 4 April 1957[6] was an attempt to put an end to the cautious but expensive policy of recent years, whereby the government had slowly shifted the balance in the armed services more in favour of new weapons and new methods of warfare without making a drastic breach with the past and present. It was not so much revolutionary as dogmatic, finalising where its predecessors had experimented and qualified. It had the certitude of the beliefs of a primitive church – with plenty of hellfire and damnation – compared with earlier Anglican subtleties or ambiguities. Its creed was the primacy of the British economy and the impossibility of fighting a major war with a hope of victory. Conventional forces would still be needed, but their roles and strength were to be more strictly limited than hitherto. The logical rigour of this policy owed much to the new Prime Minister, whose views on defence have already been noted. Sandys was also powerfully supported in favour of the nuclear emphasis by the Chief Scientist, and by government expectations that such a strategy would greatly reduce the burden of defence on the national economy.

Over the last five years defence had absorbed an annual average of 10 per cent of the gross national product.[7] It was hoped to reduce this to 7 per cent by 1962. Two-thirds of British expenditure on research had been devoted to defence. One-eighth of the produce of the metal-using industries had been for defence, a big proportion when it is recalled that these industries also produced about half Britain's exports. The services, directly or indirectly, had absorbed 7 per cent of the nation's manpower: a cut to under 5 per cent was the target for 1961.[8] British forces overseas were adding to balance of payments problems, although West Germany and the United States were to contribute about £78 million to relieve this particular burden in 1957–8. It was widely felt that Britain was trying to produce too many sophisticated weapons, Richard Stokes complaining to Parliament on 28 February 1956 that 166 aircraft projects (civil and military) had been started since 1945, of which 142 had been discontinued, 16 had partly succeeded, and only 8 had been successful – all at a cost of £1000 million. It was grimly noted that Britain spent a higher proportion of her national income on defence than any other European ally in NATO, and had the lowest rate of internal investment. Defence spending per head was nearly five times as high as in Italy, and more than twice as high as in West Germany. In 1957 Britain was devoting nearly $8\frac{1}{2}$

per cent of her gross national product to defence, and only
15 per cent to gross domestic fixed capital formation. West
Germany's percentages were $4\frac{1}{2}$ and 22 respectively. Yet
British expenditure at this level still left little for the re-
equipment of the army, for instance. Much equipment was
of Second World War pattern, or earlier. The government
itself admitted that it was trying to exhaust old arms stocks,
and was not planning to complete the modernisation process
until the early 1960s. Even these old stocks did not provide
a very large margin in reserve.[9] The expectation for much of
the 1950s that tactical nuclear weapons would dominate the
battlefield resulted in total neglect of the artillery, so that
its belated modernisation in the 1960s was dependent on
American guns for calibres larger than 105 mm.

Since no victor could emerge from a thermo-nuclear war,
it was argued that one must aim primarily at the prevention
of global war. The British contribution here was first to
be the 180 V-bombers of Bomber Command, ultimately
equipped with H-bombs, and to be superseded in time by
the British Blue Streak ballistic missile. The Avro-730 supersonic bomber was cancelled. Started as an insurance against
the failure of the missile programme, it was now felt that
when it became operational in ten years' time it would have
been rendered obsolete by offensive and defensive missiles.
This was a sound decision. Its cost would also have been
staggering. As an insurance while Blue Streak was developed,
a stand-off bomb, Blue Steel, was to prolong the credibility
of the V-bombers into the early 1960s. In addition, the Operational Requirements branch of the Air Ministry, with their
eyes on the later 1960s, though sceptical of the long-term
value of most types of manned combat aircraft, still saw the
need for a versatile strike-reconnaissance aircraft to replace
the Canberra. A highly sophisticated plane was envisaged –
although not with swing-wings, a development which was
being left to France and the United States for the time being.
Extra-European responsibilities demanded a thousand-mile
radius of action: for the European theatre a speed twice that
of sound at high level was deemed necessary, plus a near
Mach 1 performance at the lowest possible altitude. Elaborate
avionics would clearly be indispensable, especially for low-

level flight, and for good measure a 600-yard take-off capability was specified. Research and development costs were optimistically put at £90 million, with a production unit cost of £1·5 million.[10]

The government also decided in 1957 that the air defence of Britain was no longer feasible in the thermo-nuclear era, and that large cuts could be made in Fighter Command. The projected Mach 3 fighter was cancelled, the order for current Hunter fighters was cut by 100, and the immediate future was left to the Mach 2 P-1 (Lightning) aircraft. These would be required to intercept such high-performance enemy aircraft as might be employed in a variety of roles in the early stages of the missile era, and it was hoped that they would be able to protect V-bomber bases from attack by hostile aircraft long enough to enable the British deterrent to become airborne. The number of aircraft in Fighter Command was, however, to be drastically cut, and indeed according to Fred Mulley for the government on 16 December 1965 the number of aircraft was cut by seven-eighths over the whole period 1951–64. Additional air defence was to be provided by surface-to-air missiles, and these would progressively take over from manned aircraft.

Now, too, it was felt in Whitehall, was the time to proceed with cuts to British forces in Europe. British defence policy had been pointing in this direction since 1952, and from October 1956 a 'radical review' of NATO had been advocated. The four divisions in B.A.O.R. had thus been menaced long before the arrival of Duncan Sandys. Indeed, these forces were already one-third below strength, with many deficiencies in their equipment, while it was Sandys's predecessor, Antony Head, who had argued before the NATO council on 13 December 1956 that the deterrent and tactical nuclear weapons would make good any reductions in NATO's conventional forces. British approaches early in 1957 for allied consent to cuts in their forces in Europe were not, however, well received. General Norstad (SACEUR) insisted on 5 February that 30 divisions remained the 'strict minimum' target, and recalled that this estimate was based on the 1954 review of the impact of tactical nuclear weapons. Furthermore, NATO planners were now becoming increasingly attracted to the strategy of trying to 'force a pause' with conventional weapons alone against a conventional Soviet attack in the hope that diplomacy might have a better chance of averting catastrophe if the use of tactical nuclear weapons could be postponed.[11] Only the Americans, however, were maintaining forces at full strength in Europe, while the French were beginning to share the British belief that nuclear weapons would prove an effective and economical means of defence. The British felt able to ignore the protests of their allies with an easy conscience, while to critics at home the government retorted that the abandonment of nuclear arms would lead to little increase in conventional strength – given the same amount of defence expenditure. To try to provide for a long conventional war in Europe, always assuming that the Russians would agree to observe the rules, would prove exorbitantly expensive. Sandys argued on 26 February 1958 that such a strategy would add £1000 million to the estimates, and would be meaningful only if the rest of NATO followed suit. Of that there was no sign. The Secretary of State for Air pointed out a day later that for a long conventional war Fighter Command alone, to give but one example, would have to be quadrupled. The balance between nuclear and conventional expenditure over the previous decade was to be interestingly demonstrated by Christopher Soames on 1 March 1960 when he pointed out that of some £13,000 million spent on defence, only £1500 million had been devoted to the deterrent, and no less than £8000 million had been needed for service pay, food and similar running costs. Whatever the theoretical attractions of an increase in emphasis upon conventional weapons and strategy, no British or west European government has yet (1970) shown any serious inclination to move in that direction.

It was announced in April 1957 that over the next twelve months the established strength of B.A.O.R. would fall from 77,000 to 64,000, and a further 9000 would be recalled in 1958–9. Some 220 aircraft, mostly day fighters, were withdrawn from NATO's Second Tactical Air Force, while the light bomber force in Britain – another element in NATO's air power – was also cut. Overall it was intended to halve the number of aircraft for these roles, but to increase their efficacy with small nuclear weapons.[12] B.A.O.R. was to be similarly strengthened, but the first two regiments to receive the American Corporal nuclear missile did not become operational until 1959. Even some who agreed in principle with the Sandys policies questioned the pace at which they were to be implemented.[13] It was pointed out, for instance, that a vast change in artillery doctrine would be necessary, since the Corporal missile was much more than a long-range gun, and indeed had much in common with tactical bombing from the air – though with greatly increased power. Others were disturbed by the prospective loss of so many light bombers and reconnaissance aircraft, especially the latter, and in fact in 1960 a slow-down in the tempo of British withdrawals from the Tactical Air Force was to occur. In 1962 there were still five light bomber squadrons on the continent compared with the maximum of seven in 1956. On the other hand, the refusal of West Germany to assist on a large scale with British foreign exchange costs from 1958 discouraged any second thoughts that might have developed in the Ministry of Defence. After much haggling Germany agreed in May 1958 to pay only £12 million per year over the next three years, or about one-quarter of the expected cost in Deutsche Marks, though there was to be some other temporary and indirect aid. Overall this reduced B.A.O.R. of 1958–9 was expected to cost about £125 million.

Reductions were also to be made to the army outside Europe. For the first time since 1950 the international scene looked auspicious. Britain was able to withdraw her last troops from Korea in 1957. Of the overseas emergencies only that in Cyprus was to pose a serious problem in the future, and in March 1957 a temporary – and misleading – truce was in fact concluded there. Britain promised to contribute two battalions, with some air and sea forces, to the Commonwealth Strategic Reserve in south-east Asia, and would contribute to the external defence of Malaya after independence. The future of Singapore was still uncertain, but it was hoped that, with Kenya, Aden and Cyprus, it would serve as one of Britain's main bases where heavy equipment could be stored in anticipation of emergencies and the consequent arrival of reinforcements. It was believed that, with such concentrations of stores, an enlarged Transport Command would be able to ferry reinforcements at short notice to any crisis area, and that this would make possible large reductions in most British colonial and Commonwealth garrisons. Unfortunately Transport Command lacked long-range cargo-carrying aircraft, though the thirteen Britannias on order would do much to speed the movement of personnel. Overall in 1958 the carrying capacity of Transport Command had only been doubled since its low point in 1950–1.[14] Nevertheless the formation of a Central Reserve of one infantry brigade group, one parachute brigade group and one armoured regiment was to proceed, mainly from the forces recalled from overseas. This combination of garrisons and a Central Reserve was to be supplemented by naval amphibious forces, especially around the shores of the Indian Ocean. Indeed, the Defence White Papers from 1958 were to reveal an eastward shift in the balance of British naval distribution, the main reductions occurring in European waters, the less affected eastern fleet facilitating cuts in military personnel.

The navy suffered less than the other services from the manpower cuts authorised by Sandys.[15] Its personnel was to fall by only 20,000 between 1957 and 1962, a reduction of little more than one-sixth, whereas the army was to lose more than 170,000 or about 45 per cent of its strength, and the air force nearly 80,000 or 35 per cent. Sandys had originally planned to take a further 7000 off the naval establishment, but Admiralty protests finally persuaded him that the army should bear that additional cut. The Minister of Defence proved unrelenting in his determination to pare the navy's anti-submarine capability in the Atlantic and European waters, but it would seem that in the course of 1957 the Admiralty was able increasingly to impress him with the utility of that service East of Suez both on account of its ability to attract recruits and because of the many expensive ships, with plenty of life left in them, that might be profitably employed in that theatre.

An aircraft carrier could easily be spared to form the core of an all-purpose eastern fleet. None of Britain's current carriers was large enough to be really effective in a European strike role, either with conventional or nuclear bombs. To

build larger ones would be prohibitively expensive, while
the United States navy could provide all the ships of this class
that were required. The remaining British carriers could be
employed in an anti-submarine capacity in European waters.
Any carriers used in a strike role East of Suez would be able
to operate the near supersonic Scimitar from 1958. This aircraft could carry a small nuclear bomb, while the introduction
of the steam catapult meant that a carrier could provide the
equivalent of a 3000-yard runway and thereby considerably
increase the load-carrying ability of its aircraft. The eastern
fleet would also include in time a commando carrier,
equipped with helicopters, and able to transport some 600
Royal Marine Commandos. Two small carriers were to be
converted into this type of ship, another attempt to redeploy
existing resources economically. This was a useful expedient,
though in practice the converted ships were to prove expensive to operate in comparison with the forces they could
deploy, and certainly much less cost-effective than some
American ships of this type. The navy's remaining 6-inch
cruisers might also work out their useful lives in support of
the eastern fleet. Smaller supporting craft could easily be
drawn as needed from the main fleet, and the only obvious
deficiency was the absence of modern assault ships. It will be
seen later, however, that the government underestimated
both the number and the quality of the ships that would be
required in the Indian Ocean in the 1960s, and it was also to
prove reluctant to sanction such new ships as this commitment was to demand in the next decade. But at the time it
appeared to be a sensible redeployment of existing forces –
both in terms of manpower and ships which it could be
argued had no obvious role in Europe, but which, East of
Suez, would replace soldiers of an army whose manpower
would be stretched to the limit with the end of National
Service.

If the navy had achieved its most clearly defined role since
the start of the nuclear age, it was less fortunate in Europe.
Its role in total war remained 'somewhat uncertain', though
the 1957 White Paper paid lip-service to the possibility that
control of Atlantic communications might still be necessary
in some circumstances. In practice little expansion of the

active fleet was envisaged in the event of war, and the Reserve Fleet was to retain only such ships as were needed to keep the active fleet up to strength and to provide reliefs for ships being refitted. The personnel in the Royal Fleet Reserve was reduced from 30,000 to 5000. Britain no longer needed a balanced all-purpose fleet in the Atlantic and Mediterranean in view of her membership of NATO, and all but one of the remaining battleships were sent to the scrap-yard. The closing of Scapa Flow had been announced in August 1956, and that of Sheerness, with reductions to the dockyard at Portland, was to follow in 1958. Four of the ten naval air stations were to close. Marsamxett harbour in Malta began to lose its assemblage of miscellaneous naval shipping. Both British and NATO admirals tried hard to defeat this onslaught, and much publicity attended the naval exercise, Sea Watch, in September 1957.[16] Allied vulnerability at sea was emphasised. Keen submariners claimed that they had sunk both the Cunarder *Queens*, though the difficulty of re-creating warlike conditions in peacetime must be stressed here. One estimate, made in 1956, claimed that the allies were twelve times as vulnerable at sea as they had been in 1945.

Soviet interest in the sea was undoubtedly growing, with Marshal Zhukov asserting in 1956 that the oceanic struggle would be more important than in 1939–45. By 1960 the tonnage of the Soviet navy was about twice that of the British, with some 275 long-range submarines constituting the key threat. Many of these were known to have a cruising range of 20,000 miles, with high-speed capabilities, and with crews that were exercising regularly in the Atlantic and the Pacific. This fleet was, however, divided between four oceans and seas, while the Civil Lord of the Admiralty on 7 March 1960 thought that NATO would be able to deploy between 500 and 600 craft in anti-submarine operations.

Naval planners in NATO certainly continued to think in terms of a long Atlantic struggle, and some retired British admirals argued that the Soviet Union might try to use its naval powers to harass allied shipping at a time of international crisis – might perhaps even try to institute a limited blockade – to which the allies could hardly retort with nuclear weapons. Half Britain's food and three-quarters of her raw materials were imported. But the government remained singularly un-impressed by such arguments; Fred Mulley, a defence expert in the Labour party, was to agree later that if NATO were ever to face a major crisis at sea a nuclear response would be inevitable – a fact which must impress and deter Moscow.[17] Certainly the construction of a large escort fleet by Britain and her allies would have made sense only if NATO were also equipped to fight a long conventional war with land and air forces, and if one could feel confident that the Soviet Union would not itself resort to nuclear weapons. The will to prepare in such a fashion was undoubtedly lacking in NATO, while the Soviet Union seemed to be preparing increasingly for a nuclear war, despite the impressive con-ventional forces which she continued to maintain. Economic arguments complemented British strategic predilections, though one must agree that much greater integration and co-ordination of NATO's potential naval strength was needed.

Not a great deal of new building was undertaken for this dual-purpose Royal Navy. Three cruisers[18] and a carrier begun during the Second World War were being completed; other large ships had been or were to be extensively modern-ised. But this would still leave the fleet with only three medium-sized carriers, one new small carrier, and one other. Thirteen strike and/or interceptor squadrons were felt to be sufficient for this force in 1962. It had no supersonic fighters, though a formidable low-level nuclear-strike aircraft was under development for the 1960s. The cruiser fleet would in time wither away to three ships, plans for a new generation of missile cruisers being scrapped in 1957, though a new class of very large missile destroyers would partly fill the gap. Their rockets would be for use against aircraft alone, but a modest gun armament would enable them to attempt some light cruiser roles. Though individually much less formidable and versatile than a missile cruiser, it was felt that five of these would be better value than two larger ships. Even so, at £13–£14 million each they would cost nearly twice as much as a pre-war battleship. An assortment of new frigates was gradually joining the fleet, the cheapest equalling the cost of a pre-war cruiser, and big claims were being made for new anti-submarine equipment, including the use of helicopters.

A development contract was placed in 1958 for a close-range ship-to-air missile, the Seacat. Fast new submarines were in prospect, and a start was being made to the first British nuclear submarine. Radar equipment was being constantly improved, and all told the demands of naval research and development had increased Admiralty personnel in these fields from 1400 in 1938 to 7500 by 1958. The active fleet, however, had sadly diminished by pre-war standards, with three carriers, six cruisers, fifty-five destroyers and frigates, and thirty-two submarines in 1959. Only a little over one-third of naval personnel was actually afloat. Parkinsonian enthusiasts began to note that there were nearly as many admirals as front-line ships in commission. If the navy attracted less criticism than in the mid-1950s, not all were reassured by current planning.

Such, then, were the broad intentions of the Defence White Paper of 1957 – reinforced by its immediate successors. Furthermore, it was concluded that only by this policy of reliance on nuclear weapons and more mobile forces could National Service be abolished in due course, and the strength of the various Reserves reduced. National Service had already been causing some embarrassment in the mid-1950s by producing more men than the forces really needed,[19] and concentrating some 150,000 in training establishments. But to have shortened the period of service would have made it very difficult to meet overseas commitments. The Minister of Labour did refer to the possible use of the ballot on 17 April 1957 should voluntary recruiting fail in the 1960s. As it was, Sandys was prepared to run great risks in order to end conscription. The Hull Committee in 1956 estimated that a minimum of 200,000–220,000 male personnel would be required by the army even with the generous air transport. Sandys, however, took 165,000 as his minimum figure for the early 1960s, a reduction of 200,000 compared with 1957, and a figure dictated by current estimates of the size of army likely to be produced by voluntary recruitment. Seventeen infantry battalions, eight armoured and twenty-one artillery regiments would have to be sacrificed in the process.

There were those who doubted whether so small an army could possibly meet all Britain's commitments. True, more

efficient use of manpower should follow the end of National
Service, and Sandys contended that if the army could reach
180,000 by voluntary recruitment, the forces available for
extra-European operations would fall by only 5,000–10,000
below the 1957 strength of 75,000. It was also intended to raise
the 'teeth–tail' ratio in the army from 58–42 per cent to 65–35.
The critics, however, such as Sandys's predecessor, Antony
Head, came close to seeing their prophecies fulfilled several
times in the early 1960s, when the army was stretched almost
to breaking-point.[20] Contingency plans for the introduction of
selective service existed, but in the end emergency measures
were confined to the retention of 9000 National Servicemen
for six months beyond their intended date of release during
the Berlin Crisis of 1961–2. Gunners and craftsmen, however,
were to find themselves employed as infantry at times in
Cyprus and Aden in the 1960s, and there was to be much
anxious parliamentary discussion as to whether some form
of compulsory service could be avoided.

It was recognised in 1957 that merely to achieve the minimum personnel goals, especially for the army,[21] would not be
easy. More than half of the current volunteer strength of the
army had engaged to serve for only three years. Certain units,
such as the Parachute Regiment and the Tank Corps, could
recruit without difficulty, but less glamorous units, and those
in need of highly-skilled men, faced many problems. All three
services were short of technicians. For these the rewards of
civilian life were normally much higher, without the further
drawbacks of service discipline, separation from families
in some cases, unattractive postings, not to mention premature retirement by civilian standards. The government now
promised better pay, accommodation and married quarters,
and appointed the Grigg Advisory Committee in December
to grapple with long-term problems. Its report, published on
4 November 1958, concluded that if the existing recruiting
trends continued – there had been a marginal improvement
since 1956 – the intended overall strength of 375,000 men in
the three services would be attained by 1963, though some
400,000 civilians would also be needed in various supporting
tasks. Skilled servicemen would remain a problem, while
candidates for commissions in the army and navy continued

to come from too narrow a section of society. Applicants for naval cadetships in 1959 from independent schools outnumbered those from grammar schools by two to one. Sandhurst was far from filling its vacancies in the late 1950s, and the dearth of North of England and grammar school applicants continued. The air force suffered temporarily from doubts as to its future in the missile age until later qualifications made it clear that it would still be flying numerous combat aircraft in the 1960s.[22] Fortunately the navy could promise an exciting future East of Suez – this helped Royal Marine recruitment in particular – though in the mid-1960s this was to recoil on the navy somewhat, when it entailed so much service away from home, with a much higher proportion of time being spent at sea. The continual movement of units of the army's Strategic Reserve was also unpopular, and created many problems for married men. There was to be a general recruiting problem from 1963.

In the short run, however, all seemed to be going well. In 1958 nearly 60 per cent of the navy's men with twelve years of service re-engaged, a proportion that approached pre-war standards, and by 1960 it was even better. Recruiting for the army was so satisfactory that the ceiling for male personnel was raised to 180,000 in 1959. Regular reviews of service pay were promised in 1960.[23] Officers were to be treated roughly the same as comparable grades in the civil service; the pay of other ranks was to be guided by average earnings in manufacturing industry. These large increases were rather more than offset by the manpower cuts, so that by the early 1960s pay represented only 23 per cent of defence costs compared with 25 per cent in the early 1950s. The effort to offer more officers careers up to at least the age of 50 or 55 continued, though this was to be disrupted by further cuts in the size of the services in the later 1960s. Much attention had still to be devoted to the problems of attracting sufficient candidates for commissions in the army and of presenting soldiering as a worth-while career. The War Office approached educational institutions for advice in the hope that both the number and quality of candidates could be improved.

The reduction in manpower was also extended to the Reserves. No future could be envisaged for the reserve air-

crew of either the R.A.F. or the navy in a short thermo-
nuclear war. The R.N.R. and the R.N.V.R. were to be
amalgamated in 1958. The ending of National Service would
mean the ultimate run-down of the National Service element
in the Territorial Army. Its intended war strength was to be
cut from 300,000 to 123,000, and it was to be organised mainly
for home and civil defence responsibilities, though with some
elements for service overseas. Plans for the army Reservists
were finalised in July 1960, and only a few units were to be
specially trained and equipped to act as reinforcements for
B.A.O.R., and for overseas operations in general. Overall,
service Reserves were reduced from 3.5 million to 650,000
by an Act of Parliament in 1958. The Home Guard was
finally disbanded in July 1957. Such were the massive cuts
in defence personnel that were precipitated by the Sandys
White Paper of 1957. In the first year of its operation alone
(1957-8). it was claimed that defence spending had been cut
by nearly £225 million.

   This policy was forced through despite the objections of
all three services.[24] The air force protested against the idea
that missiles would, in the foreseeable future, replace both
the long-range bomber and the fighter interceptor. The army
opposed so savage a cut in its numbers. The navy objected to
the disparagement of its anti-submarine role. It would seem,
however, that just sufficient was conceded to the R.A.F. and
navy to avert resignations in that quarter, while the Chief of
the Imperial General Staff was said to have decided against
an isolated protest. All three services clearly accepted the new
policy with major reservations. A battle, not the campaign,
had been lost, and circumstances might yet come to their
rescue. The Air Staff did not abandon its belief that the
manned bomber had a future for many years to come; the
Admiralty worked assiduously and discreetly to secure a more
generous building programme, while from various sources
came the cry that the army was being starved of both
men and equipment. Rumours were also circulating of
the acrimonious atmosphere that existed between Sandys
and his service advisers. Sandys was later to describe his
tenure of the Ministry of Defence as 'very trying'; he complained of a lack of co-operation from the services, though

he and Mountbatten established a working relationship. Mountbatten himself thought this one of the most difficult periods in his life.[25]

Meanwhile a public debate was beginning to develop concerning the wisdom and morality of the pre-eminent place given to thermo-nuclear weapons in British defence policy.[26] Hitherto any nuclear controversy had been muted, with both front benches in agreement concerning the British need for such weapons. Attlee had argued in 1952 that they were needed to decrease British dependence on the United States. On 2 March 1955 he had agreed with Churchill that only the deterrent could provide Britain with the international power and influence that was rightly hers, at a cost she could afford. In 1957 John Strachey and Aneurin Bevan had spoken respectively of the danger of Britain being reduced to the level of an American 'satellite', and of British negotiators being asked to walk 'naked' into the conference chamber without such weapons. Even Philip Noel-Baker, doyen of the British advocates of disarmament, thought unilateral British nuclear disarmament would be a meaningless gesture. The government argued on parallel lines, adding in 1955 the need for British nuclear weapons to neutralise enemy targets that constituted particular threats to the nation's security, but which might not be given the same priority by the Americans. Sandys added a new dimension on 16 April 1957 with his warning that nuclear weapons would be needed by a European power in anticipation of the time when intercontinental missiles might diminish the readiness of the Americans to risk nuclear war in defence of Europe. Reginald Paget went as far on 15 March 1959 as to insist that, should NATO collapse, the British deterrent would re-create the English Channel. While this could hardly be noised abroad by the government itself, it was arguable that possession of nuclear weapons by Britain, so long as a European war had not degenerated into a nuclear holocaust, might reduce the danger of major enemy strikes against her territory, although much of western Europe might suffer severe damage at the same time. In contrast to these speculative advantages, Britain's nuclear strength certainly earned for her a relaxation of the McMahon Act in 1958, and the resultant development of the Anglo-American nuclear partnership was to reduce greatly the cost of the deterrent in the 1960s.

The dawn of the thermo-nuclear era undoubtedly spread much alarm and despondency. Churchill, despite his rolling assertion that safety might become 'the sturdy child of terror, and survival the twin brother of annihilation', also spoke out strongly against nuclear tests, and there was widespread interest in disarmament and better relations with the Soviet Union. But of those who regretted the decision to manufacture the H-bomb only Sir Richard Acland left the Labour party in protest, and the question failed to arouse much interest in the 1955 general election. Nevertheless the Labour party continued to be riven by debate over foreign and defence policies. While the Labour front bench merely persisted in its opposition to tests and accused the government of undue reliance on the deterrent as explained in the 1957 White Paper, a cacophony of dissident voices was to be heard in the background. The Liberal party also opposed the separate manufacture of H-bombs by Britain. From 1957, and more particularly from the first months of 1958, various organisations and individuals began to make strong protests against the British deterrent, and the Campaign for Nuclear Disarmament(C.N.D.) was born. Its leading members included the philosopher Bertrand Russell, Canon L. J. Collins of St Paul's Cathedral, the scientific journalist, Ritchie Calder, novelist J. B. Priestley, and Michael Foot, editor of the Left-wing journal, *Tribune*. The first of the famous fifty-mile Aldermaston marches took place over the Easter week-end in April 1958, Aldermaston being the Atomic Weapons Research Establishment in Berkshire, and over 5000 were present when the march ended on 7 April. Soon afterwards 618 scientists and many academics urged the government to seek further talks with the Soviet Union to bring nuclear tests to an end. The same year saw the publication of Sir Stephen King-Hall's interesting plea for non-violent resistance as Britain's only defence against the Soviet Union. Better this than the reduction of the country to 'a smoking radio-active charnel-house'. In 1959 the distinguished British mathematician and student of war, Professor Blackett, urged that Britain should become the founder of a non-nuclear club.[27]

C.N.D. flourished, and its annual marches reached their climax on 18 April 1960. The Labour party was being thrown into confusion over the issue – it was both a cause of and an occasion for dissension – and in the autumn of that year both the Trades Union Congress and the Labour Party Conference voted in favour of unilateral nuclear disarmament.

The Labour leadership had already been forced to modify its position of the late 1950s. Ambivalence was to be detected in its statements as early as 1958, though by and large it had preferred to concentrate its attack upon the government's undue reliance on nuclear weapons, and to plead for the end of nuclear tests. In June 1959 there appeared a joint Labour–T.U.C. statement in favour of a British renunciation of nuclear arms should all nations save the United States and Russia agree to do the same. This was unlikely, and Hugh Gaitskell's true position was made clear in a speech of 1 March 1960 when he argued that Britain required the deterrent in case the United States should fail to act in defence of Europe in certain circumstances. Forty-three Labour members openly opposed him on this score, while opinion polls suggested that between one-quarter and one-third of the population apparently opposed the continued manufacture of British H-bombs. A major reconsideration of Labour policy was facilitated by the cancellation of Blue Streak, which appeared to place the viability of a British deterrent in doubt. A joint Labour–T.U.C. statement recommended in June 1960 that the deterrent should become the sole responsibility of the United States and that Britain should concentrate, as Richard Crossman had long been arguing, on conventional arms. It was asserted that the British contribution to NATO could be increased without resort to conscription (here public opinion polls demonstrated the unpopularity of its renewal without a shadow of doubt) by cutting outdated overseas commitments. Labour came to argue for a B.A.O.R. of 77,000 troops – its old strength – with modern equipment. This new approach to defence regained the support of the Trades Union Congress and the Labour Party Conference for the leadership in 1961, the latter arguing fiercely against any withdrawal from NATO, as some of the extreme critics of the deterrent were also advocating. C.N.D. was by now losing ground, partly as a result of its own inner divisions, the extremism of some of its supporters and the public reaction to the bullying tactics used by Khrushchev over Berlin. There had, in any case, always been a strange mixture of motives inspiring the movement. In many ways it had been a protest, especially of the young, against current society. Frank Parkin also described the Aldermaston march as 'a yearly catharsis for the middle-class conscience'.

Criticism of the deterrent, however, was not confined to C.N.D. or the Labour party. On 11 March 1959 a former C.I.G.S., Field-Marshal Lord Harding, was to oppose a separate British nuclear force. Peter Thorneycroft, shortly after his resignation as Chancellor of the Exchequer, in January 1958, told an audience in Newport that Britain should not try to duplicate the American deterrent: a British nuclear force was 'a questionable policy . . . Our prestige will be rated not by the bombs we make nor by the money we can spend, but by the contribution we can make to Western solvency and economic strength.' Antony Head, Nigel Birch and later Aubrey Jones among Conservatives, and several of the quality press, all thought there was too much emphasis on nuclear weapons. Montgomery now argued that to reply to a Soviet conventional attack with nuclear weapons would be 'national suicide'. This, nevertheless, remained government and NATO policy. Britain's most distinguished military theorist, Liddell Hart, favoured the abandonment of the British deterrent, if proliferation could thereby be avoided, while a leading military historian, Michael Howard, believed in 1959 that the nation was following a strategic doctrine which, 'judged by other than fiscal considerations, is of highly debatable value'.[28] He agreed with Americans, such as Henry Kissinger and Hubert Humphrey, that Britain was grasping at the shadow and not the substance of power with her nuclear policy. The latter would not increase her influence with the United States, and she would be saddled with a virtually unusable weapon. Later an American student of British post-war defence policy was to conclude of this era: 'Britain's doctrines seemed to imply a deliberate courtship of suicide.' Howard averred that Britain could do more for western security by the maintenance of strong forces for limited war and miscellaneous operations outside Europe. He wrote: 'It may well be the minor campaigns fought by the British Army during the nineteenth century whose study will yield the most useful results to strategists of the future.'[29] But even here, as we have already seen, many dangers lurked, not the least being the total transformation of the political and consequently the military environment outside Europe since the nineteenth century. The small wars of the past could be as deceptive a guide as current British doctrine concerning the deterrent. Meanwhile an important step towards the more systematic study of nuclear questions outside government circles had been taken in 1957–8, when a meeting in Brighton in January 1957 to discuss the implications of Russo–American nuclear parity had led in November 1958 to the formation of the Institute for Strategic Studies, with its headquarters in London.

The basic principles of the 1957 Defence White Paper were to remain unquestioned by the government until about 1962–3, though several changes of detail were to occur in the interval. Although from 1963 the Conservatives were to place great emphasis upon the 'independent' deterrent, they were also to take a few steps towards its close integration in NATO. More striking about this time was to be the growth of doubts concerning the utility of tactical nuclear weapons in the defence of western Europe, while in 1962 it was admitted that Aden and Singapore might in time become unsuitable, for political reasons, for their current role as Britain's main bases East of Suez. The break in British defence policy around 1962–3 must not be over-emphasised, but it will be convenient to review the fortunes of Sandys's policies down to that date.

With respect to the deterrent, the main feature of these years was the close Anglo-American co-operation.[30] This was a paradoxical sequel to the crisis in their relations occasioned by Suez, and to the growing fear that the Soviet nuclear threat to the United States might make the latter less willing to defend western Europe. Britain's first H-bomb test took place in May 1957, and she had high hopes that a successful thermo-nuclear programme would lead to closer collaboration with the United States. American assistance with Britain's missile programme was already saving much expenditure. The announcement of the H-bomb programme had been well received in the American press in 1955, and the new Macmillan government was determined to make good Anglo-American relations the basis of its foreign policy. Eisenhower and Macmillan were old friends: the former rated the British far above America's other allies. Soviet technological advances provided material justification for such sentiments, and the Americans were soon prepared to proceed beyond the existing levels of nuclear co-operation. Impressed by Soviet thermonuclear and long-range bomber progress in the mid-1950s, shaken by the launching of the first Russian earth satellite or Sputnik on 4 October 1957, and with their own missile programme clearly lagging, the Americans believed that close co-operation with the British would be to their advantage. There might even be some financial savings. Washington also believed that through co-operation their control over British nuclear forces would be increased, and they sought to integrate the latter as far as possible into their own deterrent. This is understandable, but circumstances were undoubtedly helping to give the British a favoured position.

As early as January 1957 the United States suggested that a number of intermediate-range ballistic missiles (Thors) be deployed in Britain, under joint Anglo-American control, but operated by R.A.F. personnel. As Soviet claims concerning their intercontinental ballistic missiles grew, so the Americans sought to enhance the credibility of the western deterrent by the interim deployment of I.R.B.M.s in Europe. But apart from Britain, only Turkey – and later Italy – responded favourably. An Anglo-American agreement to station sixty Thors in Britain was negotiated in 1957–8. A year later, in 1959, when Franco-American relations were deteriorating, France demanded the removal of 200 American fighter-bombers, equipped with tactical nuclear weapons, from her soil. Most of them were moved to Britain. In 1960–1 Anglo-American co-operation was further extended by their agreement to work together in two new warning systems against Soviet missiles, BMEWS and MIDAS, the former including the establishment of a large radar station at Fylingdales in Yorkshire. This system was expected to give the United States fifteen minutes' warning of a missile attack. Britain might receive as little as four minutes, but in that awesome interval it was claimed that V-bombers on special alert could be flown off to retaliate. In November 1960 Britain permitted the Americans to station a depot ship in the Holy Loch, near Glasgow, from which nuclear submarines equipped with Polaris missiles were to operate. Since the range of the Polaris missile was only about 1250 miles at this time, these facilities in western Scotland greatly reduced the passage time of submarines from their base to the zone of operations.

The above agreements were to the advantage of Britain as well as the United States, with the possible exception of the Thor rockets. These were vulnerable, slow-reacting liquid-fuelled missiles, which many feared would be unusable – a danger rather than an asset to the West. If the Soviet Union were to resort to nuclear weapons first, the Thors might be destroyed before they could be fired. Their very vulnerability might give rise to Soviet fears that they would be fired near or at the outset of a major war, and this might tempt them to strike first. In other words, they might both increase the danger of nuclear war and the danger to Britain in a time of crisis. At best they were interim weapons, designed to help deter the Soviet Union in a rather primitive fashion and to complicate Russian targeting problems until something better could be put in their place. From this point of view the arrival of the Polaris submarines was a great step forward, since these, normally hidden in the depths of the ocean, were invulnerable in the early 1960s, and could hold back their missiles until it was clear that Doomsday had arrived.

More particular advantages were gained by Britain from the American decision to revise the McMahon Act in 1958, so that all types of nuclear information could be supplied to any ally who had made substantial progress in that field. As early as 1956 the United States had been supplying information on various military power reactors, especially for use in submarines, and in 1958–9 they agreed to sell a Westinghouse submarine atomic reactor of a type already used in the American *Skipjack* class, which was greatly to hasten the construction of the British nuclear submarine, H.M.S. *Dreadnought*.

More dramatic was the agreement of Washington in June 1960 to sell 100 Skybolt stand-off bombs to Britain, following the decision of the latter that it was no longer expedient to proceed with its own cherished long-range missile programme. The ballistic missile in question, Blue Streak, was already indebted to the United States, where expenditure on rocket technology was thirty or forty times as great, as in Britain. Sandys, as Minister of Supply, had been promised American aid from June 1954, and the Blue Streak rocket motor was in fact based on the American Atlas liquid-fuelled missile, Rolls-Royce manufacturing it under licence. In 1959 the American Secretary of Defence, Thomas Gates, had considered the sale of Polaris missiles to allies who were prepared to assign them to NATO. Duncan Sandys explained to Parliament in the defence debates of 25–6 February that Blue Streak would have a longer range, would carry a larger warhead, and would be capable of greater development. In this respect he certainly underestimated the potential of Polaris, whose range was soon to double to 2500 miles. On the British side in 1959 there was also the attraction of building their own rocket, whatever its debt to American technology. It would have some civil potential, as well as the promise of greater military independence than, say, Polaris. The Royal Navy was in fact closely following the development of the latter missile, but the Civil Lord of the Admiralty pointed out on 9 March 1959 that any British move in that direction would entail a radical recasting of the naval estimates. Sandys himself doubted if Britain could develop a Polaris-type submarine before the 1970s. The future of another American project, the long-range stand-off bomb, Skybolt, that was to be launched from aircraft, was also in doubt, and Sandys claimed that he was advised by Washington in September 1958 to continue Blue Streak for the time being as an insurance. Government statements in 1959–60 certainly leave the impression that to some extent they were waiting on events, and were continuing with Blue Streak as the best available option pending the outcome of American work on Polaris and Skybolt.

At the same time the existence of a strong school of thought in Britain in favour of Blue Streak is quite evident. Labour

tended to regard Sandys himself as its main champion, but
the Minister of Supply, Aubrey Jones, was another avowed
supporter, as was Sir Frederick Brundrett, chief scientific
adviser to the Ministry of Defence until the end of 1959, and
who was deeply involved in the project from the start.
Remarks by Jones, Brundrett, and by Sir Arthur Vere
Harvey, all show that there was a serious clash of opinion
between the rocket enthusiasts and those who wished to
retain manned bombers, equipped with stand-off bombs.[31]
The Air Staff had also been remarkably frank in their struggle
to retain a manned strategic deterrent, notably at the 'Prospect Conference' for the press on 6 May 1958.[32] The Assistant
Chief of the Air Staff, Air Vice-Marshal Kyle, who had a
special responsibility for operational requirements, argued
emphatically that Britain would need another generation of
manned strategic weapons. This would not necessarily entail
a super-bomber, but an airborne launcher of stand-off bombs
that could strike from outside an enemy's defensive peri-
meter. A military version of the VC-10 was apparently one
of the possibilities that the Air Staff had in mind, though
they were also in quest of a delivery vehicle that was not
dependent on vulnerable airfields. George Brown claimed on
27 April 1960 that the hostility of service chiefs to Blue
Streak, with its vulnerable fixed firing-sites, was such that
they

> spoke in public, against all our traditions, taking that risk
> in order to get round the Ministers whom they could not
> persuade in private. There was virtually nobody in the
> Service Departments at that time who was not taking the
> trouble to tell anybody about it who would listen. I have
> minuted notes of receptions and conversations in which
> leading Service men made only the reservation, 'Do not
> quote me.'

Certainly Harold Watkinson, who succeeded Sandys as
Minister of Defence, admitted that expert examination of
the future of Blue Streak in November 1959 had resulted in
only a 'narrowly balanced' decision in favour of its continuance.

Critics of Blue Streak had been appearing from 1958.

George Brown was vaguely critical on 26 February of British development of a 1500-mile missile, if serious development of stand-off bombs was proceeding in the United States. There were several pleas for a British Polaris programme, while Geoffrey de Freitas insisted that the nation must seek solid-fuelled missiles, either for installation underground, or in submarines. Critics became more numerous in 1959, and were joined by the newly-established Institute for Strategic Studies. Not surprisingly, therefore, many thought that when Blue Streak was finally cancelled in April 1960 the decision had been taken up to two years too late. The government tried to defend itself by arguing that Blue Streak had been an insurance policy, pending the development of an American alternative that the British would be permitted to use, and certainly it was only in February 1960 that a firm American decision was taken to develop Skybolt. British objections to Polaris have already been noted, though these were to prove even more short-sighted. The government also came to recognise early in 1960 that whatever decisions were taken in the United States, Blue Streak was doomed by reason of the growing accuracy of Soviet missiles. Watkinson conceded on 29 February 1960 that Soviet missiles were experiencing a margin of error of a mere one and a half miles over ranges of up to 6500 miles. Blue Streaks, being liquid-fuelled, could not be fired at short notice – and a four-minute warning might be the limit – nor could their launching sites hope to survive a missile attack. Blue Streaks, like the Thors, would therefore be usable only as first or pre-emptive strike weapons, whereas V-bombers, equipped with Skybolt, would still be viable second-strike – and therefore less provocative – weapons for some years to come. This latter combination would also be much cheaper than Blue Streak, whose final cost was expected to be in the region of £600 million, nearly £100 million of which had already been spent. As a further insurance in 1960 the Admiralty was to make 'an urgent study' of the requirements for a British Polaris programme, but for the immediate future the V-bomber–Skybolt combination was to provide the British deterrent. This would exploit an existing asset – the £500 million V-bomber force – while the agreement of June 1960 to purchase 100 Skybolts from the United States was expected to prove much cheaper than any Polaris purchases. Labour and other critics of the government in April 1960 were bitter and sweeping, but the latter was able to save face up to a point by the current expectation that the British deterrent could be prolonged through the 1960s at a more than bearable cost to the taxpayer.

Nevertheless there were those who argued that the cancellation of Blue Streak meant the end of Britain as an independent nuclear and rocket power. This line of argument overlooks the existing British debt to the United States for help with that missile. But certainly the Skybolt agreement included clauses binding Britain to joint consultation with the United States before this weapon was used, and carrying further the integration of Bomber Command with the Strategic Air Command. There was also the further problem – would the United States carry the Skybolt programme through to completion? Sir Solly Zuckerman, Chief Scientific Adviser to the government, was among those who doubted whether the government had made the right choice in June 1960.[33]

Meanwhile another aspect of British defence policy was coming under increasing fire. This was the reduction of B.A.O.R. to barely 50,000 by the end of the 1950s, although the strength agreed with NATO was 55,000. Even that was considered too small. The growing reliance of B.A.O.R. on tactical nuclear weapons was similarly being attacked, and there were further complaints of its lack of mobility and the inadequacy of some of its equipment. Exercises, war games, and actual weapon tests were convincing more and more experts that tactical nuclear weapons were too destructive to use on the heavily urbanised Central Front, and if used would cause such casualties that even a defending army would require large numbers of troops. Tactical nuclear weapons would not save manpower in the manner expected. Zuckerman himself adopted this line of argument,[34] but the army chiefs responded slowly and reluctantly. Corporal missiles had become operational with the army in Germany only in 1959. Given B.A.O.R.'s weakness in men and some forms of equipment their attitude is not surprising. Might they not also have felt that the government, by its policies since 1957, had left them with no option? Most of their allies in NATO, despite much new thinking at SHAPE, were doing little or nothing to strengthen their conventional forces. If there were 'serious deficiencies' in B.A.O.R., an American observer admitted that the French were still less co-operative, providing only two out of a nominal contribution of ten divisions to NATO.[35] West Germany had contributed seven out of a promised twelve, and the forces of the Low Countries had also fallen below expectations. B.A.O.R. at 60 per cent strength no longer looked so bad, especially with its formidable array of tanks. The military could also plead the difficulty of preparing simultaneously for conventional and atomic warfare, and at this time published Soviet military doctrine gave them no reason other than to expect a war in Europe to be an all-out struggle with nuclear weapons used from the outset.

Nevertheless criticism of this view – that early use of nuclear weapons against a major conventional Soviet attack was inevitable – was mounting, notably in the United States, but also in Britain.[36] In 1960 Liddell Hart produced his *Deterrent or Defence*. In this he pleaded: 'There is urgent need for a better kind of deterrent that does not impale us on the horns of the dilemma: "Suicide or Surrender".' He argued that the Soviet Union could not pour troops into central Europe on the massive scale so often suggested. Given the danger of nuclear escalation he thought that the Soviets would attempt nothing more than 'a sudden pounce of a limited kind', using at the most forty divisions. To counter such a threat NATO required, not its present assortment of divisions and tactical nuclear weapons, but forces of high quality and mobility. Twenty-six Regular divisions, or twenty such divisions reinforced by about ten good West German militia divisions, should suffice to contain such a threat. NATO lacked quality rather than quantity, and in particular it required more professional volunteer soldiers and fewer conscripted men. Alastair Buchan was also developing a similar line of argument. A variety of views – all critical of undue reliance on nuclear weapons – was presented by the Army League, *The Times* and *The Economist*, the Labour party, and even Conservatives such as Antony Head and Aubrey Jones. But the plea of Labour, for instance, that

NATO should deploy sufficient conventional forces so that it would not be forced to use nuclear weapons before an attacker did so, was not very realistically backed up by the suggestion that B.A.O.R. should be restored to its former strength of four divisions. These would have been a mere gesture without large increases by other NATO states, while for Britain it would have been an expensive – indeed an impossible – gesture without recourse to conscription, unless most of Britain's extra-European commitments were abandoned. Quite apart from the problem of increased foreign exchange costs the additional troops would have had little meaning without equipment, and the deficiencies of B.A.O.R. at its current level have already been noted.

Further pressure in favour of increased conventional forces was soon coming from the United States, once the Eisenhower administration had given place to that of John F. Kennedy, with Robert McNamara as his Secretary of Defence. On 10 April 1961 Kennedy told the NATO Military Committee that the alliance 'needs to be able to respond to any conventional attack with conventional resistance which will be effective at least long enough . . . to force a pause'. This was not a new idea within NATO. SHAPE and Norstad had been thinking on these lines since 1956–7. Norstad had referred in November 1957 to the value of an option, 'more useful than the simple choice between all or nothing'. But fifteen months later he had been obliged to admit that NATO was still dependent on nuclear weapons, even in limited war or in any 'significant situation'. Now, however, he had a President who was ready to make a radical departure, and who was encouraged to do so by the mounting crisis with the Soviet Union over Berlin. 1961 was to be the year of the Berlin 'Wall', and was to see the despatch of two extra American divisions to Europe. But a Washington appeal to London for two brigades was to fall on deaf ears, and Britain found it necessary to hold back about 9200 of the last of her National Servicemen in 1961–2 in order to meet her commitments – the Kuwait crisis also occurring in June–July 1961.

Meanwhile the British Minister of Defence, Harold Watkinson, had shown himself unsympathetic to the new American thinking at the Western European Union Assembly

on 1 June 1961. Indeed, his room for manœuvre was limited,
since Britain was in the grip of an economic crisis that
summer, and the Chancellor of the Exchequer was insisting
that the nation could not afford the foreign exchange costs of
B.A.O.R. at even its current strength. Overall Britain's commitment to NATO was costing her some £80 million in
foreign exchange, and in July she appealed to her allies for
relief. The West German contribution was in due course to
be stepped up from £12 million to about £50 million, but it
was doubtless the financial situation which helped discourage
the Prime Minister's initial inclination to call up reserves
and place B.A.O.R. on a war footing. American interest in
larger stocks and reserves for a war of more than thirty days
was also not reciprocated. B.A.O.R. in 1961 remained committed to its current bases, which were too far back from the
frontier to make a firm, forward defence easily practicable,
and to the strategy of a fighting retreat covered by generous
use of tactical nuclear weapons. Anthony Verrier departed
from Exercise 'Spearpoint' at the end of 1961 dismayed by the
apparent addiction of the British to the almost automatic use
of nuclear rockets. The Director-General of Military Training protested that Verrier was reading too much into the
exercise, which was intended to give officers training against
all eventualities, and was not designed to prove or disprove
any special tactical theories. Verrier remained unconvinced
and unrepentant, and he was not alone in his view.[37] A correspondent of *The Economist*, on 29 October 1960, had
reported B.A.O.R.'s enthusiasm for tactical nuclear weapons,
and their desire to use them at the outset of a major
emergency.

British thinking, however, was at last on the move, if not
very eagerly or swiftly. American pressure won acceptance
of the 'pause' concept in theory before the end of 1961. The
1962 Defence White Paper[38] was somewhat equivocal, talking
simultaneously of the need for an adequate B.A.O.R., the
need to respect balance of payments problems, and of the impossibility of a major war remaining a conventional conflict
for any length of time. There was, as we shall see, a great deal
of emphasis on Britain's extra-European responsibilities, but
it was claimed that the Strategic Reserve in Britain could also

be deployed in Europe. The training of B.A.O.R. from 1962 began to take account of NATO's hopes of forcing a 'pause' in the event of war with Russia,[39] and Peter Thorneycroft was to explain to Parliament on 3 March 1965 how Britain had joined with NATO in the *study* of 'variable options' from 1964. But Britain still thought American insistence on supplies for a ninety-day war excessive; thirty days would be more than enough. Both Peter Thorneycroft, and Denis Healey after him, left Parliament in no doubt as to their expectation that any major conventional collision must soon become nuclear. Indeed, Healey was to tell the Commons on 4 March 1970 that he had been advised by his first Chief of the Defence Staff, Lord Mountbatten, whom he had inherited from the Conservatives, that the only final answer to a 'deliberate major attack was strategic nuclear retaliation . . .'. The forces of NATO were designed to contribute to the overall deterrent by stopping small attacks, and by forcing the enemy to mount a major attack if they wished to make any serious move against the West. In addition, 'to deter minor incursions I was told that NATO needed sufficient tactical nuclear weapons so as to make the risk of escalation a real one. . . . I was told strongly that tactical nuclear weapons could not be used to fight and win a war or defend an area in the classical sense, like a sort of superior artillery. Their role was to strengthen the credibility of the deterrent.'

The British continued to believe that nuclear weapons would have to be used in a war at a much earlier stage than did the Americans. Meanwhile the Army Reserves Act of March 1962 was intended to improve the flexibility and efficiency of the heterogeneous reserve forces, with the particular aim of providing a speedily mobilisable force of up to 60,000 men. As Thorneycroft, the latest of the many Conservative Ministers of Defence, was to claim on 17 September 1962, 'we could pretty well double . . . [the strength of B.A.O.R.] in a matter of days'. Reinforcements, however, would be sent out individually or in small units, the last two T.A. divisions no longer being earmarked for NATO from 1961.

The Reserve problem, indeed, had yet to be solved. The War Office complained early in 1965 that there were still ten different types of reservists, costing about £24 million and all governed by different rules, and that only the small Territorial Army Emergency Reserve (the 'Ever-Readies') of 6000 men was speedily available. These could be called out for up to six months' service without a proclamation, but the remainder of the Reserves lacked modern equipment and did not provide that flexibility or efficiency that would be demanded almost immediately in the event of a conventional conflict in Europe. Nor could B.A.O.R. always look to the Strategic Reserve in Britain for relief. By the summer of 1964 extra-European commitments had reduced it below the brigade group strength which was intended to serve as the very minimum reinforcement for B.A.O.R. Finally the Defence White Paper of 1962 had eliminated any hope that British forces would be significantly strengthened with its insistence that not more than 7 per cent of the gross national product should be devoted to defence. Thus the beginning of the retreat from the almost automatic use of nuclear weapons in 1962 was to take place without any change to existing force levels, and to the accompaniment of a relatively slow rate of re-equipment. Fortunately the army could expect more air support than had once seemed likely, now that Britain's contribution to the tactical air power of NATO was to be cut less drastically than had originally been planned. The Sandys policy in Europe was definitely becoming blurred at the edges.

Meanwhile doubt was being cast on the 1957 calculation that much reliance could still be placed on fixed bases to support Britain's Far and Middle Eastern interests, despite the growing emphasis on mobile reserves and amphibious forces.[40] Sandys thought about 70,000 troops would be needed for the Strategic Reserve and extra-European role. At first all had seemed to go well, with the unhappy crisis in Cyprus finally being resolved in February 1959. True, in the second half of 1958 no less than 25,000 British troops had been hard put to control the situation. Finally, at the cost of 104 servicemen's lives, it was agreed that Britain should retain sovereign rights in two areas of the island alone, with such other rights as were needed to maintain the effectiveness of her bases, which were to be used mainly to provide air support (including

nuclear bombs) for CENTO (lately the Baghdad Pact) and
NATO's southern flank. A garrison of about 5000–6000 was
planned for normal times, though with facilities for about
20,000 in an emergency. Malayan independence had been
accompanied by the defence agreement of 12 October 1957,
which permitted the stationing of Commonwealth forces in
that country, while Article VII provided for co-operation in
the defence of Malayan and British territories in the Far East.
The 1959 defence agreement with self-governing Singapore
also embraced Britain's responsibilities under SEATO. Singapore's importance was further enhanced by its possession of
the only dry-dock between Japan and Sydney large enough to
hold an aircraft carrier. More than 10 per cent of the island
was being used by British forces for various purposes, including the storage of heavy equipment. Not surprisingly Sandys
described this island as 'the pivot of our military situation in
the Far East'.[41] Gan served as an air-staging post between it
and Aden, while Kota Belud in North Borneo was being
developed as a jungle training area. Among economies were
the closing of Hong Kong dockyard as too small and vulnerable, and the halving of the Malta dockyard personnel to
3000. Political reasons had removed the British from Jordan
and Iraq in 1957–8, and Aden was now being built up in
compensation. The army had taken over responsibility for
the security of Aden and the Protectorate in April 1957, and
a steady build-up had followed. Given the possibility that a
Middle Eastern crisis would find Cyprus and Aden with no
direct means of communication, the latter was being developed into a fully-fledged base, as well as an air-staging post
to the Far East. For the same reason a battalion of the Strategic
Reserve was sent to Kenya, and there was a further reinforcement following the Congolese disorders from 1960. An expensive building programme was needed in both Kenya and
Aden, War Office works expenditure increasing eight- or
ten-fold in 1958–61. The Templer barracks at Kawaha,
Kenya, alone cost £3.5 million, with their accommodation
for up to three battalions. But as Kenya moved towards
independence it was clear that their utility would be
short-lived.

Many circumstances therefore combined to increase British

interest in Aden from 1957. It was variously called 'a stepping-stone' to the East, or 'a spring-board' for the defence of the Middle East and of local British oil interests. But it would not be long before 'quagmire' would prove the best simile. Admittedly, down to the late 1950s tribal incidents within the protected states of the hinterland and frontier disputes with the Yemenis had, like incidents in Muscat and Oman on the Persian Gulf, suggested a nineteenth- rather than a twentieth-century political environment. Nevertheless there were already those who believed that even this remote region of the world could not long be insulated from the upsurge of Afro-Asian nationalism. Above all the radio knew no boundaries, and could speedily revolutionise the political thinking of its listeners. As early as 23 January 1957 a *Times* correspondent thought that only a rearguard action was possible in the area, while in 1958 the Governor of Aden himself, Sir William Luce, warned London that the region was likely to become politically untenable within ten years.[42] Two students of strategy in 1959, one a Briton[43] and the other an American,[44] variously described British strategy in general with respect to bases in the East as 'increasingly precarious', and as vague and short-sighted. The American thought the British too steeped in past history and past methods; too little disposed to weigh current resources against possible hostile pressures in the near future. In fact, however, with the loss of the bases in Iraq, Britain was intensifying her build-up of strength in Aden, and was apparently banking on a twenty-year stay at least. Soviet military aid to the Yemen was disturbing, and it seemed vital to ensure that Aden, one of the world's main bunkering ports and commanding the southern approaches to the Red Sea, should not fall into hostile hands. The ability of Egypt, the Yemen and Iraq to withstand Soviet influence was in doubt.

Of course the American alternative of a leased base was not yet feasible in Aden, and would only have been feasible with the emergence of a politician and party with the ability and local influence of Lee Kuan Yew and his supporters in Singapore. Imitation of the almost self-sufficient American carrier and amphibious forces would have been prohibitively expensive, so that Britain's freedom of choice was virtually non-existent given the government's belief that a Middle Eastern presence was vital.

When Aden was added to the Federation of South Arabia in 1963, Britain insisted on her right to create sovereign bases if necessary, with ultimate responsibility for defence and internal security. About £8 million was being spent on Aden as a long-term base between 1962 and 1966, although an element of ambiguity was creeping into British policy with the Chancellor of the Exchequer's announcement on 25 July 1961 that a thorough review of British defence policy had been launched, which would embrace the possibility of a cut in the nation's world commitments. The Minister of Defence himself, on 5 March 1962, admitted that it would be unwise in the long run to place too much reliance on Aden and Singapore as bases. Various islands in the Indian Ocean were now being examined as potential substitutes, but for the moment the executants of policy appeared in no doubt as to the immediate relevance of Aden. In contrast articles were appearing in *The Times* which described such bases as 'wasting assets', while Liddell Hart had argued in 1960 that they were no more than 'crumbling sand castles', and that Britain could best protect her interest in Middle Eastern oil by taking up the 'detached role of "the good customer" '.[45] The 'East of Suez' debate was beginning.

In the meantime, however, Britain's armed forces had enjoyed no small success in their extra-European role since the Suez fiasco. An interesting, if minor, episode occurred in 1957. On 19 July the Imam of Oman revolted against the Sultan of Muscat, who promptly requested British aid. Three companies of Cameronians were flown in from Kenya, while Venom fighters from Sharjah, Shackletons and some transport aircraft lent support. The British troops acted in support of the Sultan's own forces and the British-officered Trucial Oman Scouts, but it was left to the R.A.F. to soften up any serious opposition. The most notable resistance occurred on 10 August when the rebels tried to hold a line in front of the village of Nizwa, but this was soon smashed. In general the rebels were flushed from villages by Shackletons dropping fragmentation bombs after forty-eight hours' warning by leaflets. Venoms shot up the rebels, their forts and villages with rockets and cannon, while other planes air-lifted supplies into the inhospitable terrain of north-eastern Muscat. Off the coast naval frigates patrolled to stop further arms smuggling. The rebellion was crushed by 12 August, though in January 1959 further British aid was required against the rebel stronghold on the 9000-feet Jebel Akhdar. Rebels were also becoming more active in the Aden Protectorate from December 1956 to February 1957, and again from December 1957 until May 1958. Yemeni aid was increasing, the Yemenis themselves being allied with Egypt and receiving arms from Russia. The fighting at times became fairly serious, the relief of Fort Affarir in the Jebel Jihaf hill country in April 1958 involving action against 600 men.

In July 1958 a military coup overthrew Britain's allies in Iraq, and it was feared that King Hussein of Jordan would be the next victim. The usually stable state of the Lebanon was also in turmoil. But in this crisis Britain could count on the support of the United States, so that when London agreed on 16 July to respond to Hussein's appeal for help it encountered none of the problems of 1956. American support helped to persuade the Israelis to grant overflying rights to British aircraft proceeding from Cyprus to Jordan. An American 'air-lift' provided oil from Bahrein for British forces in Jordan at a time when the closing of the frontiers of neighbouring Arab states were creating logistic difficulties.[46] Meanwhile 37 British aircraft moved 1500 troops, 120 vehicles and 111 trailers, and 150 short tons of fuel and stores from Cyprus to Amman in twenty-four hours. In all, two parachute battalions were flown in, while the navy had brought the 1st Battalion, the Cameronians, from Kenya to Aqaba by 7 August. A brigade was flown from Britain to Cyprus to act as a strategic reserve. These forces had sufficiently stabilised the situation for a withdrawal to become possible at the end of October.

The events of 1958, however, had indicated that Transport Command was still too small for Britain's needs, while the revolution in Iraq was lengthening the space between the stepping-stones on the air route to the East. Aircraft now had to fly via Malta, Nicosia, Turkey and Iran to Bahrein, or from Malta via El Adem in Libya, Khartoum and Aden. Fortunately Britannias were to join the Command in 1959, and by the end of that year its capacity had increased to about 150 million passenger-nautical miles compared with an average of 50 million or so in the early 1950s. Long-range air freighters were not ordered until 1959, the ten Belfasts having an expected capacity of about 35 tons each, which could include armoured cars, helicopters and guided missiles. The supply of more air-portable equipment to the army would further increase their value, but many of these expected increments would be lost should Afro-Arab hostility become such that the Middle Eastern and central African air routes proved unusable, and a diversion via Ascension Island and Salisbury to Aden became necessary.[47] Nor was the Estimates Committee as late as 1963 convinced that the R.A.F. was giving sufficient attention to Transport Command. Only two of the ten types of aircraft in service were truly modern, despite the purchase of 316 planes since 1953 at a cost of £145 million, 87 of these being for the strategic role. Fortunately, at sea, Britain's forces East of Suez were strengthened by the commissioning of the first of the converted commando carriers in 1959.

The biggest test of the 'new look' forces to date was to occur in June–July 1961. The newly-independent state of Kuwait appealed for British aid against a threat to its independence from neighbouring Iraq.[48] The British embassy in Baghdad reported a number of ominous military movements. In the first two weeks of July some 6000 British troops, with stores and equipment, arrived in Kuwait, mostly by air. Two squadrons of Hunter fighters and some Canberra bombers also appeared in the Gulf. V-bombers were ready to operate from Malta, while the navy contributed a commando ship and later a fleet carrier, as well as smaller ships. Just how impressive and effective a demonstration of force was this? To begin with, the British may not have been entirely unprepared for this eventuality, and they were certainly not averse to making a show of force in the Gulf. George Wigg claimed on 23 November 1962 that he had 'direct evidence' of anticipatory plans and preparations. Certainly the commando carrier, *Bulwark*, was very conveniently placed at Karachi for a speedy move, though she was unsupported by frigates and small craft. The political conditions were also right, with Saudi-Arabia disputing the Iraqi claim to Kuwait, and with President Nasser also quietly disapproving. The Suez Canal was thus open to British warships: there were no over-flying problems. If Arab feeling was generally cool towards Britain, there was no question of support for Iraq.

These political advantages were important in that some observers were not convinced that the British military position was as strong as it appeared, even against an opponent such as Iraq. Certainly it could be argued that there were important lessons to be learned. The operation was assisted by the existence of many important facilities in Kuwait itself, and by the fact that other British bases were not too far distant. The actual forces sent had a rather heterogeneous appearance about them. The tanks arrived in obsolete landing ships, and were not abundantly supplied with ammunition. Deficiencies in artillery and anti-tank equipment were also reported. There was too little air-portable equipment. Almost the whole of Transport Command had been involved, and half the Strategic Reserve had had to be sent to the Middle East. The acclimatisation of troops had also been a problem, though troops would not often be required to operate in a temperature of 115° F. As one brigadier put it: 'They were living, working and digging in the red-hot wind – burning, hot, stinging sand.' There was a great deal of heat exhaustion, and much had to be learned concerning operations in such conditions.[49] It was an operation on which the services could look back with some satisfaction if not with complacency. It was certainly an operation worthy of the closest study – from the political as well as the military point of view.

There existed many temptations in 1962 for the government and services to survey with some pride their achievements in limited and policing operations outside Europe since 1950. Earlier, Britain had been unable to avoid heavy loss of life among Indians and Pakistanis with the grant of independence, and had failed to control the situation in Palestine. But since 1950 Suez had been the only disaster, even if in Cyprus several tragic years had elapsed before sound sense had been able to prevail. In contrast, in both

Malaya and Kenya military action had helped to create a suitable environment for constructive political action, while it had been able to protect British interests in many parts of the Middle East – outside Egypt – at only moderate cost. Although the greater part of Britain's colonial empire had been given independence by 1962, many dangers and much turbulence were still anticipated. The anarchy in the Congo had been a fearful warning. Harold Macmillan had spoken of the 'Wind of Change', but should it rise to hurricane strength there were many in Britain who hoped that small but efficient forces might successfully 'seed' and at least moderate the storm. In the Middle East they pointed to the threat from President Nasser and his admirers, with their outspoken determination to expel British political and military influence, and their supposed threat to British oil interests. Malaya and Singapore could hardly be described as stable, and racial conflict in the region was much feared. Less clear, but possibly the gravest threat of all according to Kennedy and Macmillan when they met at Nassau in 1962, was that from Communist China, with her teeming millions, and her revolutionary creed. Not surprisingly there were many who saw Britain's main military role in the 1960s moving increasingly from Europe to the East. Denis Healey, in 1969,[50] was to speak of a crucial paper produced by the Chiefs of Staff in 1962 which, if it failed to predict the precise crises that were to arise in the next few years, at least foresaw with 'uncanny precision' the nature of the joint operations that would be undertaken outside Europe. Montgomery, for one, was most emphatic on this point, and he spoke of the army becoming more and more a marine force, working with joint service mobile task forces, and finding profitable occupation outside Europe where the nuclear deadlock prevailed. Such a vision even began to infect many in the Labour party, especially after the death of Gaitskell in 1963.[51] But all this would cost money, as well as the ability to retain suitable bases. And one of the most disturbing facts of the early 1960s was the degree of re-equipment required by all three services, but especially in terms of cost by the navy and air force, if they were to carry out this extra-European role effectively. Already the estimates for the TSR-2 were escalating; a successor to the Hunter and many new transport aircraft and helicopters were also required. The navy needed new carriers and new assault ships to maintain one or perhaps two amphibious task forces. Guided missile ships were at last being completed, but more were required. By the early 1960s it was becoming only too clear that the East of Suez role could not be upheld indefinitely with essentially Second World War or Korean rearmament equipment.[52]

6 Illusions of Grandeur: 1962–6

The average life expectancy of each defence review since 1945 had been a mere two and a half years. This was far too short, given a usual gestation period for each new weapon of from two to four times that figure. But things were to get worse, not better, in the mid-1960s, with doubts and dissensions developing at almost every level of British defence policy, with strategy, fundamental weapons and administrative methods all being thrown into the melting pot. Denis Healey, Labour's talented Minister of Defence from 1964, declared that he had inherited 'a runaway train' from the Conservatives, but in the next three years, despite several sudden applications of the brakes, the train was not brought under control. Finally it was hopefully diverted on to a new line altogether from January 1968. Recurrent economic crises and internal Labour divisions were ostensibly responsible for this erratic progress, but more fundamental was the accumulation of past mistakes, misconceptions and misfortunes whose implications could no longer be avoided. Many observers were becoming persuaded that the post-war policy of piecemeal adjustments to meet Britain's changing position in the world was no longer enough, and that even so drastic a transformation of policy as had occurred in 1957 had been less radical than it appeared on the surface.[1] Britain, after 1957, was still trying to remain a nuclear and world military power, based on limited resources for which the welfare state and private consumption at home, and various overseas interests, were also competing. No proper priorities for arms procurement existed – merely a hotchpotch of individual service requirements that had received the government's blessing. According to one estimate made in 1967, if all the programmes of the late 1950s had been allowed to continue, 'it could have amounted to an over-commitment of double the Research and Development funds available during the early 1960s'.[2]

As the last chapter set out to show, various qualifications had been creeping in since 1957 to blur and alter the character of defence policy as set out in that year. Thus, on 8 March 1961, Julian Amery expected no further cuts in R.A.F. aircrew over the next decade. The downward trend in the number of aircraft was to be halted – and even briefly reversed in 1962. It was also becoming evident in the early 1960s that the financial savings to be secured from the policy decisions of 1957 were at an end, and that henceforward defence spending must either rise or policy be changed yet again.[3] Since 1952 the services' share of the gross national product had fallen sharply, contributing in no small measure to government tax-cuts, and helping to make possible considerable increases in personal consumption despite the nation's sluggish economic growth. By the early 1960s such bonuses had been exhausted. Indeed, some questioned the adequacy of the manpower levels within which the government had chosen to operate. Certainly the nation was to be hard put to find all the manpower she required to meet her many commitments. More savings had been achieved at the expense of the re-equipment of several important arms of the services, and by 1962–3 it was clear that this must come to an end, especially if Britain's reluctant admission that less reliance should be placed in nuclear weapons for western defence was to be taken at all seriously.

Some small savings were still being implemented in 1962. The run-down in manpower with the ending of National Service was not quite complete. Cyprus was losing much of its British garrison now that it was to be used mainly by the R.A.F., and by personnel running the NATO early-warning and radar installations. Gibraltar and Malta were to provide no more than forward operational facilities for the air force and navy, the ships of the Mediterranean Fleet becoming interchangeable with those in the Home Fleet, and using British ports for their main repairs. Air-staging facilities were being retained in Libya, and a small military force was also to stay there, but in general the early 1960s witnessed a marked fall in British interests in the Mediterranean theatre.

If necessary it could be reinforced from Britain. Over-flying problems, however, necessitated a physical presence East of Suez, though the emergence of independent states in East Africa was leading to a British evacuation from there too. Westward, the small British garrisons were quitting Jamaica and Trinidad as those islands became independent. Some strengthening of the Strategic Reserve was envisaged (to about 15,000 men), while hopes of stability in the East were reflected in the government's intention to cut the Gurkhas from 14,000 to 10,000. Furthermore, with an eye to the more distant future various Indian Ocean islands were being studied as potential bases in case Aden and Singapore should prove untenable.

Conservative estimates of the strength needed East of Suez were soon to be rudely upset by the concurrent challenges of Arab and Indonesian nationalists, the one in the Protectorate of Southern Arabia, and the other in Borneo.[4] As if this were not sufficient, clashes between Greek and Turkish Cypriots required the despatch of some British troops to that island, so that in 1964, with the army 5 per cent below its intended establishment, the Strategic Reserve was fully committed, B.A.O.R. was below strength and possibly threatened with further cuts to meet these emergencies. There was renewed talked among some Conservatives of a revival of National Service. The government had certainly prepared contingency plans for selective service. These unexpected calls had added heavily to the foreign exchange costs of the services deployed overseas. Between 1956 and 1964 these had more than doubled to £250 million, about two-thirds of this sum being expended outside Europe. Building programmes to improve accommodation for Regulars and their families in Kenya, Aden and Singapore had helped to inflate costs. There was also an improbable British promise early in 1964 to raise B.A.O.R. from its current strength of 51,350 to about 55,000. The situation in Germany was further complicated by the unsatisfactory working of the 1962 Deutsche Mark agreement. Fortunately, after much hard bargaining, a revised and extended agreement was forthcoming in June 1965 whereby West Germany agreed to pay about two-thirds of Britain's foreign exchange costs in Germany from 1964 to 1967. Some

American aid was also provided. Nevertheless the overall increase in these costs was alarming, especially in view of the catastrophic balance of payments crisis that was developing from 1964.

But even without these emergencies Britain had reached the point by 1962–3 when either her commitments in the world had to be cut or her defence spending sharply increased. If a plateau in manpower had been reached, service pay would still have to rise both to counter inflation and to offset the rapid growth of civilian wages and salaries. Nor could the remorseless advance of weapon technology be ignored, although the British government had no intention of supplying forces of the quantity and quality envisaged by the Americans for their dream strategy of 'flexible response'. If one British battalion had been assigned to the Allied Command Europe (ACE) Mobility Force in 1961, new orders for helicopters and cross-country supply vehicles fell short of the scale needed to revolutionise the mobility of B.A.O.R. Fortunately the mid-1960s were to see the arrival of the formidable new Chieftain tanks, the Abbot self-propelled 105-mm. guns, armoured infantry-carriers and Stalwart cross-country vehicles, mortar-locating radar and much other radio and electronic equipment, a variety of rockets and other arms. Naturally there was a bill to be met, the Defence White Paper of 1965 estimating that the cost of an armoured regiment would double between 1963 and 1968 (in real prices alone); that of an artillery regiment would treble, and that of an infantry battalion would increase sixfold! Pride in the new Chieftain tank was tempered by doubts as to whether Britain would be able to afford a successor. At least General Lord Bourne could note in 1966[5] that for the first time for many years British artillery and infantry need no longer feel that much of their equipment was inferior to that of the enemy and some of their allies – much of it being purchased from the latter.

The needs of the air force and navy had also to be considered, and here, in contrast to the army, a great deal of the new equipment had not advanced beyond the design stage. Work was, of course, proceeding steadily on the TSR-2, though it has been argued that Treasury parsimony was slowing its progress unnecessarily. Its cost mushroomed re-morselessly, and there were cancellation rumours in the early 1960s. The supersonic Lightning, and Mark II versions of the Vulcan and Victor, were entering service, together with some aircraft for Transport Command.[6] Nevertheless some frightening gaps were beginning to develop, mainly as a result of the 1957 decision that the future lay with missiles rather than manned warplanes. Two British missiles (in addition to Blue Streak) were in fact cancelled in the early 1960s when it was recognised that no foreign sales, unlike those for the Bristol-Ferranti Bloodhound, would be forthcoming and that the cost of such weapons for Britain's own forces alone would be prohibitive. With tactical nuclear weapons declining in favour, more accurate and discriminating delivery systems than rockets would be required, and so there was renewed interest in tactical strike aircraft. A successor to the Hunter was clearly needed before the end of the decade, and the Air Staff's insistence on a supersonic capability ruled out – for the time being – the one aircraft that might quickly and cheaply have met their needs at least in part by the late 1960s – the trans-sonic, vertical take-off and landing (V.T.O.L.) Hawker P-1127. Hence the start of the supersonic P-1154 project, which – in the interests of economy – the government hoped would also be purchased by the navy. Unfortunately the navy was mainly interested in an interceptor, whereas the R.A.F. was most anxious to find a close-support successor to the Hunter. The P-1154 was therefore to be developed for the R.A.F. alone from 1963, but was now unlikely to be operational before the 1970s, while £375 million was soon being mentioned as its possible cost. Coastal Command would be in need of a new long-range aircraft before the end of the decade, while at the beginning of 1962 it was calculated that two-thirds of the R.A.F.'s 120 transport aircraft would require replacement before the 1970s. The Belfast strategic freighter, and various civil designs, such as the VC-10, would fill some roles, but a versatile tactical aircraft, with short landing and take-off (S.T.O.L.) capabilities, was badly needed, and to meet this need the Hawker-Siddeley 681 was ordered in 1964. But this was only at the development stage, and could hardly be ready before the 1970s. It too would cost a lot of money.

Yet another increase in defence costs had to be faced in the winter of 1962-3. This arose from the American decision to cancel the Skybolt missile which the British had been hoping since 1960 would greatly prolong the life of the V-bombers, and so increase the return on that considerable investment. Anglo-American relations had become increasingly intimate in the last years of Eisenhower's presidency, and the British position had seemed assured as a junior partner of the United States in the provision of the western nuclear deterrent. The cost of the British deterrent was greatly reduced by American assistance – the latter bearing the research and development costs of the next generation of delivery vehicles. This really was too good to last, as a new American administration under John F. Kennedy, with a human computer – Robert McNamara – at the Defence Department quickly demonstrated. Kennedy and McNamara initiated a much more complex and sophisticated approach to defence questions.[7] They wished to strengthen the western deterrent, but they believed also that it should be used more flexibly. This implied not only more nuclear power, but also more conventional power and more centralised control of western nuclear forces. Nuclear weapons could not be used selectively in a major conflict unless Washington monopolised control. Logically, too, if the United States were to spend more on nuclear forces, the European states should concentrate on conventional strength. Public criticism by McNamara in June 1962 of European nuclear forces brought protests from Britain. Washington replied that the Secretary's remarks did not apply to Britain since her nuclear force was not being operated independently. Nevertheless the British government remained fearful that the United States would try to subordinate the British deterrent still more to Washington, or end it altogether. The 'independent' deterrent was cherished by many Conservatives, and no government could lightly ignore this feeling, especially when the 'Super-Mac' image of the Prime Minister was becoming somewhat tarnished.

The American decision to cancel Skybolt was taken on grounds of cost-effectiveness – the rigorous test that McNamara had hopefully introduced into all aspects of American defence policy.[8] Technical difficulties, escalating costs and the success-

ful development of more attractive missiles were all endangering Skybolt. The solid-fuelled Minuteman and Polaris
missiles represented an important breakthrough. They could
be fired at short notice: they could be rendered almost invulnerable on land or at sea, and their use could therefore
be delayed – if desired – until an enemy's determination to
risk all in a nuclear holocaust had been demonstrated beyond
doubt. This second-strike capability cancelled out the one
possible advantage of Skybolt over earlier (and vulnerable)
missiles – its launching aircraft could be recalled at a late
stage in a sortie. Otherwise Skybolt would share the vulnerability of its launching aircraft on the ground; its slower speed
would render it more vulnerable to anti-missile missiles than
ballistic missiles. Finally Skybolt would lack the payload and
accuracy of the bomber. From the American point of view it
appeared the least attractive of the possible weapon systems
of the 1960s. British needs, however, were less sophisticated.
With four minutes' warning some at least of its Vulcan
carriers would become airborne; British Skybolts would not
be directed at Soviet missile sites or other targets where
accuracy would be at a premium, but against huge cities.
Missile defences would remain a problem, but an enemy
could hardly expect complete success against such a form of
attack in the immediate future. Thus as a relatively simple
form of deterrent – to be used in a single convulsive response
– the V-bomber–Skybolt combination did not lack credibility
from the British point of view. The United States, however,
could hardly be expected to bear the research and development costs – perhaps a further $2500 million – for the sake
of the British.

At least three main ingredients were responsible for the
crisis that occurred in Anglo-American relations at the end
of 1962 over the cancellation of Skybolt. The British outcry
was, in part at least, tactical, in order to secure the best
possible compensation. The Kennedy administration was not
immune to the hope that the 'independence' of the British
deterrent could be diminished. But thirdly there was a very
real lack of understanding on both sides; a failure of communications so real that President Kennedy commissioned
Professor R. E. Neustadt to make a special and confidential

study of the whole crisis. Robert Kennedy also underlined this point, while Henry Kissinger has argued that Americans tend to see problems in technical terms and logical abstractions, whereas the European mind is guided more by history and intuition – the British in particular being swayed by national pride. Certainly feeling in the Conservative party made it essential that Harold Macmillan should return from Nassau in December 1962 with at least the appearance of an 'independent' deterrent. Conservative emphasis on this weapon in the 1964 election affords further proof of this feeling, although the electorate was more interested in bread-and-butter issues. The Americans should have recognised that they could not hope to scrap Skybolt without the offer of a satisfactory alternative to soothe Britain's injured pride unless they were prepared to face a major crisis in the Atlantic alliance. This it is clear they were not prepared to do.

In the course of 1962 several hints floated across the Atlantic that Skybolt might be cancelled. More frequent and obvious were the intimations that the British deterrent should be merged even more totally into the alliance. In February Kennedy warned Macmillan privately that the British deterrent might encourage France and West Germany to seek a similar status. France was indeed already doing so, while the United States was hoping to blunt nuclear proliferation in Europe with a multilateral nuclear force (M.L.F.) of mixed-manned merchant ships, armed with Polaris missiles, in which the European states should participate, and which should be controlled by NATO. Lord Mountbatten, Chief of the Defence Staff, and the Admiralty were reported to be derisive; the Foreign Office was more diplomatic, but in general the proposal evoked little interest in Britain, none in France, and not much in the rest of Europe outside West Germany. M.L.F. would have been essentially a political instrument, expensive, and of little value militarily even if satisfactory manning and command procedures could have been devised. But more than that, the British government felt that all the nation's nuclear power must not be internationalised in this fashion. Its reaction to McNamara's proposal on 11 December 1962, while on a flying visit to London, that Britain should receive Polaris missiles instead of Skybolt, and assign them to the M.L.F., was consequently violent. British opinion was still recovering from Dean Acheson's assertion of 5 December that Britain had lost an empire and had yet to find a new role. *The Times* defence correspondent further reported on the 13th that he believed many key Americans viewed Britain's nuclear pretensions as 'ridiculous'. Nevertheless when Kennedy and Macmillan met at Nassau on 18–21 December it was soon clear that the main problem was not Skybolt at all, but the terms under which Britain should receive a substitute.

Kennedy was torn between indifference to the British deterrent and the desire to avoid a serious clash with this ally. His concern for the latter left him a remarkably weak hand to play in the circumstances. It was as if he held many high cards only to see them trumped by Macmillan's warnings of the threat to the Anglo-American alliance if no satisfactory alternative were offered. The British at Nassau were bent on securing Polaris missiles to preserve the 'independent' deterrent into the 1970s. Thus, although the Polaris submarines which Britain was to build were to be assigned to NATO, and although reference was made to a future British contribution to M.L.F., the latter clause was ambiguously drafted and committed the British to little or nothing, while a further clause gave them the right to withdraw the submarines from NATO in certain critical circumstances. Admittedly this was unlikely, but this clause formed the essence of the 'independent' deterrent, and satisfied Conservative pride. Britain even acceded to the American desire to reverse the usual descriptions of the alliance's deterrent and conventional forces by calling the former 'the shield' and the latter 'the sword', yet this concession had no noticeable impact on defence policy. Meanwhile the United States would bear most of the costs of the Polaris programme, would service the missiles, would provide facilities for test-firing, and would even provide part of the warhead, though this apparently could be manufactured at no great extra cost in Britain. The nuclear submarines themselves were to be largely of American design, and the missile-compartments mostly American-built. All this, of course, meant that Britain could remain a nuclear power for some years at comparatively low cost, the govern-

ment claiming that to have developed Polaris in Britain
would have cost another £1000 million. The capital cost of
Polaris for Britain finally proved to be some £350 million,
with annual operating costs in the early 1970s of some £32
million.[9] These low costs were, however, palpably dependent
on American goodwill and assistance.

The Nassau agreements evoked much criticism in Britain.[10]
Speculation that the nation might want to use Polaris missiles
'independently', say in defence of Kuwait, was ridiculed by
Socialists, Liberals and some defence writers. Aubrey Jones,
a Conservative M.P., insisted that the deterrent was a cause
of British estrangement from Europe – de Gaulle having
recently vetoed British entry into the Common Market – and
that it no longer secured Britain any special influence in
Washington. Sir John Slessor also agreed with those who
thought that Britain should abandon the 'independent' deterrent, and devote the resources saved to more conventional
forces for the security of Europe. The Opposition denounced
it as a 'costly pretence' and urged that the current nuclear
force should be allowed to run down without any provision
being made for a replacement. Labour in office, however,
were to proceed more cautiously, and in an undemonstrative
fashion were to keep open the nuclear option. This was really
what their Conservative predecessors had been doing, in that
the purchase of Polaris missiles and the construction of four
or five nuclear submarines were the cheapest long-term
method of keeping Britain in the nuclear field, with the
option in the 1970s of doing more or less – or much the same
– according to circumstances. Party feeling, however, compelled them to trumpet their policy, whereas Left-wing
pressures obliged their successors to refer to nuclear matters
sotto voce.

It was, in fact, hardly conceivable that any British government would have sacrificed this instrument, save in return for
equally remarkable sacrifices by other states, so long as it
could be maintained as cheaply as had been arranged at
Nassau, and so long as its existence was not obviously and
undoubtedly meaningless. One may doubt whether it continued to buy much influence in Washington, outside joint
targeting arrangements, but Sir Michael Wright, a British

G

disarmament expert, Denis Healey and Joseph Grimond all agreed that it had secured for Britain a place at the test-ban negotiations in 1963. On the other hand, the Nassau agreement undoubtedly contributed to de Gaulle's veto of the Common Market talks early in the same year. The agreement was coldly received in western Europe as another sign of the privileged position enjoyed by Britain in Washington. Yet Britain would have received no credit, certainly not from France, had she decided to opt out of the nuclear race. To have entered into a new nuclear partnership with France, had it been possible, would have been much more expensive. Such a decision would have been a most remarkable 'leap in the dark' given all the circumstances of 1962–3. In any case, the course of events for the remainder of the decade was to remove the question of the British deterrent progressively from the limelight. The possibility of its independent use was becoming increasingly hypothetical. In May 1963 the British V-bomber force was officially assigned to NATO, but it is doubtful if this was much more than an exercise in semantics, given the pre-existing close association with the American Strategic Air Command.

Meanwhile the Polaris force had yet to be created, and it was feared that before its completion the V-bombers would have lost their ability to penetrate the ever more sophisticated Soviet air defences. The Blue Steel stand-off bomb, with a range of at least 100 miles, was operational by 1963, but its efficacy in the later 1960s was seriously in doubt. The government revealed its anxiety lest the credibility of the British deterrent should soon be lost, and the defence statements of 1963 referred vaguely to the TSR-2 equipped with a new missile bomb as a stop-gap measure. This was greeted with considerable scepticism by non-official air experts, and the following year the Defence White Papers spoke of the conversion of some V-bombers to low-level flight to complicate their detection and interception by an enemy, though the radius of action of these aircraft was now probably cut from about 2000 to 1500 knots. There were also further reference to the strategic and nuclear potential of the TSR-2.

The decision to transfer the British deterrent to the Royal Navy, coupled with the growing emphasis on amphibious forces East of Suez, led to a steady increase in the naval estimates so that in three years the navy moved from being the least expensive of the services – a position it had held continually since the war – to the most costly. This was a dramatic transformation compared with its uncertain fortunes in the 1950s, yet its costs would have risen still higher had all the original plans of the Conservatives been implemented. The important East of Suez fleet was still mostly made up of modernised or converted ships, and there was a limit to what could be achieved by such improvisation. True, some of the carriers were well worth modernising, but even here a start would soon have to be made to a new generation. A new strike carrier was in fact authorised in July 1963, and a start made in her design. Ideally one or two sister ships would have to be laid down before the end of the decade. Two new assault ships – each able to carry up to 700 troops – were under construction to supplement the commando ships which could not carry tanks or heavy equipment; the first of the new guided missile destroyers joined the fleet in November 1962; naval fighters were being equipped with air-to-air missiles, and a formidable new strike aircraft, the Buccaneer, became operational in 1963. The helicopter threat to submarines was being increased with dipping sonar equipment and with homing torpedoes; more frigates from which helicopters could operate were coming into service. Another 500 men were being added to the establishment (9000) of the Royal Marines, and recruiting was good, while the commando ships had been refitted so that each could carry 700 or more men, and a battery from the Royal Artillery. Sufficient ships would be forthcoming to make possible a permanent force, based on Singapore, whose main offensive strength would be supplied by one or two strike carriers, one commando ship and one assault ship. One critic,[11] however, argued in 1962 that at least three ships of each of these types would be required to afford an adequate margin for refits and reinforcements. It seemed likely that such strength was to be maintained only in strike carriers. Even this would be expensive, given the need for at least one new ship, the cost of modernising others,[12] the expense of the new Buccaneers, and the decision in 1964 to buy Phantom fighters from the United States to replace the sub-sonic aircraft currently used. None of the existing carriers could operate Phantoms without a 'face-lift', but given Soviet exports of supersonic aircraft to several Asiatic states it was clearly essential to provide the navy with the means to hit back. Unfortunately not even modernisation would enable the existing carriers to carry all the aircraft and helicopters that a task force ideally required. They were also required to help cover the fleet against Soviet submarines and missile-firing patrol boats in the hands of states such as Egypt and Indonesia. Hence the Admiralty's bid, with the support of Mountbatten as Chief of the Defence Staff, for new large carriers.

Against the growing sophistication of certain air forces the R.A.F. looked to the TSR-2 for mastery of the air. It was hoped that these aircraft would menace enemy airfields, and prevent or deter air strikes against concentrations of British land or naval strength. They would operate from Aden and Singapore, and perhaps also from Indian Ocean airfields. Nevertheless carriers would still be required to provide close cover for task forces and to support opposed landings by amphibious forces. An effective East of Suez strategy also pre-supposed many new aircraft for Transport Command, more air-portable equipment for the army, and the maintenance of expensive bases in Malaya, Singapore and Aden, or failing them a string of small bases on Indian Ocean islands, with a new main base in Australia as suggested by Lord Montgomery. Finally there was a repeated cry from all the services for more helicopters, but whose role with the army, for instance, had often to be confined to that of supply through sheer lack of numbers and from fear of irreplaceable losses if used operationally.

A series of crises in the early and mid-1960s seemed both to justify the British East of Suez role and to underline the question marks against its long-term wisdom and prac-ticability. Although the main flood of criticism of Britain's aspiration to remain an eastern power did not develop until 1965, the foundations of this case were being laid long before this, and the ranks of sceptics and critics were being steadily reinforced in the early 1960s. Kenneth Younger[13] in 1964 likened the British preoccupation with eastern bases to a

'White Knight mentality', and doubted the feasibility of a long-term eastern role. Elizabeth Monroe criticised British Middle Eastern policies in 1963, while in the same year Christopher Mayhew became privately convinced that a military presence in the Persian Gulf no longer made sense.[14] On the other hand, the official policy of the Labour party following the death of its leader, Hugh Gaitskell, in 1963, tended to move in the opposite direction. Its pleas for reduced overseas commitments began to be displaced by the desire to play a leading part in United Nations peacekeeping missions, and to support India and other eastern states against the threat from Communist China. Denis Healey[15] argued on 26 February 1964 that mobile peacekeeping forces would be the most likely requirement for the later 1960s and 1970s. Montgomery, impressed by the supposed military stalemate in Europe, argued that Britain's armed forces would find themselves progressively employed in the East. Circumstances also tended initially to favour the eastern enthusiasts, although those with direct experience of the financial implications of the following crises were soon to take a more sceptical look at these policies. The burden of the Far East showed itself interestingly in the navy even before the crisis with Indonesia had reached its peak, naval personnel on that station growing from 8500 in 1960 to 13,000 in October 1963.

The first emergency was small and fairly quickly brought under control. Rebellion broke out in Brunei and Sarawak at 2 a.m. on 8 December 1962: by 11 a.m. British troops were ready to move out from Singapore. Aircraft quickly flew several companies to the scene of the trouble, while a battalion was flown out from the United Kingdom to Singapore as a replacement. No commando ship was in the vicinity on this occasion, but one reached Singapore on the 13th, and was able to assist in the final stages of the operation, especially with its two helicopter squadrons. The main trouble was over by 31 December, by which time 2000 rebels had been rounded up or disposed of at a cost of 35 casualties to the British forces. Even so observers thought that some lessons might be learned from this successful operation. The communications network during the first days of the crisis left room for improvement, and it was argued that more service integration and preparation in anticipation of such emergencies was desirable. Major-General Moulton complained in 1965 that British forces were not organised or trained functionally for rapid overseas deployment, so that there was too much reliance on last-minute improvisation.[16]

Another useful operation in support of British interests took place in January 1964 when aid was promptly given to three newly independent East African states that were menaced by mutinous troops. They appealed for help on 23–4 January, and aid was speedily given to Uganda, Kenya and Tanganyika by means of a carrier (H.M.S. *Centaur* with 45 Royal Marine Commando), air transport, and the troops still stationed in Kenya. Almost bloodless operations quelled the mutinies, which, although not very formidable in themselves, were disturbing in the context of such newly-formed states, and with memories of the Congo still fresh in people's minds. Yet valuable as British aid was, it was doubtful whether any long-term precedents had been established. Julius Nyerere of Tanganyika in particular was sorely embarrassed by his appeal to his recent masters, so easily was the taint of neo-colonialism acquired. As he said at a meeting of ministers of the Organisation of African Unity in Dar-es-Salaam on 12–13 February 1964: 'Already it is clear that there are some people who will seize this opportunity to play upon the natural fears of neo-colonialism in the hope of sowing seeds of suspicion between African states.' Nigerian troops in fact replaced the British Marine Commando as soon as possible in Tanganyika. Therefore the claim of the 1966 Defence Review that 'Recent experience in Africa and elsewhere has shown that our ability to give rapid help to friendly governments, with even small British forces, can prevent large-scale catastrophes' was an over-simplification, and already circumstances in the Protectorate of Southern Arabia were demonstrating the difficulty of trying to maintain a friendly régime in territories bitterly riven by dissension.[17]

The traditional tribal dissensions of the Protectorate were being intensified by more modern political troubles, while in Aden itself opposition was mounting against the town's inclusion in a federation with the rulers of the hinterland. The main disturbances in 1964 were centred in the Radfan, where British forces found themselves engaged in a sizeable police operation in a most inhospitable terrain against a tribal foe strengthened by revolutionary Arab forces. The difficulties in Radfan were well explained by Brigadier G. S. Heathcote, who pointed out that the British were not only chasing an elusive enemy in territory that favoured him, but were continually hampered by political considerations. A quick, clean and decisive victory was needed, yet too ruthless methods could lead to embarrassment in an age when anti-colonial currents ran so strongly. It was necessary to take account of divided opinions in Britain, where many questioned the morality or wisdom of such operations, and it was essential to avoid heavy British casualties for political and military reasons. Overall the 1964 Radfan operations succeeded in checking insurgency until the British withdrawal from the area in June 1967. Meanwhile it had been necessary to proclaim a state of emergency in Aden itself in December 1963 as the local nationalists stepped up their campaign against the federation and the British.

Another federation was also running into trouble, though here the ultimate outcome was to be more satisfactory from the British point of view, despite the departure of one member from the federation. Malaysia, a conjunction of Malaya, Singapore, Sabah (ex-British North Borneo) and Sarawak, came into being on 16 September 1963, but whereas the British saw this union as a stabilising force in south-east Asia, Indonesia was denouncing it as a neo-imperialist organisation. The Philippines, too, though to a lesser extent, were critical. 'Confrontation' initially helped to maintain the tenuous national unity of Indonesia, but that country's economic decay continued, while the ambitions of the Indonesian Communist Party soon carried the racial and political divisions to boiling-point. The failure of the attempted Communist coup of September 1965 was to undermine the power of Indonesia's demagogic leader, Sukarno, and bring the clash with Malaysia to an end. Britain had been fortunate that on this occasion she was dealing with an opponent who had over-reached himself, who had over-played the nationalist card, and who, unlike President Nasser in 1956, had failed to retain a sufficient breadth of support among his people. Similarly in Malaysia itself, although the Chinese of Singapore and the Malays on the mainland proved incompatible partners and had to separate in August 1965, support for the Indonesian case remained small, and sufficient inner cohesion existed to enable the fighting forces of Britain and her allies to concentrate on the enemy without. The conflict itself was strictly limited in character: it remained essentially a test of nerve, of will and political unity.[18]

'Confrontation' cost few British lives, but in other ways it was an expensive contest.[19] Contrary to original expectations, the formation of Malaysia led to the despatch of British reinforcements and not to service economies. In all, service personnel in the area increased by more than 50 per cent to some 60,000 between 1963 and 1966, including much of the Strategic Reserve, additional warships and even a number of V-bombers. These, with a carrier, were to deter Indonesian use of their supersonic aircraft, missile-firing patrol boats and submarines, which had been supplied by the Soviet Union. There was a sharp increase both in the amount of foreign service and of sea-time for naval personnel, and this probably contributed to the navy's mounting recruitment problems in the mid-1960s. The financial cost of British forces in Malaysia was put at about £250 million, nearly £100 million of which was in foreign exchange. Not surprisingly the early stages of 'confrontation', before the inner tensions in Indonesia gave hope of speedy relief, prompted some pessimistic feelings in Britain that the nation was committed to a long conflict, to which there was no obvious solution, and one in which Britain's neo-colonial image might be heightened. Only in the longer run did it become clear that she was performing what could be described as an invaluable short-term stabilising operation for the whole of the region, though perhaps a generation would have to elapse before it could be said with any assurance that the local beneficiaries had profited from this respite.

The main tasks facing the British and Commonwealth forces were the defence of the 1000-mile common frontier and border villages of Sabah and Sarawak with Indonesia, and the 3000 miles of Malaysian coastline against infiltration by sea and air. Small Indonesian units were reinforced by

Indonesian-trained Sarawak-born Chinese. Hostilities mostly took the form of fleeting brushes with an elusive enemy in deep jungle, though there were engagements with parties of 100 or more. About 13 Commonwealth infantry battalions were deployed in Sabah and Sarawak, with various supporting forces. The only deep-water port, Labuan, was some 900 miles from Singapore: few roads pierced the mountainous and jungle terrain, and 90 per cent of the service supplies within the territory were carried by air. Some seventy helicopters (forty too few according to the local commander, Sir Walter Walker) and forty fixed-wing aircraft provided the main mobility against the more numerous enemy, with his many advantages of surprise, space and concealment. Air superiority was used only for reconnaissance, mobility and supply, to discourage escalation, the basic fighting being the work of well-trained, well-handled infantry, who set out to out-guerrilla the guerrilla. Helicopters were used to land troops, not amid the enemy, but near the scene to set up ambushes or outflanking moves in secrecy. Good intelligence was of course vital. The Commonwealth forces also took care to win 'the hearts and minds campaign' among the local population – the first objective according to General Walker, who directed operations with some twenty years' experience of Asian warfare behind him, having fought against a variety of foes from Pathan tribesmen to Chinese Communist insurgents. The enemy was never in a position to 'swim like fish' in the friendly pool of an indigenous population. The British also had the delicate task of co-operating with Malaysia as the sovereign power: they had to act by influence and not by fiat.

In 1964 the Indonesians endeavoured to extend their operations to Malaya and Singapore, attempting first espionage and sabotage, and later small-scale infiltration by air and sea. Commonwealth air and sea patrols achieved a high interception rate, and those who escaped the net were soon rounded up by ground forces, aided by the local population. In the three years of 'confrontation' some 1500 casualties were inflicted on the enemy, mostly in killed and captured, against some 300 Commonwealth losses, of which 114 were fatal. In general the British forces had performed well in trying conditions, though their efficiency would have been increased had more helicopters been available. A helicopter could fly as far in one hour as a patrol could march in five days in thick jungle. Lighter equipment, especially weapons and radios, and dehydrated food, would have eased the army's task. Some unfavourable comparisons were also drawn between some British warships and the ex-Soviet vessels, with their surface-to-surface missiles. British experiments with hovercraft in the region were a promising step into the future.[20]

It was fortunate that these eastern crises were accompanied by an easing of relations with the Soviet Union in Europe from 1963, otherwise it is difficult to see how some form of National Service could have been avoided, unless Britain was prepared to risk the displeasure of her allies, and the decline of her influence in NATO. Three battalions had to be removed from B.A.O.R. and at times further cuts seemed likely in order to meet the extra-European demand for troops. And while the existing forces were stretched to the utmost, defence costs once more began to cause concern. True, the government hoped to limit the rise in defence spending to $3\frac{1}{2}$ per cent per year over the four years following 1963, whereas it was asserted that the national economy should grow at the rate of at least 4 per cent. Defence should therefore be kept quite comfortably within the official target of a maximum of 7 per cent of the gross national product.[21] Lord Home, the Foreign Secretary and Leader of the House of Commons, was not, however, disposed to treat that ceiling as sacrosanct, as he said on 14 March 1963, and certainly the government was to exceed its target increase of $3\frac{1}{2}$ per cent a year in its estimates for the period 1963–5, even if defence's share of the gross national product was still marginally falling.

These trends were watched in alarm by some observers, and by some in government, not least since the most expensive stages of the new carrier and aircraft programmes had yet to be reached. As the defence correspondent of the *Financial Times* noted on 23 March 1964: 'For a long time the maximum allowable spending was said to be £2000 million a year, that beyond that we would not, could not go. But £2000 million has now been reached. It may only be a ques-

tion of time before the limit is raised to £2500 million.' As
Britain's economic problems mounted from the second half
of 1964, so too did the criticism of the current arms policy.
The Economist of 28 November 1964 feared that the nation's
balance of payments might have entered a period of long-term
disequilibrium, a state of affairs that had apparently been
developing since 1955, and certainly from 1960. It concluded
on 16 January 1965: 'The defence budget is strained beyond
endurance by costly weapons and this year something has to
give, either the budget or the weapons.' Subsequent critics
of the government's economic strategy as a whole in the early
1960s included an O.E.C.D. report of 27 July 1965 and the
last Conservative Minister of Defence, Peter Thorneycroft,
both complaining of over-confidence and excessive expenditure. Specific critics of defence policy included those who
were dismayed by the escalation in foreign exchange costs
arising out of Britain's foreign commitments. These had
apparently doubled to £250 million since 1957, a serious
matter given the sensational balance of payments deficit of
1964. There were rumours and rumblings in Whitehall of
civil servants' alarm at the financial implications of the
defence programme as it stood in the autumn of 1964.[22] The
Chief Scientific Adviser, Sir Solly Zuckerman,[23] was certainly
troubled by the burdens imposed upon the economy by
defence. He calculated that it was absorbing about 1,400,000
of the nation's manpower, about one-fifth of the scientists and
engineers employed in research and development, and nearly
two-fifths of the national expenditure upon the same. Concern
was being expressed in other ways. The House of Commons
Estimates Committee reported on 24 August 1964 that expenditure on overseas bases reflected too little calculation
of long-term value and heavy building programmes whose
future value might well be questioned. Colin Jackson, M.P.,
retailed a current army joke that the construction of permanent buildings was a sure sign of imminent withdrawal,
and he concluded that the British seemed belatedly bent on
raising edifices to emulate the ruins of the Roman Empire.
Others asked if sufficient account was being taken of the
possibility of air reinforcement, and were dismayed to learn
that current services accounting provided no means of

accurately ascertaining the cost of overseas bases. Singapore, in 1964, was *thought* to be costing about £70 million a year.

As the economic crisis deepened in the winter of 1964–5, so more and more people were becoming cost-conscious, and were beginning to look to more efficient management and accounting techniques to make better use of the nation's resources. A start had already been made with respect to defence by the Conservatives in their last years, and Denis Healey, Minister of Defence in the newly-elected Labour government, gladly acknowledged these advances by his predecessors on 23 November 1964. Once the dust had begun to settle following the reorganisation of the Ministry of Defence in 1957–8, critics such as Aubrey Jones, Zuckerman and Shinwell had soon been at work again. Thus Aubrey Jones asserted on 27 February 1961:

> It would, I think, be less than patriotic if we did not concede that the weapons programme as now constituted does not, in fact, conform with an objectively shaped plan. To the best of my opinion, it is a sum of items, a large number of them designed for no better purpose than to promote the interest of an individual Service. There is nothing more tragic, to my mind, than the spectacle of the R.A.F., . . . now seeing its whole purpose threatened with destruction and reacting, as I see it, with extravagant claims and advocacy.

The critics had friends in high places. Lord Mountbatten outlined his own feelings to the defence representatives of certain developing countries in September 1961 when he urged them to seek the advantages of a single defence college, a strong defence ministry, and the minimum of service separatism. His thinking had been evolving on these lines since 1941. The Prime Minister, Macmillan, as we have already seen, was a firm supporter of a strong Ministry of Defence, and was later to speak on 9 September 1969 of his five-year struggle against 'terrific resistance' to carry his point. Peter Thorneycroft as Minister of Defence was another ally, and the intentions of this powerful trio were finally backed by Lord Ismay and Sir Ian Jacob, with their formidable experience of defence administration.

The government announced its quest in July 1963[24] for a unified Ministry of Defence that would be able 'to strike a correct balance between commitments, resources, and the roles of the Services'. From 1 April 1964 there was to be a Secretary of State for Defence, the service ministries and their political chiefs being downgraded to the level of service boards and ministers of state, and confined to administrative matters. The 1958 Defence Board now became the Defence Council, chaired by the Secretary of State for Defence, and attended by the Ministers of State, the Chiefs of Staff, the Chief Scientific Adviser and the Permanent Under-Secretary of State for Defence, with the Ministers of Aviation and Public Building and Works as required. Cabinet oversight of defence was to be provided by the Committee on Defence and Oversea Policy, chaired by the Prime Minister, and including the relevant ministers, the Chiefs of Staff and the Chief Scientific Adviser. Within the Ministry of Defence continuous efforts were to be made to organise service needs on a centralised and functional basis, so that a single Defence Staff at last emerged, together with unified Operational Requirements, Signals and Intelligence staffs. The centralisation process was to be carried further in 1967 when the Ministers of State for the three services were replaced by two functional Ministers for Equipment and Administration, the service Permanent Under-Secretaries following suit in 1968. Functional defence accounting was promised to Parliament for 1970. This new structure still had its critics, such as Charles Douglas-Home,[25] who doubted if the system could be really effective until the Chiefs of Staff were also functionally replaced, or others such as Christopher Mayhew[26] and Sir Maurice Dean[27], a former Permanent Under-Secretary of State for Air, who feared that centralisation on the present scale would stifle the unorthodox and decrease flexibility and military dynamism, especially in time of war. The return of a Conservative government in June 1970 was indeed to check the functional tendencies to some extent. A Parliamentary Under-Secretary was retained to look after each of the services, whereas Healey had been fusing those appointments into the functional, inter-service structure.

Much else was needed for the efficient management of

defence policy. One elementary need was for more durable heads of the Ministry of Defence. Peter Thorneycroft was the ninth Conservative occupant since 1951, and Lord Attlee in 1963 likened the ministry to 'a siding' for ministers on the way up or down in their careers. Lord Kilmuir[28] also thought some of its occupants in the 1950s had treated it as a stepping-stone to better things, and that defence had sometimes been treated in 'an off-hand manner'. By the later 1950s it had become a rather bad parliamentary joke as successive ministers introduced defence statements with profuse apologies for their ignorance. Fortunately the turnover in ministers was to slacken from 1957, and was to stop altogether from 1964 to 1970.

Firmer and more consistent direction from the top had also to be supplemented by more professional management throughout all ministries connected with defence. Important steps had been taken at the macro-financial level in 1958 and 1962, and shortly before the fall of the Conservatives in October 1964 a start was made in micro-financial management with the introduction of computers, functional costing techniques, and professional economists. The need for these new techniques and highly qualified specialist personnel was to be highlighted by the subsequent 'scandals' over the excess profits earned by Ferranti and Bristol-Siddeley on government contracts relating to the period before 1964. Indeed, the conclusion drawn by committees of inquiry into these affairs, and by the Fulton Committee's (1968)[29] examination of the civil service in general, was that further improvement in government techniques and in the use of specialist personnel was essential. Thus the Wilson Committee concluded concerning the Bristol-Siddeley contract, when a profit had been made by the company of no less than 74 per cent (although the Treasury permitted no more than 14 per cent profit on the capital employed), that the government departments responsible 'fell seriously below a reasonable level of competence'. It was remarkable, for instance, that the Ministry of Aviation's Directorate of Technical Costs had failed to note that Rolls-Royce had quoted much lower prices for similar work. The Committee of Public Accounts in 1967[30] blamed both the Ministry of Aviation and the contractors for the failure to record and appraise the escalating costs of the TSR-2 and its engine. The latter, indeed, escalated fourfold in under five years, with the Ministry virtually immobile on the sidelines. Not all cost escalation was blameworthy; much was inescapable in an age of inflation and rapid technological change. Expensive mistakes were inevitable when working near the frontiers of knowledge. On the other hand, deceptively low estimates were sometimes submitted initially in order to wring approval from the Treasury. But whatever the prospects the attempt had to be made to supervise and control costs as effectively as possible, and to lessen the very real waste of public money that had been taking place, especially since 1950.[31]

Widespread agreement existed in the mid-1960s that the civil service overall was short of some types of specialist personnel – notably accountants – nor was it always making the best use of many of the specialists it already possessed.[32] It was noted, for instance, that two-thirds of the higher civil service consisted of specialists, but that 33 of the 36 permanent secretaries came from the non-specialist administrative class. Few of the Ministry of Aviation's 3000 scientists were to be found at or near the top of its administrative tree. The Fulton Committee, and other critics, concluded that not only were greater specialist, including managerial, skills needed by leading civil servants, but that the true specialists must themselves be integrated into the top planning and policy bodies, and not left in separate and subordinate hierarchies. The 'cold war' between specialists and generalists must end, with power, status and influence more fairly distributed among them. Such integration would not be easy. Different training, background, modes of thought, experience and interests created many barriers between the groups, including even that of simple communication. The French, however, had achieved some common understanding between the products of the École Polytechnique and the École Nationale d'Administration. Nor could the infallibility of the specialists be assumed. The historically minded could point to the notorious Cherwell controversies of the 1930s and early 1940s, when scientists had argued in a far from scientific manner. Where scientists had grievances against senior civil servants

and serving officers, engineers complained of neglect at the
hands of the scientific civil service. The influence of two Chief
Scientific Advisers, Brundrett and Zuckerman, on government defence policy was felt by many to have been excessive.
It was contended that undue deference to the scientist led to
decisions which paid too little attention to economic costs,
technical feasibility, production problems and general
political considerations. Zuckerman's concern for a sensible
division of labour between British and American defence
industries and his belief that 'the best is too often the enemy
of the good' were held by some to be utopian, and innocent
of the competitive realities of both business and politics.[33]

Clearly there was no simple solution. It was not enough to
advance one specialist at the expense of others. The theoretical goal must remain effective teamwork between a range of
specialists, so that operational needs, financial costs, scientific
and technological feasibility and production problems could
all be reconciled in the most satisfactory way possible. If this
was asking for the moon, it was also evident that the imbalance
that existed between the various interested parties in the
development of the ill-fated TSR-2 could not be allowed to
continue to that degree. As the Select Committee on Science
and Technology concluded in its report on 7 May 1969, recent
defence projects had not been based sufficiently on 'a deliberate structure of informed decision-making, nor is it sufficiently
accessible to all potential participants'. The government
claimed in reply[34] that these defects had been put right, and
that the services, government departments and industry were
all now collaborating closely. Changes were also beginning
to take place within the civil service itself, with specialists of
all kinds being increasingly allowed to compete for the top
posts.

Other measures to try to control defence costs included the
addition of 'equality of information' clauses to arms contracts
from 1968, plus recognition by contractors of the government's right to post-cost contracts in an effort to protect the
public purse. Already the Hawker-Siddeley Nimrod £100
million contract had been drawn up with unusual stringency,
the company promising delivery within three years, and
giving the government the right of cancellation should the

contract be not fully met. The credibility of such clauses was not, however, to be tested, the Nimrods barely exceeding the original estimate. This was a useful though not an extreme test, since the aircraft was a development from a proven type, using an existing engine design.[35] The successful completion of the Polaris programme, on schedule, and roughly in accord with the original estimates, was also aided by pre-existing American experience in the building of such submarines.[36] True many British contractors had to raise their standards and improve production methods in order to reach the exacting requirements laid down in the American plans, but again they were working within known fields. Success with the Nimrod and Polaris programmes was no guarantee of comparable success with contracts that entered into wholly new fields, such as the Anglo-German-Italian M.R.C.A. aircraft project.[37] Early estimates of the latter's expected cost were greeted with widespread scepticism, even if unlike the doomed TSR-2 it had the advantage of being designed primarily for the European rather than for the eastern theatre as well. On the other hand, American experience with a multi-purpose, swing-wing aircraft, the F-111, was not encouraging. Indeed, nearly a decade of systems analysis, cost-effective studies and other techniques that had been given prominence by the American Secretary of State for Defence, Robert McNamara, had brought much disillusion in their wake by 1969. Many Congressmen were in full cry against escalating costs and unfulfilled specifications. In general, as the TSR-2 warned only too clearly, it seemed likely that any government that approved a service demand for a revolutionary, or near-revolutionary, weapon had to be prepared for many unpleasant shocks, financial and otherwise. A government could protect itself only by demanding that every major innovation seemed likely to justify its cost with comparable operational gains, and by recognising that the finest analytical techniques could still be upset by human subjectivity and a host of other imponderables. One could hardly hope for more than educated guesses when embarking on advanced weapons projects with gestation periods of a decade or more.[38] Above all, one had to recognise, as the Assistant Chief Scientific Adviser (Projects), Ministry of Defence, told the Royal United Service Institution in 1969, 'military science has now outstripped resources'.[39]

Labour's narrow victory in the election of October 1964 had thus coincided with a period when criticism of existing machinery for the formulation and administration of defence policy was mounting rapidly; when many new ideas and techniques for efficient management were being suggested; and when it was clear that, whichever party won the election, the time had come for some hard thinking about the current cost and prospective trends in British defence policy.

It was quickly evident that the Wilson government from October 1964 hoped to follow much the same defence policy as their predecessors, though at much less cost. While Labour had been in opposition, there had been some talk of reviewing the Polaris submarine programme and the whole future of the 'independent' deterrent if and when they won the election. The party had also argued in favour of the strengthening of British conventional forces with NATO to support the Kennedy–McNamara thesis that the threshold when nuclear weapons would have to be used in defence of Europe should be raised as high as possible. In practice, however, Labour was to do no more than cancel the fifth of the Polaris submarines, endeavour to conceal the British elements in the deterrent as far as possible under the guise of NATO – to reassure some elements in the Labour party – and continue with the re-equipment of British forces with NATO on much the same lines as their predecessors. Certainly there was no dramatic breakaway in principle from Conservative policy, while the new government even took up the East of Suez role with as much enthusiasm – at least on its front bench – as its predecessor. Labour's victory at the polls had in fact coincided with the first Chinese nuclear test – on 16 October 1964 – and this, following so soon after the Sino-Indian war of 1962, gave rise to fears of further Chinese threats to the sub-continent. Harold Wilson, as Prime Minister, was for a time attracted to the idea of using some of the V-bomber force as part of an external nuclear guarantee of India against aggression. He spoke of Britain as a world power or nothing. 'We have always been a world power, we should

not be corralled in Europe.' The Defence Review of 1966
affirmed:

> It is in the Far East and Southern Asia that the greatest
> danger to peace may lie in the next decade, and some of our
> partners in the Commonwealth may be directly threatened.
> We believe that it is right that Britain should continue to
> maintain a military presence in this area.

The government viewed the economic crisis of 1964 as a
temporary problem and one which required no drastic reappraisal of Britain's world commitments – economic, political or strategic. All that was needed of the services was a
firmer ceiling on defence spending – namely £2000 million
at 1964 prices – in contrast to the more flexible ceiling of the
Conservatives of about 7 per cent of the gross national product, a ceiling ironically criticised by George Brown on
6 March 1962 for its rigidity. The services would be required
to meet roughly the same roles at less cost – an optimistic
requirement, presumably based on the arrogant assumption
that Labour could manage both foreign and defence questions much more skilfully than their predecessors. Yet, as we
have seen, the Conservatives had already placed themselves
in a position where only sharp increases to the defence
estimates seemed likely to enable the services to meet the
roles mapped out for them by the government.[40] They had
consequently committed themselves to heavy new programmes
in 1962–4, but from the rumours circulating in Whitehall
and Parliament by October 1964 it would seem that some of
these decisions had been taken with reluctance, and that all
doubts had not been eliminated.[41] When the Labour assault
on the Conservative air programme began in the winter of
1964–5, Sir Roy Dobson, chairman of Hawker-Siddeley,
claimed that the Conservatives would have liked to do much
the same, but 'they just waffled'. Instead, projects had been
delayed by lack of funds. Christopher Soames admitted to
the Commons on 13 April 1965 that the TSR-2 and HS-681
would have been the last generation of military aircraft built
to purely British requirements by his party. Another Conservative minister, Hugh Fraser, had argued against the
carrier programme, insisting that land-based aircraft could

do the same work at less cost.[42] Certainly in the winter of
1964–5 the feeling was not confined to the Labour party that
British defence costs were rising too rapidly. What had also
to be recognised was that to attempt the same responsibilities
at even less cost could only be described as a very considerable
gamble.

The new government was particularly troubled by the cost
of new warplane projects for the R.A.F., and by the overall
burden imposed on scientific and technical resources by the
British aircraft industry. The Conservatives had been striving
to rationalise and revitalise this industry since the late 1950s,
especially by the formation of the Ministry of Aviation in
October 1959, with Duncan Sandys, the government's
'trouble-shooter', as its first minister. Repeated cancellations
of aircraft projects by the government itself in the 1950s had,
of course, caused many of the industry's current ills, but it
was certainly a step in the right direction to encourage the
formation of two major airframe and two leading aero-engine
manufacturers, with Westland for the production of helicopters. The Conservative government had made great use
of its position as the main purchaser of aircraft to hasten these
mergers. Contrary to expectations, however, the labour force
of the industry did not decline by anything like the expected
30 or 40 per cent from the 290,000 at which it stood in 1960–1,
and by 1964 there was a widespread feeling that the British
aero-industry was larger and more costly than the nation
could comfortably afford. It was said to be earning one-fortieth
of the nation's foreign exchange while absorbing no less than
a quarter of spending on research and development. If its
considerable import-saving contribution – overall aerospace
sales averaged some £450 million a year – had also to be
borne in mind, there still remained the remorseless rise in the
overall cost of each new aircraft type, and the imperative need
for foreign sales of such aircraft to make the cost tolerable.
Britain's recent experience here had not been encouraging,
none of her military aircraft enjoying the success of the Canberra and Hunter with foreign powers. Complaints might be
made of unfair American competition, but France, with an
industry little more than one-third the size of Britain's, was
exporting nearly as much by 1964, in particular the versatile

supersonic Mirage III fighter. Dassault had successfully produced this aircraft with less government outlay and control
than was normal in Britain. When the Swiss, in 1960, were
examining various models to form the core of their air force
for the later 1960s, no British aircraft was in the running. A
supersonic Hunter might have been a real competitor. It was
poor consolation when the Swiss Mirage programme ran into
difficulties in 1964, and it was being attacked as unrealistic
and ill-administered. Australia, too, had bought Mirages, and
was seduced away from the British TSR-2 by attractive
American terms for their F-111. There were no other prospective purchasers of the TSR-2, nor for the other new Conservative projects, the P-1154 or HS-681,[43] though the last
two might have evoked interest in due course had they
attained their ambitious specifications.

Britain's world-wide commitments and interests imposed
a heavy strain on the British aircraft industry. Exceptionally
sophisticated aircraft were required that could operate almost
anywhere in the world. No other country save the United
States had such exacting requirements, and consequently few
were interested in paying the extra cost for capabilities they
did not always require. The British aircraft industry, in any
case, was competing for foreign sales against the United States
whose firms were backed by a vast home market. The latter
made possible longer production runs, with consequent
savings in unit costs, and overall productivity in the American
aerospace industry was said to be about three times as high
as that of Britain. As early as December 1961 the Zuckerman
Committee, inquiring into the control and management of
research and development, had concluded that Britain should
try to co-operate with rather than compete against the
Americans. This was an important step towards a less ambitious air policy. Indeed, as the 1964 election approached there
were many unrealistic hopes afoot that talent and resources
could easily be extracted from a reputedly overgrown industry, and put to more profitable use elsewhere. Aerospace
had become a popular target for abuse.[44]

The first British aircraft projects to be cancelled were the
P-1154 and HS-681.[45] The government made much of the
claim that neither aircraft would be operational, in all prob-

ability, until the early 1970s, some years after the aircraft they
were scheduled to replace – the Hunter, Hastings and
Beverley – were due for retirement. Certainly the previous
government had, through want of funds, seriously delayed
the start of these projects. Labour also argued that the replacement aircraft would not only be operational sooner, but
would prove less costly. Credit arrangements with the United
States would also alleviate the immediate defence burden.
Some concrete points can be made about this change of plan.
The American C-130 (Hercules) substitute for the HS-681
was certainly cheaper, perhaps by as much as two-thirds, and
arrived sooner. It required twice the runway length of the
other, though Healey claimed that it would be able to land
within 100 nautical miles of most likely ground operations,
and noted the rapid proliferation of suitable airstrips. The
HS-681 was undoubtedly an exciting idea, but probably not
one that Britain could afford. The V.T.O.L. P-1154 was to be
replaced by two aircraft, a developed British version of the
V.T.O.L. P-1127 (the future Harrier) incorporating many of
the P-1154 specifications, and the formidably versatile, but
conventional, American supersonic Phantom. The choice of
the 'bird-in-hand' Harrier was a good one, especially since
exceptional speed did not seem an indispensable requirement
in a ground support aircraft. The Phantom was an excellent
aircraft, well suited to a variety of roles, and the British services might have accepted it 'off the peg' with only minor
alterations. The government, however, decided that the fitting of a British engine, the Spey, was vital for the future
development and prosperity of Rolls-Royce. Unfortunately
this was to prove one of the main causes of the doubling of
the cost of the Anglicised Phantom compared with the
American model. The cost of the engine itself was to increase
by some 40 per cent between 1965 and 1968, and further
expenditure was incurred in adapting the Phantom to its new
power-plant, and to the British navigation-attack equipment.[46] These modifications would, however, increase the aircraft's endurance and its strike capability.

These changes of policy naturally evoked controversy, but
among the new government's initial champions was *Flight
International* which, on 18 February 1965, thought it detec-

ted a more professional approach by the new Ministers of Defence and Aviation. It complained sharply of their predecessors' 'shillying and shallying', especially over the P-1154, and of a 'complete failure to control cost and delivery time'. Nevertheless an even greater storm was to break over the government's head when it decided in April 1965 to cancel the TSR-2.[47] It was contended that the expected cost of 150 of these aircraft had risen to prohibitive heights – to £750 million at the very least, and with the manufacturers still unable to bind themselves to a fixed price. It was some time before the government's final plans became clear, but in 1966 it was announced that the tactical reconnaissance-strike role would be taken over at the end of the decade by fifty American F-111s – revolutionary swing-wing aircraft – supplemented by Vulcans. In the longer run, in anticipation of the withdrawal of the Vulcans in the mid-1970s, Britain was to co-operate with France in the development of her own swing-wing aircraft, smaller than the F-111, but still highly versatile, and with a useful range that would be relevant to Britain's needs both in Europe and the East. This two-string policy would, it was claimed, prove cheaper than the Conservative TSR-2 programme, a claim that was fiercely contested by the government's critics.

Although the TSR-2 controversy often generated more heat than light, some points of substance have emerged. Close questioning by the Committee of Public Accounts in 1967[48] elicited three important admissions from the permanent secretary, Ministry of Aviation. The project had been too ambitious in relation to the cost levels originally envisaged; so complex a project should have been investigated more thoroughly before starting; both government and contractors lacked adequate control procedures. It had also been unfortunate to start the TSR-2 at a time when the airframe contractor, the British Aircraft Corporation, was still in process of formation, and was striving to fuse the disparate skills of English Electric and Vickers. Bristol-Siddeley, the engine contractors, was also a recent merger of two firms. In retrospect it was widely agreed that too many technical breakthroughs had been attempted simultaneously, and despite the refinement of procedures since the disappointments of the

1950s both technical problems and costs had been grossly underestimated, especially of the plane's avionics and engines. A Conservative spokesman, Mr F. V. Corfield, accepted much of this criticism on 7 March 1968. The situation was made worse by the maze of government committees involved in the project, and by hesitant government financial support. This owed much to the Treasury's serious doubts about the project as a whole, and there were sceptics or opponents in other government departments, including the Ministry of Defence. Mountbatten, Zuckerman and other scientific advisers were said to be hostile. Certainly the TSR-2, even under the Conservatives, was never pursued with single-minded zeal, and its survival probably owed much to the persuasive powers of the Minister of Aviation. It had many critics outside government, and cancellation was strongly supported by Sir John Slessor as a wise acknowledgement of ambition in excess of the nation's resources.

Meanwhile the government set out to prove that its alternatives to the TSR-2 would prove cheaper in the long run. Healey asserted on 1 May 1967 that over the period from April 1965 – that is, after excluding the £125 million or so already spent on the TSR-2 – to March 1976 fifty F-111s would cost only £336 million against £610 million for a similar number of TSR-2s. To Conservative complaints of 'Buying American', Healey retorted that the dollar cost of the F-111 would be fully covered by dollar offset orders, either in the United States or in other countries, such as Saudi-Arabia's purchase of Lightning aircraft. There was further controversy over the comparative performance of the two aircraft, Conservatives insisting that the F-111 was an inferior plane. Labour was certainly to be spared much embarrassment by its decision – on non-technical grounds – in January 1968 to cancel the American order: the F-111 was to fall well below the expectations of its designers. On the other hand, and this was apparently an accidental result, the government gained financially when it decided, also in January 1968, to abandon a specific capability for operations East of Suez. The F-111 cancellation charges came to a mere £13.5 million, whereas the cost of the TSR-2 was said to be running at £4 million a month in 1965. Of course the TSR-2 might have been continued, and the government would have been saved the collapse of the A.F.V.G. project in 1967. The R.A.F. would have possessed a new tactical-strike-reconnaissance aircraft in the early 1970s. It seems clear, however, that the main justification for the enormous expense of this aircraft would have been its East of Suez capability.[49] It would have been of value in Europe, but was not irreplaceable. In the longer run its cancellation facilitated the quest for a European swing-wing collaborative project whose initial disappointments nevertheless paved the way for the highly promising Anglo-German-Italian M.R.C.A. design for the later 1970s, an aircraft of great commercial as well as military promise – though no final judgement on this project may be possible until about 1980.

The Wilson government in 1965 had certainly taken risks with the future of British air power. Claims that the new policies would prove £1200 million cheaper over ten years than those of their predecessors were speculative in the extreme, and were perhaps designed for Left-wing Labour consumption as much as anything. The morale of the British aircraft industry was risked. Some loss of valuable expertise to America followed. Yet it was clear that the time had come for a long hard look at British air policy overall. By any test the industry had been devouring a great deal of the nation's resources, and it was now necessary to measure pretensions and performance against material requirements and expected returns. This exercise was attempted in particular by the Plowden Committee in 1965. If its resultant Report concerning the industry was to prove too pessimistic, at least in the short run, it spelled out much that was wrong both in the industry itself and in government handling of air policy. Many experts, without necessarily agreeing with all its conclusions, reinforced the core of its verdict.[50]

A major target for the critics proved to be the Ministry of Aviation. Lord Plowden told the Lords on 1 March 1966 that one of its main effects had been to keep profits low and costs high in the aircraft industry. The Plowden Committee concluded that its interference, which was both excessive and often ill-informed, had been an obstacle to efficient management. The ministry was in fact to be abolished in February 1967, and its duties taken over by the Ministry of Technology.

The Commons Select Committee on Science and Technology in a report of 7 May 1969 agreed that manufacturers should be consulted as a matter of course when the specifications for a new project were drawn up, in order to give advice as to feasibility and likely costs. In this way the service and ministerial weakness for over-ambitious specifications might be checked. The negative, penny-pinching approach of the Treasury also had unfortunate effects, in that projects were often badly delayed or upset by financial delays and parsimony. Departments were said to resort to deliberate underestimates of likely expenditure in order to overcome initial Treasury resistance. The sum total of this vacillation and tortuousness in government departments resulted in bad relations with industry, a basic lack of trust, and often, in the long run, a waste of resources, when escalating costs or incipient obsolescence – arising out of repeated delays – brought cancellation. All these conditions were bad for industrial morale, efficiency and economy – dangers of cancellation, for instance, discouraging investment in modern capital equipment. As Aubrey Jones remarked, it was essential that the government should act as a responsible customer, and this it had clearly not been doing of late years. Fortunately in the later 1960s the importance of effective control of projects was recognised, and the main responsibility for this was being placed increasingly in the hands of the contractors – or so the government claimed.

The industry itself was also the object of much criticism. French aircraft firms were, in some respects, more efficient, Sud Aviation for instance being ahead in the use of certain new management techniques. The Elstub Committee, set up in 1967[51] to push further the work of the Plowden Committee, concluded in 1969 that while American firms were superior in a variety of respects, most notable was their efficient and economical control of production, with a smoother flow of work, shorter delivery time, and better use of capital. The Elstub Committee noted that British aircraft firms were modernising their management techniques in the later 1960s, but even Rolls-Royce remained less productive than its great American rival, Pratt and Whitney, not least because the latter was building larger numbers of fewer types of engine.

Finally, early in 1971 Rolls-Royce's desperate gamble with the RB-211 to remain in the forefront of civil aero-engine technology came to grief, necessitating nationalisation of that great firm.

In the last analysis it was clear that modern aircraft were becoming so complicated and expensive that a nation of the size and with the resources of Britain had to think increasingly in terms of international co-operation – especially in military aircraft. The Plowden Committee indeed recommended that Britain should buy her most advanced military aircraft from the United States, and limit herself to one medium-sized project in the 1970s, or two in conjunction with European partners. The Conservative party in 1965[52] acknowledged that it was not far from this position, differing from Labour only with the argument that the P-1154, HS-681 and TSR-2 projects should have been completed before turning to European co-operative ventures. Indeed, the Conservatives in office had already made a start towards the latter, notably with the Concorde and with some preliminary steps in the case of warplanes. The Wilson government preferred to forgo this last generation of British aircraft for the reasons already mentioned, and to meet short-term needs with American purchases – Phantoms, Hercules and F-111s – with British Harriers and Nimrods[53] for two specialist roles, while seeking co-operation with France to provide long-term replacement aircraft in the 1970s. These co-operative ventures with France included helicopters, and a supersonic light strike/trainer to be known as the Jaguar. More important were the Anglo-French negotiations to produce a swing-wing or variable geometry aircraft, the so-called A.F.V.G. which the 1966 Defence Review was to describe as 'the core of our long-term aircraft programme'.

What interim verdict, then, can be suggested concerning Labour's air policy of 1965-6? The prophets of gloom and disaster were to be disappointed in the short run at least by the overall buoyant performance of the industry in the later 1960s, though the immediate impact of the cancellations had been bad for morale and efficiency. Some experienced aircraft designers were lost to the United States, and not absorbed, as hoped, by other industries in need of highly-

trained men. As for defence, the government had undoubtedly saved some money – however speculative its own
estimates of the actual savings – while its American purchases
provided the R.A.F. with some new aircraft sooner than
would have been the case under the Conservative programme,
though with some loss of capabilities in the process. Against
this, in the same time scale, could be set the advantages
offered by the Harrier and Nimrod – the latter apparently
replacing a Conservative interest in fifty Breguet Atlantiques
or Lockheed Orions. The gap left by the TSR-2 cancellation
was not in fact to be filled, since the decision to give up a
specific capability for operations East of Suez was accompanied by the cancellation of the American F-111s. Instead,
and at a much later date, the service could look forward to a
partly British-built swing-wing aircraft, versatile though
smaller than the F-111. The air force was undoubtedly being
required to sacrifice its longer-range strike-reconnaissance
powers in the 1970s, and indeed to subsist in the early part
of that decade with essentially non-revolutionary aircraft –
apart from the Harrier. If, on the one hand, the 1965 cancellations had released resources for further British participation
in the exciting field of swing-wing aircraft, there could be no
disguising the fact that, in contrast to the TSR-2, this would
involve delay and a much greater gamble as to ultimate value
and performance. Success in the swing-wing field would, however, represent a very real advance on the TSR-2, and there
was the further attraction in that a co-operative venture with
continental partners in the production of so versatile an
aircraft carried with it the promise of a long and perhaps
expanding production line – possibly into four figures –
whereas there was an uncomfortable finiteness about that of
the TSR-2 – a mere 150 or so. There could, therefore, be no
disguising the fact that Labour had embarked upon a risky
venture in 1965–6, one that could have led to serious embarrassment had it not ultimately been followed by a new
East of Suez policy, and by the discovery of new partners after
the A.F.V.G. fiasco. Yet, once the essentially European policy
had been adopted, the combination of Phantoms, Harriers,
Nimrods and Hercules, followed by the Jaguar and a swing-
wing aircraft, made a good deal of sense.

The other major attempt by the Wilson government to follow broadly the same objectives as the Conservatives at less cost was the decision at the beginning of 1966 to build no more aircraft carriers, and to phase out the current ships by 1975.[54] Healey was later to describe this as 'possibly my most controversial decision in the equipment field'. Certainly to have tried to provide a carrier force beyond the 1970s – or even to provide a viable force in that decade – would have been a costly undertaking. There was a limit to the number of face-lifts – currently running at about £30 million a time – that could be given to existing ships, while fewer and fewer of the most modern types of aircraft could be carried, even in the *Eagle* and *Ark Royal*. The smaller *Hermes* could operate so few that she could hardly be classed as an effective carrier. In terms of simple cost comparisons there could be no doubt that carrier-borne aircraft were much more expensive than land-based ones. Healey put it as high as two and a half times, but it is difficult to make a realistic comparison. In some circumstances the extra cost of carrier-borne aircraft might be more than justified. But the navy also agreed that carriers would need the support of F-111 type aircraft East of Suez. To provide all that was desirable was becoming intolerably expensive.

Only one new carrier had been ordered by the Conservatives, which meant that three carriers would be operational in the later 1970s. Thus only one carrier's presence could be guaranteed East of Suez at any one time. The Conservatives had been hoping for two. Would the presence of one ship, carrying an average of forty strike-interceptor aircraft, justify the expenditure of £1400 million over ten years? The editor of the *Journal of the Royal United Service Institution*[55] thought that nothing less than the much more expensive programme of building four carriers over the next ten years would be worth attempting as a viable policy. The current war in Vietnam suggested that aircraft attrition rates in modern war would soon exhaust the resources of a single carrier.

The Ministry of Defence argued that substitutes for all carrier roles East of Suez could be found save that of covering an opposed landing beyond the reach of friendly land-based aircraft. Such an operation was no longer envisaged by Britain alone without the aid of allies. Assurances that land-based aircraft, ship-borne missiles, and helicopters would be able to cover the fleet against all likely forms of air, surface or submarine attack were greeted with much scepticism in the service. Memories of the early war years, when the fleet was 'naked under heaven' off Crete, Malaya, and *en route* to Russia, were still vivid. Sailors with long memories could be forgiven for recalling the fate of the *Prince of Wales* and *Repulse*, sunk by Japanese aircraft off Malaya in 1941 before land-based aircraft could intervene. Exercises in July 1968 off Norway[56] and in October 1968 in Far Eastern waters underlined the value of carriers and the uncertainty of land-based air support. Troubling too was the fact that Soviet-built warships, large and small, some in the possession of Arab and Asian navies, were equipped with long-range missiles against which the navy had hitherto relied for protection on carrierborne strike aircraft. Such had been naval policy since the 1950s, and so central had been the carrier in British naval thinking for the last generation or so that no easy adjustment was possible.

Some critics of the government suggested the construction of cheap 'Woolworth' carriers to operate V.T.O.L. aircraft as an economical alternative. Traditionalists argued that large carriers were essential – to service the aircraft, provide air control, and to carry all the necessary radar and other equipment. A carrier had provided radar control for fighters during the Kuwait crisis. It was also pointed out that the *Ark Royal*, which was to be refitted to operate Phantoms, and possibly the *Eagle*, had a decade of useful life left in them. The government was being unnecessarily precipitate, and should at least retain the carriers until effective missile or V.T.O.L. air defence systems had been perfected. The government, however, was adamant, insisting that carriers were too expensive in relation to their probable utility. In the Far East F-111s would be present to deter an enemy from interference with maritime forces. Ships other than carriers could provide air control. Furthermore, to provide the necessary personnel for the operation of the carriers beyond 1975 would require either an increase in the navy's manpower beyond the intended level, or the sacrifice of some other ships, a point on which the navy itself was said to be divided.

In the last resort the government's decision was not an ideal one. The act was deemed essential in 1966 to maintain the defence ceiling of £2000 million at 1964 prices. A reduced role for British forces East of Suez was already envisaged, and it was hoped – and much emphasis must be placed on the word 'hope' – that a combination of allies, F-111s and ships equipped with missiles and helicopters would provide sufficient security for British shipping in the later 1970s. Perhaps the best logic lay with those who argued that unless Britain was prepared to provide adequate forces for her East of Suez role she should cut her losses, and abandon these pretensions altogether. It was on this basis that Christopher Mayhew, Minister of State for the Navy, resigned in February 1966. The First Sea Lord did likewise, but these resignations had no effect, and may have persuaded other senior officers to soldier on later in the decade in the face of further service cuts. But strict logic is not always feasible in politics, and the government had yet to persuade itself that it was attempting too much. Indeed, it intended to make full use of carriers in the interval in the hope that 'confrontation' with Indonesia would soon be ended, and that the states bordering the Indian Ocean would have been stabilised as far as possible by 1975. There would thus be further carrier refits, and the Fleet Air Arm was still to be reinforced with such formidable aircraft as the American Phantoms and British Buccaneer Mark IIs.

In the meantime the Wilson government had been building upon the Conservative policy with respect to the Indian Ocean, encouraged by the American desire for such a British role and by hopes of American aid in the financing of new bases. In November 1965 a new colony, the British Indian Ocean Territory, was proclaimed. This was composed of a number of tiny islands, some of which might be developed into small air bases. Some interest was also being displayed in the possible establishment of a base in northern Australia in case Singapore should prove untenable. Aden, at least, was being written off in the winter of 1965-6 in view of the hostility of many of the local population, and a total British retreat was to accompany the grant of independence in 1968.

There were apparently doubts even about the retention of Singapore beyond the end of 'confrontation', but American and Australian protests won a British promise to stay as long as local conditions permitted. Certainly by the beginning of 1966 the government's enthusiasm for an East of Suez role was no longer quite so great as a year earlier. The cost of the Indonesian crisis was particularly sobering, and it was anxious not to repeat the experience. Overall extra-European military responsibilities were eating up about £190 million in foreign exchange, not to mention 136,000 service personnel by 1966. The Defence Review of February 1966 therefore insisted that there must be more equitable sharing of responsibilities among Britain's partners in the East – a remark especially directed at Australia. Britain would and could fulfil her defence commitments only if her friends provided the necessary facilities: she would and could fight no major war without allies, and it was her intention to rely increasingly on air reinforcements from Britain to strengthen the forces normally deployed East of Suez. These would be smaller, though, as the government stated: 'We cannot forecast with any confidence how Britain's forces will be deployed outside Europe at any given time in the 1970s. . . .'

Nevertheless, both in the 1966 Defence Review and during a visit to Canberra in February 1966 Healey strove to spread the conviction that Britain would remain 'in a military sense a world power' in the 1970s and possibly into the 1980s as well. The Defence Review also included this affirmation of faith:

Much of Africa, the Middle East and Asia, is going through a period of revolutionary change, which may sometimes spill across national frontiers. . . . When such instability leads to open war, it may imperil not only economic interest in the area, but even world peace. . . . On more than one occasion in the recent past, we have seen how local conflict in a faraway country has threatened to embroil the major powers in a direct confrontation, directly endangering world peace. . . . Recent experience in Africa and elsewhere has shown that our ability to give rapid help to friendly governments, with even small British forces, can prevent

large-scale catastrophes. In some parts of the world, the
visible presence of British forces by itself is a deterrent to
local conflict.

Special emphasis was laid on the dangers of war and instability in the Far East in the next decade, and on Britain's
contribution against such eventualities. In the absence of a
date on this paper one might have attributed it to a Conservative minister. Healey assured the Commons on 7 March
1966 that for the time being an independent capability to
mount 'small-scale military operations . . . to prevent large-
scale disaster' was to be maintained. On the other hand, he
revealed the following day that the government looked to
the end of 'confrontation' in the near future as a means of
achieving a further cut of £100 million in manpower and
equipment in order to achieve its defence ceiling of £2000
million at 1964 prices. It is interesting to note, however, that
Healey also claimed that these prospective cuts would bring
Britain's eastern forces back to the level intended by the Conservatives before the start of the crisis with Indonesia.

The need to economise meant that there could be no question of an enlargement of B.A.O.R., for which Labour had
displayed no small enthusiasm in the early 1960s. Less had
been heard of this as the general election approached, and
once in office the new government argued bluntly in the
winter of 1964–5 that NATO planning should be based on
existing force levels, not on unattainable force-goals. Account
should be taken of Soviet intentions, a point made as early
as December 1958 by Duncan Sandys, as well as of their
military capabilities, while it was unnecessary to prepare
stocks for more than a conventional conflict lasting a few days.
A major collision, which was dismissed as most improbable,
could not fail to escalate almost at once into a nuclear conflict.
Conventionally, one should prepare for no more than a clash
arising by mistake or some misunderstanding. With some
variations this was very much the line of policy followed by
the Conservatives. They, in their turn, as early as 1963 had
begun to follow the American lead in giving more emphasis
to the tactical training of B.A.O.R. for a conventional conflict. In May 1964 exercises were held east of the Weser in

H

accord with the new NATO strategy of fighting conventionally in a forward position. This gesture to McNamara, however, carried with it no expectation that such fighting could
last for more than a few days. The Labour–Conservative con-
vergence in practice was thus quite remarkable, though in
appearance they were to exchange policies in the mid-1960s
as they had exchanged seats in Westminster in 1964. For
Healey's new-found emphasis in office on nuclear weapons was
complemented by growing Conservative enthusiasm for conventional forces, an enthusiasm which fired some back-
benchers in particular, since it provided a useful rationale
for their defence of the Territorial Army against iconoclastic
Labour reformers.

Labour, in office, proceeded with the re-equipment of
B.A.O.R. with a wide range of new and highly effective conventional weapons, such as the Chieftain tank – which was
entering service two years late in 1965 – and a variety of guns
and missiles, programmes mostly initiated by the previous
government, and now reaching fruition. Old-fashioned 25-
pounders and 5.5-inch guns were at last being replaced by
British and American self-propelled weapons; the Corporal
tactical nuclear missile was withdrawn, and battlefield nuclear
firepower confined to the Honest John rockets and 8-inch
howitzers. Healey also accepted his predecessor's planned war
establishment for B.A.O.R. of 120,000 men, or about twice
its current strength in West Germany. But, while on the one
hand this was to be a firm target, anything beyond that target
was to be cut. Hence Healey's eye fell on the rambling army
reserves and Territorial units as they existed in 1964. These
heterogeneous forces, with their variegated liabilities for service, their deficiencies in organisation and equipment, called
for a new Haldane. Others, such as *The Times* and *The
Economist*, and Lords Montgomery and Sandon, agreed that
a drastic remodelling to meet the needs of the later 1960s and
1970s was essential, though this did not preclude the criticism
that Labour, in hacking away dead wood, was leaving too
little from which new growth might spring according to
need.[57] Much of the opposition showed less discrimination,
and the passing of the Territorial Army in 1966 was accompanied by protests that recalled Conservative objections to its

formation in 1908. The Conservative front bench, with Enoch Powell as Shadow Defence Minister, placed much emphasis on the government's neglect of the possibility of a longish conventional war and the virtual scrapping of home defence forces.

Healey in reply on 16 December 1965 argued that he had inherited costly and ineffective reserves, several of whose intended roles had become superfluous or too costly a form of insurance in relation to probable risk. Soviet and allied spokesmen were agreed, he insisted, that a long conventional war in Europe was impossible. An attempt to fight at length with tactical nuclear weapons, without recourse to strategic nuclear devices, would necessitate a 50 per cent increase in NATO manpower, and to fight with conventional force alone – assuming that the Russians did the same – would entail a doubling of current forces in Europe, the revival of A.A. Command, the expansion of Fighter Command in Britain, and the creation of a larger escort fleet to fight a third Battle of the Atlantic. Even if Britain was prepared to vote a doubled arms budget, together with conscription, her allies in NATO would not follow suit. In these circumstances one should concentrate on the provision of small but efficient reserves, for the speedy reinforcement of the Regulars, and especially of B.A.O.R. The government also envisaged the need for reserves in the event of their offer of logistic units in support of a United Nations peacekeeping force being taken up. Government plans were to be somewhat buffeted between 1966 and 1968, with first the fierceness of the Opposition to their proposals leading to the creation of an additional reserve force of 23,000 with a purely home defence commitment, and later the shock of successive economic crises leading both to the elimination of that force, and to further cuts in the reserves in 1968.

In 1966 the Territorial and Army Volunteer Reserve was set up to replace the Territorial Army and Army Emergency Reserve. The Volunteers, or T. and A.V.R. I and II, included an 'Ever-Ready' element of some 8600. A further 42,000 could be called out when 'warlike operations are in preparation or progress', a more flexible commitment than that undertaken by such reserves in the past. The Territorials, or T. and

A.V.R. III, of 23,000 were purely for home defence, especially Civil Defence. The latter's establishment was also being cut in 1966 (from 122,000 to about 75,000), but work continued on the thirteen emergency regional governments, on plans for the dispersal of the population, and on the provision of Civil Defence equipment in anticipation of a nuclear attack.

In two years, therefore, the new government had considerably modified the detail and cost of their predecessors' defence policies. True, in February 1966 Healey was as yet able to claim that solid progress had been made towards only three-quarters of the planned £400 million saving by 1969. The achievement of the whole target must await the end of 'confrontation'. Claims that military capabilities had been little affected by these savings were widely disputed, notably by Christopher Mayhew, who observed that the main cuts were being directed against equipment, so that the loss in capabilities must in fact exceed the intended cut of one-sixth in the overall estimates. More disappointing from the government's point of view was the fact that, given the sluggish performance of the economy as a whole, defence spending was apparently continuing to absorb much the same share of the gross national product as under the Conservatives. The high hopes of 1964 were not being fulfilled. In consequence the services were soon to be called upon to bear further cuts.

7 An Exercise in Optimism: 1966–70

Until the end of 'confrontation' in 1966 the government was unable to complete the main part of its defence review, which aimed at a defence expenditure by 1969–70 of no more than £2000 million at 1964 prices. The end of the crisis with Indonesia made it possible to make projections concerning both Britain's immediate roles East of Suez and the forms they might take in the 1970s. The discussions that took place within the machinery of government leading up to the defence policy announced in July 1967, and to the final revision of January 1968 that was made necessary by the devaluation crisis in the autumn of 1967, will, in time, make fascinating reading. But it is already clear that some of the most powerful figures in the Wilson Cabinet, including the Prime Minister himself, came to revise their East of Suez policy with the utmost reluctance, and only under acute economic and political pressures. One may also guess, in the light of the evidence that has emerged concerning the role of the Treasury in the 1950s, that the latter was a severe critic of the defence estimates given the recurrent economic crises and the steady refusal of the economy to grow at the pace so optimistically envisaged by the government in 1964–5.

From 1965 Britain's strategic role East of Suez became the subject of fierce debate. It had been questioned before, as we have already seen, but only from 1965 was a sustained attack launched by many Labour back-benchers, the Liberal party, some Conservatives, and by some political and military commentators. The sorry finale to British rule in Aden, the end of 'confrontation', the relative – though possibly temporary – calm around most of the Indian Ocean and Persian Gulf, and the apparent inability of Britain to influence events in Rhodesia, Vietnam and the Middle East, were all cited in support of a policy of retreat. Enthusiasm for the Commonwealth was waning; Britain's internal problems seemed to be mounting on all sides; doubts were growing as to the actual degree of national progress and strength enjoyed in the 1950s; and, in so far as Britain could afford to be outward-looking, Europe appeared to be the most relevant focus of her attention. The nation was becoming more introspective, more selective, more convinced that her resources were limited, and that her fields of action must be chosen with greater care and discrimination than in the past.

Certainly there remained a strong body of opinion that there were things that Britain could not afford *not* to do. Yet since Churchill had begun to review the Korean rearmament programme in 1951 hardly a year had passed without some major weapon being cancelled or some overseas commitment reduced or given up. In this longer perspective the decisions that were to be taken in 1967–8 were less dramatic than they appeared at the time.[1] Repeatedly even sophisticated arguments – and not all were sophisticated – had succumbed to the belief that the cost was exorbitant. Considerations of cost were to prove a powerful ally for the East of Suez critics after 1966.

The two most dramatic events in the debate were a speech in October 1965 by the Conservative Shadow Defence Minister, Enoch Powell, and the resignation of Christopher Mayhew from the government in February 1966. Powell, addressing the Party Conference in Brighton on 14 October 1965, questioned the long-term value of Britain's eastern bases, and argued that the states of Asia must in time establish their own local balances. Sir Alec Douglas-Home, with general responsibility for the party's overseas policies, hastily added that no eastern political vacuum could be allowed to develop that might be used against the West, though he gave it as his personal opinion on 26 April 1966 that future British forces in the region should be mainly drawn from the R.A.F. and navy, especially the latter. The *Economist* took a similar line, while expecting Japan, Indonesia and India to be strong enough to fill any vacuum by the 1980s. Powell was not without supporters in the Conservative party, who seemingly favoured a more precipitate retreat,[2] and Labour critics steadily became more vociferous. Reinforced by Mayhew

from February 1966, they seriously embarrassed the government at a Parliamentary Labour party meeting on 25 May,
so much so that a second meeting was addressed by the Prime
Minister on 15 June, and his speech justifying Britain's
eastern role was published. Fifty-four members still dissented,
and attributed more than half of the pro-government vote to
the latter's powers of patronage. At the Party Conference in
October a half-million majority voted in favour of drastic
eastern cuts, the Foreign Secretary's protests against irresponsible 'scuttle' notwithstanding.

The debate also raged in the press and some serious periodicals, with two of Britain's most noted defence analysts,
Michael Howard and Alastair Buchan, making important
contributions in *International Affairs*.[3] Both agreed on the
need to withdraw in the long term, but not over the timing.
Howard thought it should take a generation; Buchan suggested from five to ten years. Some, like the editor of the
Royal United Service Institution Journal in May 1966,
thought that economic stringency might soon leave the
government no choice, but in general the critics and defenders of an East of Suez role debated the issue on much broader
grounds than this. Thus the critics argued that a British presence could act as an irritant to local nationalists and revolutionaries rather than as a stabilising force. It might discourage
existing governments from implementing necessary political
and military policies for their own stability and security. A
large British presence might be out of all proportion to the
interests to be protected, yet still inadequate or ineffectual
against serious indigenous opposition. A small presence would
still be a commitment which, once honoured, could grow
through force of circumstances into a major one. Economic
self-interest in the various regions would be the best guarantee that their doors would remain open to Britain, supplying
crucial raw materials and buying her goods in return. Both
Powell and Mayhew made much of the commercial success
of West Germany and Japan although they maintained no
foreign military presences. And over all hung the shadow of
the American experience in Vietnam, and their failure to
impose their will despite all the power at their disposal.

In contrast the East of Suez champions emphasised the

danger that a precipitate British withdrawal might cause power vacuums into which the enemies of Britain – and here they had Nassar, Arab revolutionaries as well as Communists much in mind – would rush, overthrowing friendly régimes. Much was made of the Indonesian defeat in 'confrontation', and the scale of British investments and trading interests in politically vulnerable areas East of Suez. Thus Britain still drew about 60 per cent of her oil from the Middle East, especially from the Persian Gulf. It was argued that nationalist xenophobia might prevail over economic self-interest. More than £1000 million of foreign investment could easily be put at risk by a policy of too hasty retreat, Sir Alec Douglas-Home was to tell the Commons on 31 October 1968. At the very least, it was argued, if such interests could not be directly protected by military force, a presence would contribute to the general political stability of certain areas, and thereby afford indirect protection. The mere hint of weakness or retreat would, in contrast, encourage the enemies of Britain and antagonise her friends, and cause the situation to deteriorate, as was occurring in the mid-1960s in and around Aden, with Nasser and Arab revolutionaries exploiting to the utmost the announced intention of the British to leave by 1968. A retreat from the Persian Gulf would also let loose a variety of local and traditional rivalries which had long been inhibited by the British presence, not least the differences between the local Arab rulers themselves, and the long-standing disputes between Iran and the Arab states. Communists in and around Malaysia would be encouraged; dissension between Chinese and Malays might increase; there might be further trouble with Indonesia. Soviet ambitions in the Indian Ocean would undoubtedly grow. In short, it could be argued that a British presence was a massive stabilising and mollifying force throughout the region.

A hint of the official mind is to be found in the guarded conclusions offered to the public in 1966 by Sir Philip de Zulueta, private secretary to three prime ministers between 1955 and 1964.[4] Concerning the Middle East he noted: 'Small wonder that unhappy politicians at Westminster are left feeling that Britain can afford neither to stay in Arabia nor to go away.' He also thought that the most formidable pressure

for the British to stay East of Suez had come from the United
States – the least from British businessmen. Indeed Aubrey
Jones suggested to Parliament on 3 March 1965 that the
Wilson government was using the East of Suez presence rather
than the nuclear deterrent to perpetuate the 'special relationship' with the United States and to keep a seat at the international top table. 'Good, true-blue stuff,' he remarked.

The government itself was also reviewing its East of Suez
policy in 1966 and the first months of 1967. It had already
decided to abandon Aden, and more attention was being paid
to the potential of island airfields in the Indian Ocean. The
Prime Minister, defending his policy before his party in June
1966, placed great emphasis upon these in a long-term policy
for a reduced presence relying heavily upon air reinforcement
from Britain. The end of 'confrontation' in August 1966 gave
the government further elbow-room, but account had still to
be taken of American and Australian objections to too extensive a reduction. Furthermore, too precipitate a run-down of
the bases in Singapore might well undermine the political
stability of that island whose economy was heavily dependent
on the British presence. The government received a sharp
reminder in January–March 1967 of the delicacy that was required in such matters. A British move to cut their forces in
Malta by two-thirds by the end of 1970 evoked such protests
that it was finally agreed to slow the rate of withdrawal during
the first eighteen months. Mediterranean cuts had already
made redundant one of the most famous appointments in the
Royal Navy – that of commander-in-chief in the Mediterranean.

The Defence White Paper of February 1967 made no more
than an interim reference to policies East of Suez, promising
only that forces in Singapore and Malaysia would return to
their pre-confrontation level by April 1968. Long-term prospects received little attention, though neither this, nor the
great play made by the White Paper as a whole that Labour
defence spending would fall by 1969–70 by no less than £400
million (at 1964 prices) below Conservative plans, satisfied
the many Labour critics of government policy. Sixty back-
benchers refused to support the government when the House
divided.

Nevertheless more radical decisions were in the process of being taken, the second stage of the much-vaunted Defence Review being completed around Easter. The Cabinet was now being converted to the idea of a second attempt to enter the Common Market, the formal decision being made on 2 May 1967. The diplomatic dividends to be earned from a British presence East of Suez seemed to be declining. Certainly it was bringing Britain no influence upon events in Vietnam; rather the opposite, since it seemed to encourage some Americans to feel that British units should be fighting on their side. India was taking no interest in a possible British contribution to an international nuclear umbrella against China. Russia, not Britain, had presided over the discussions that had ended the war between India and Pakistan in 1965. Britain's balance of payments remained obstinately in the red, and hopes of rapid economic growth seemed no nearer to fulfilment. Even British successes East of Suez did not necessarily point to a major continuing presence. The end of 'confrontation' could be said to afford a convenient pause during which some measure of disengagement might occur. The time for the East African type of intervention of 1964 might have passed, while the eastern policing role had lost much credibility following the successful defiance by Rhodesia.

The Australian Prime Minister, Harold Holt, visited London in June 1967 in a vain effort to arrest the new trend in British policy. The Wilson government's intentions were made plain in a defence statement of 18 July 1967. Its optimistic assertion that this would provide a firm guide to British defence policy over the next eight or ten years was to prove valid for only four months. But in July the government proudly hoped to combine a military capability to operate East of Suez within an ultimate defence budget ceiling of £1800 million at 1964 prices. It was bluntly stated that the great bases in Malaysia and Singapore were too costly in proportion to their value to Britain, and if circumstances permitted these would be evacuated by the mid-1970s. Healey told the Royal United Service Institution in October 1969 that the earliest evacuation date envisaged in the summer of 1967 had been the end of 1972.[5] This should save £100 million in foreign exchange, 75,000 in service personnel, and 50,000 in overseas civilian manpower.

There was not, however, to be a complete retreat. The continuation of the F-111 order, and renewed reference to possible island airfields, such as Bahrein, Masirah, Gan, Cocos and Aldabra, suggested that an air-strike force would be available for many years to come. It was also possible that a naval-amphibious force would be maintained East of Suez, using Australia as its main base, and there would certainly be a three-service Strategic Reserve in Britain, with a strengthened Transport Command to make possible the speedy, if limited, despatch of reinforcements. Current plans for Transport Command suggested that one brigade, or thereabouts, depending upon the amount of equipment to be carried by air, could be flown East at short notice. The three brigades of the Strategic Reserve were to be reinforced with a fourth. No date was given for a British retreat from the Gulf or Hong Kong – indeed the former presence was to be strengthened following the evacuation of Aden at the end of 1967 – while the government insisted that it would continue to honour its commitments to SEATO, Malaysia and other eastern members of the Commonwealth. The Prime Minister claimed on 27 July 1967: 'What we shall maintain is not a military presence but a military capability based on the ability to get there to fulfil our remaining commitments.' In contrast the Conservatives argued that sufficient forces should remain 'until there is stability in the area', while many Labour back-benchers complained that the new policy was nothing but an unhappy half-way house that would continue to waste the country's resources.

One eastern commitment was to be extinguished rather more rapidly than the government had anticipated. This was the obligation to provide temporary protection against external attack for the South Arabian Federation that was due to become independent in 1968.[6] Conservative promises of a long-term defence treaty with the Federation had already been watered down by Labour in 1966 to no more than air and naval support in the first months of its independence, plus some help in the development of the Federation's armed forces. Much has been made of the argument that the prospect both of early independence and the withdrawal of British protection deprived the local peoples of any incentive to work against the Arab activists. They could not afford to offend the possible rulers of the morrow. Thus the British found it increasingly difficult to gather intelligence, and so the effectiveness of their counter-measures declined. Certainly these British political decisions aided the extremists, but it is worth noting that earlier attempts to stand firm politically in Cyprus had been dismal failures. Unless effective local allies could be found, as in Malaya, the British were doomed to defeat. Their only allies in the region were shadow politicians, the British alone providing any substance. From June 1967 the local revolutionary movement, the National Liberation Front, began to make rapid progress, winning over most of the federal army, and completing their seizure of power by the beginning of November. Hasty negotiations brought the People's Republic of South Yemen into existence on 30 November following the departure of all British forces, save for a naval task force. Since the start of the emergency in December 1963, 129 British servicemen had lost their lives.

British forces in the Persian Gulf were now doubled to about 7000, Sharjah becoming the main base with its neighbouring training and practice grounds. Bahrein was less important now, since its use as an air-staging post had been closely linked with Aden as a base. The size of the British oil investment in the Gulf (about one-third of the total for the whole region), the fact that it earned about £200 million in foreign exchange, and the fact that Britain drew about half her oil from the Gulf all seemed to make considerations of defence costs irrelevant – if one assumed that a British presence somehow contributed to the security of these economic interests. Arms, however, had not prevented the oil stoppage during the Arab–Israeli war of June 1967, and it was commercial considerations that had restarted the flow. It was possible that a British presence would act as a cushion, preventing collisions of interest between the various Gulf rulers, but equally it might act as an irritant to local dissidents and contribute to a second Aden-type situation. It is noteworthy that some firm advocates of withdrawal from Singapore, such as *The Times*, hesitated before making a similar recommendation concerning the Gulf. Healey himself argued that British forces should remain so long as they clearly acted as a tranquilliser.[7]

The government's decision to wait upon events in the Gulf was speedily upset by the economic crisis of November which resulted in the devaluation of the pound on the 18th. Further savings in government spending overseas were said to be essential, as well as the release of more resources from defence to promote exports. The Ministry of Defence endeavoured to rescue its current policy with a promised saving of £100 million, which included the phasing-out of one carrier earlier than expected, and the cancellation of a proposed £20 million airfield on the island of Aldabra. This was to have been part of the island staging-post chain across the Indian Ocean, Aldabra attracting particular attention since it would have facilitated the movement of air reinforcements to the East in the event of over-flying rights being denied to the British in the Middle East and over 'black' Africa. The proposal had, however, provoked a storm of protest from biologists, the Royal Society sending a delegation to the Ministry of Defence in June. The ecology of the island was said to be unique, and of vital importance in the study of evolution. The cancellation was therefore welcome, not least because, like so many British defence projects, it might have been abandoned within a decade, but only after irreparable damage had been inflicted on the island's natural life.[8]

The Ministry of Defence admitted that these cuts so weakened Britain's posture East of Suez that only the improbability of a long struggle could justify this latest gamble. An ex-Cabinet minister[9] thought that the government had for some time been subconsciously moving away from an East of Suez presence, so that when all the political and other implications of the devaluation crisis came to be considered the balance finally tipped against its continuance. The Prime Minister was later to admit that he was one of the last to be converted. Denis Healey spoke of himself as more of a penultimate convert, inclined to stay in Malaysia and Singapore as long as those states desired a British presence, though more doubtful of the wisdom of a lengthy stay in the Gulf.[10]

George Brown, the Foreign Secretary, was later to make no secret of his misgivings over the speed of Britain's withdrawal from the Middle East, whilst Ivor Richard, Parliamentary Secretary to the Secretary of State for Defence, wrote in *The Times* with undisguised frankness: 'I was one of those who felt it to be hasty and unjustified. There seemed to be no long-term interest, either economic or political, which would be served by a total withdrawal by 31 December 1971. I felt also a sense of almost personal obligation to Australia and New Zealand. . . .'[11] Conservatives described the decision as a sell-out to Labour back-benchers to win their consent to blows against the welfare state, and certainly the Prime Minister thought it judicious to place the defence cuts first in his parliamentary statement of 16 January 1968. At the same time it is difficult to avoid the conclusion that there had been a general shift in the government's priorities. Its enthusiasm for the East of Suez role had rapidly waned since 1966. The irrelevance of Britain and her forces during the Arab–Israeli war in 1967 must have given food for thought. The Prime Minister's hopes before the war to maintain freedom of navigation through the Straits of Tiran by international action had been coldly received by Washington and many of his Cabinet colleagues.[12] As attention turned to Europe, as the economic dilemmas of the government became more pressing, so the East of Suez presence not merely lost its appeal but began to look expendable. Certainly to do so would increase the government's freedom of manœuvre not only for domestic purposes but also with respect to Europe. Some slack would be created in Britain's over-stretched armed forces; some diversion of forces to Europe would be possible within a more limited defence budget. It was a very tempting prospect, and Lee Kuan Yew, the Prime Minister of Singapore, flew unavailingly to London in January 1968 to try to qualify the decision.

On 16 January 1968, therefore, Harold Wilson announced to the Commons that the British retreat from Singapore, Malaysia and the Persian Gulf would be complete by the end of 1971. British forces would remain in Hong Kong, and the staging posts of Gan and Masirah would be retained. No special capability for operations East of Suez would be pre-

served, which meant that the order for F-111s – now expected
to cost £425 million over ten years – could be cancelled.[13]
Pleas were to be heard outside official circles, and undoubtedly there were others within, for the retention of these aircraft to provide Britain with a medium-range capability in
Europe in the later 1970s. With the phasing-out of the V-
bombers around 1975 the R.A.F. would possess no strike and
reconnaissance aircraft with more than a very modest range.
The government was adamant, and in view of the later
chequered history of the F-111 they were wiser than they
knew. It was later announced that in place of the F-111 the
R.A.F. was to receive twenty-six Buccaneer aircraft in addition to those to be transferred from the navy as the carriers
were phased out in the early 1970s. The navy was now to cease
operating carriers and fixed-wing aircraft in 1972 – not 1975
as originally planned. An expensive refit of the *Eagle* was
cancelled. Overall, a saving of 75,000 service personnel and
80,000 civilians could be expected by 1972–3. Defence spending should drop to about £1650 million at 1964 prices, and
about £100 million should be saved in foreign exchange each
year.

Future British involvement in the Far East was not wholly
ruled out. Aerial tankers (ex-Victor bombers) would facilitate
the speedy movement to the East of such combat aircraft as
the government might choose to spare in any emergency.
Transport aircraft would be able to fly out some ground
forces, and naval units might be on hand. The efficiency of
such aid, if sent, would be heavily dependent upon local
facilities, and upon the availability of the various routes to
the East. Naval reinforcement, for instance, would be slow
so long as the Suez Canal remained physically closed – it
might also be politically shut at some future date. No stockpiles of equipment and stores were to be left to assist any
'fire-brigade' force. It would be dependent on its local allies,
and on supplies sent out by air and sea. Healey promised that
small British units would be training regularly in the area,
and that larger forces would be sent out occasionally to participate in large-scale exercises. Nevertheless many experts feared
that British skills in jungle warfare and other types of eastern
operations would soon decline. 'Confrontation' had shown

how quickly the lessons learned during the Malayan emergency had been forgotten. The acclimatisation of troops to
tropical conditions would be a further problem. Apart from
the material problems, many questioned whether, once the
withdrawal had been effected, a British government could
find the will-power to intervene again, despite the current
protestations. Finally the government stated in 1968 that the
Gurkhas would be cut to 6000 over the next three years, and
thereafter their future would be subject to review.

The new policy was bitterly debated, though with some
embarrassment on the Conservative side so long as Enoch
Powell remained Shadow Defence Minister – which he did
until 1968. Among the press *The Economist* bitterly opposed
the retreat. On 16 December 1967 it argued that Britain's
military record over the past ten years had been surpassed
only by the Israelis. Did the United Kingdom, it asked, wish
to become an 'Iceland with fifty-five million people'? The
fifty-five million, however, seemed bent on a record Christmas
shopping spree. The *Daily Telegraph* was another outspoken
critic; the *Glasgow Herald* and *Financial Times* only a little
less so. *The Times*, however, insisted on 10 January 1968 that
Britain could not 'nurse-maid' states such as Singapore indefinitely. It was less happy about a precipitate retreat from the
Persian Gulf. The *Spectator* on 5 January remarked bluntly
that the overseas bases should have gone long ago, and had no
possible economic justification. Left-wing critics rejoiced,
although they were disappointed that the arms cuts had not
gone further. Much moderate opinion, however, was more
concerned over the timing of the withdrawal rather than the
principle, Sir William Luce, for instance, later arguing that
a delay of five years in the Gulf would have given valuable
time in which to harmonise the relations of Iran, Bahrein,
the Trucial States and others interested in the future of the
Gulf.[14] He disliked the arbitrary date imposed, a product of
internal circumstances in Britain and not related to the necessities in the Gulf. Yet he felt that the British military presence
could not defend the nation's economic interests – at least not
directly – but could only contribute to the political stability
of the region. This thoughtful criticism might be compared
with the rhetoric of the Air League, which asserted in its

journal, *Air Pictorial*, in March 1968: 'If British forces were still a powerful influence in the Suez Canal Zone, there could have been no Arab–Israeli wars or Middle Eastern crises capable of interrupting our oil supplies. . . .'

Almost immediately events seemed to play into the hands of the East of Suez enthusiasts when within one week of the Prime Minister's statement British aircraft were flying troops from Malaya to Mauritius to assist in the maintenance of order on that island against rioters. Troops remained there until November. Fears of racial conflict and a serious resumption of Communist terrorism in Malaysia persisted. The political future of the Persian Gulf remained uncertain. Yet the most dramatic event of 1968 was the Russian intervention in Czechoslovakia, while in the longer run the most serious military development that would affect Britain was the growing tendency in the United States to review the scale of its presence in Europe, and to incline towards a policy of partial withdrawal. In this context the declared intention of Britain to concentrate her forces in Europe was most welcome to those whose main concern was the future of that continent. In practice, however, Europe's gains from Britain's East of Suez withdrawal would not be all that extensive.

Apart from the defence cuts specifically aimed at Britain's forces East of Suez, some other reductions or adjustments were made. Britain intended to reduce her air strength based on Cyprus, and while at a meeting of the CENTO members in London on 24–5 April 1968 she promised to operate Canberras and Vulcans from that island in fulfilment of her treaty obligations, she could make no commitments once those aircraft had been phased out of service by the mid-1970s. No successor aircraft had been or seemed likely to be ordered, future British combat planes being designed mainly for Europe (apart from the long-range anti-submarine role), though usable elsewhere given Britain's flight-refuelling capability. A very disappointing feature of the latest defence review was the slowing down of the nuclear hunter-killer submarine programme. As late as July 1967 these vessels had been described as the main striking force of the fleet (apart from the Polaris submarines in the deterrent role). The Chieftain tank programme was also being slowed, while the extinction of a number of army regiments and other units would be correspondingly hastened.

On the home front the government also decided in January 1968 to reduce the various components of the Civil Defence forces to no more than a care and maintenance basis.[15] Some tentative cuts had been made two years before, when emphasis had been shifted from rescue to the survival of those outside the main areas of devastation and radio-activity. Greater de-centralisation had been envisaged.[16] But now a cut in expen-diture from £25 million a year to about £7 million by 1970 was envisaged. About 84,000 volunteer personnel would be disbanded, though small local nuclei would be retained, and the Home Office's scientific training school would provide refresher courses. Although much equipment was to be moth-balled, the elaborate control system, the emergency communi-cations network, the monitoring and warning systems were to remain, together with special police and fire-service plans and stockpiles. Nevertheless, a fundamental change of policy was being introduced. Whatever the inadequacies of the previous policies, it was now estimated that in future it would take at least six months, not seventy-two hours, to activate the nation's Civil Defence organisation. If past policies had appeared about as useful as a life-jacket to a round-the-world yachtsman – one could imagine its utility in some circum-stances – the new approach left him with a jacket that would take a long time to inflate. That the government itself believed that Civil Defence was not wholly useless is sugges-ted by a Home Defence Review in 1965 with its estimate that in some circumstances as many as one-third or one-half of the nation's population might survive a thermo-nuclear attack. According to its own professed beliefs, therefore, the govern-ment's new policy could only be justified on the ground that there would be ample warning of any major deterioration in East–West relations. There was also the probability that even the equipment, personnel and organisation that were to be maintained would be allowed to decline in quality over the years.

The government was to make many optimistic projections as to the future course of defence spending. If all went well, the nation's arms budget per head of the population should be as low as that of the much-envied West Germans by 1973. Denis Healey claimed[17] that by the end of 1972 defence spending would have been cut by one-third in real terms, commitments would have been halved, and manpower reduced by one-sixth. His attempts to gloss over cuts in new equipment by emphasis on increased efficiency were not wholly convincing. All these hopes, too, could be undermined by a change in the international situation. On the other hand, Britain had chosen a European orientation at a most opportune moment, given the growing possibility of American cuts to their forces in Europe, the actual withdrawals by Canada in the near future, the uneasiness introduced in East–West relations by the Soviet intervention in Czechoslovakia, and the fact that Britain's application to join the Common Market required a display of as much European-mindedness as possible.

Indeed, until recently Britain had not seemed a very enthusiastic partner in NATO, with vague and maladroit threats in 1967 that her forces in Europe would have to be cut unless West Germany provided more relief in foreign exchange costs. One of B.A.O.R.'s six brigades was indeed recalled to Britain to save Deutsche Marks, though its heavy equipment was left in Germany, and it was to return there for exercises. The British threats were not very credible, in that facilities did not exist in Britain herself for the housing and training of large modern military formations, while further cuts would have undermined British influence in NATO, as well as diminishing the credibility of the nation's candidature for admission to E.E.C. Yet the negativeness of the British attitude was apparent, with Healey insisting that a major Soviet attack on western Europe was the least likely of contingencies, and that if it occurred NATO would, in a matter of days, be forced to use nuclear weapons for its own survival. NATO's current strength was therefore, he insisted on 27 July 1967, about right, and there would be ample warning of any change in Soviet attitudes that might necessitate a reconsideration of the western posture.

Complacency concerning the balance of forces in Europe was not confined to Britain. Already some in the United States were asking whether so large an American presence was necessary. One expert, Carl Kaysen,[18] thought that a cut of at least one-third should be possible. Among the NATO commanders the fear was growing that the alliance might be on the brink of all-round reductions, and they protested that the military strength at their disposal was barely adequate. Indeed, only if they could be sure of the prompt despatch of reserves to the front by all the NATO partners in any crisis could they feel at all satisfied with the current situation. Many units were below strength, especially in terms of efficiency, given the rapid turnover in conscripted men. B.A.O.R. at least provided a professionalism, and consequently a proficiency and versatility, that was out of all proportion to its size. The uneasiness among the military was unmistakable. The politicians, they felt, were thinking too much in immediate political terms. They were dismayed, too, by the decision of the NATO ministers of defence in December 1967 to adopt a full forward strategy for the defence of West Germany, with as much delay as possible in the use of nuclear weapons in any crisis. Sir John Hackett,[19] commander of the Northern Army Group, was to describe this as 'a simple absurdity' so long as nothing was done to increase NATO's conventional forces.

Some of this alarm began to penetrate the Ministry of Defence, for on 17 and 25 July 1968 – that is before the Czech crisis – a less complacent Healey challenged American estimates that a satisfactory balance existed between NATO and the Warsaw Pact. The latter, he insisted, had twice as many tanks on the Central Front in normal times, and could double this advantage in thirty days. Soviet capabilities in the rapid movement of forces were indeed to be only too impressively demonstrated in the following month, when no less than 300,000 troops were redeployed during the Czech crisis in a few days. The extensive modernisation of Soviet conventional forces had been in progress for some years, especially since the removal of Khrushchev in 1964. Furthermore, some Soviet military thinking and practice was being directed towards non-nuclear operations, at least for some days at the start of an emergency.[20] Most notable had been the 'Dnepr' exercise in 1967, which had included armoured and motorised thrusts over distances of 800 kilometres. Supporting air and parachute units were also being strengthened.

After the Czech crisis it was claimed that Soviet forces were established in eastern Europe in greater strength than at any time since 1945, and that as many as eighty-five divisions might be assembled in East Germany within two weeks. Healey stated in Munich on 2 February 1968:[21] 'The figures . . . show that nuclear escalation would be the only alternative to surrender in case of a major Soviet attack [after the first few days]. . . . NATO is outnumbered by the Warsaw Pact on the central front by more than two to one in infantry formations and nearly three to one in armoured formations. The Warsaw Pact superiority in aircraft is nearly two to one.' Air-Marshal Sir Christopher Foxley-Norris, commander of the British air units in Germany, not only referred to the 'critical' Soviet tank advantage, but thought the problems of establishing air superiority 'under some of the circumstances that might face us are frightening, to put it mildly'.[22] NATO commanders doubted, too, whether their political chiefs – and especially the Americans – would agree to the sufficiently early use of nuclear arms to avoid complete collapse. Sir John Hackett thought the most likely strategy would be a conventional defence in depth for an uncertain period of time, almost certainly longer than a few days. He noted that 'Staff colleges were permitted to teach (and the Rhine Army to plan and exercise) on the assumption that a conventional phase might last for as long as a week or ten days'.[23] If such assumptions were correct, NATO could not afford any further cuts to its active forces; indeed more reserves – especially from Britain – would be required, and the tactical air forces should be increased.

The British and West German governments, agreeing that the conventional prospects were not good, led the way in a new examination of the possible use of tactical nuclear weapons, not as a means of winning a campaign, but of buying time, warning and deterring an aggressor. In 1968 NATO governments entrusted Denis Healey and the West German Defence Minister, Dr Gerhard Schröder, with the preparation of draft proposals. By the beginning of 1970 good, though not complete, progress was claimed for this bid to find political guidelines for the use of nuclear weapons both for military purposes on the battlefield and as a warning to an aggressor

of the determination of NATO to resist without necessarily
launching the world into a general nuclear war. Healey explained to Parliament on 19 February 1970: 'The purpose
of nuclear weapons as we see them is to restore the credibility
of the overall deterrent in a situation in which a large-
scale conventional attack shows that that credibility has dis-
appeared.' Knowledge of NATO discussions to this end had
already given rise to controversy in Britain in 1969, but now
it became a major issue in both press and Parliament in
February–March 1970. Reference to agreed political guidelines for the initial use of nuclear weapons in the Defence
White Paper for 1970 precipitated a critical amendment by
thirty Labour members of the 'Tribune' group. The debate
on the White Paper itself produced a majority of only twenty-
one for the government on 5 March, a measure of Labour
disaffection.

Nor were the Conservatives in an entirely happy or consistent position, for while many of their number attacked the
government for neglect of conventional forces and undue
emphasis on nuclear weapons, their leader – conscious of
his possible responsibilities in the near future – agreed on
5 March that escalation from the use of tactical nuclear
weapons to that of strategic ones was not inevitable. This was
a rare remark of interest in a generally unedifying debate,
with members' thoughts more on electioneering than on
defence. Some attempts were made to put the case for more
conventional forces, and if this tempted Labour members to
ask whether the Conservatives wished to restore conscription,
it was certainly hard to see how voluntary recruitment could
be so improved as to make a significant difference in the
strength of British forces available for the immediate defence
of Europe. If Lord Wigg of the Labour party made a strong
appeal in *The Times* for the return of conscription, most of
Healey's critics were content to talk vaguely about increases
in conventional strength, or to assault the wisdom of his
professed faith in the tactical use of nuclear weapons in the
early stages of a conflict. Harold Watkinson, an ex-Minister
of Defence, wrote that studies in the early 1960s had left him
convinced that any nuclear detonation would result in 'a
massive and probably total reaction'.[24] Lord Mountbatten

declared that he had always opposed the use of tactical nuclear weapons when he was serving on the NATO Military Committee in the early 1960s.[25] Sir John Hackett thought that in 'North Western Europe nuclear weapons are virtually unusable. The implications of this conclusion are not easily digestible in either party.'[26] A neat finishing touch! Sir John Crowley, the *Daily Telegraph* and *The Times* took a similar view, while the *Observer*[27] and *The Economist*[28] insisted that reliance on nuclear weapons should not be used as a justification for conventional cuts. Nuclear arms must not be regarded as a panacea or allowed to create a Maginot Line mentality, and ultimately lose all credibility.

There were defenders of the new course, too. Brigadier Kenneth Hunt,[29] Leonard Beaton[30] and L. W. Martin[31] supported it broadly in principle, pointing out that a return to a Second World War type of conflict was unthinkable, that the Warsaw Pact might be able to offset any western conventional increases, that Britain's NATO partners were averse to any increased conventional effort on their part – while the United States might very well reduce her contribution, that conventional increments in Europe could lessen the chance of a *détente* with the Soviet Union and the hopes of mutual arms reductions in Europe. In short they argued that anything that increased the overall credibility of the nuclear deterrent was to be welcomed in an imperfect world. Beaton further praised Healey for facilitating a process whereby the United States and the European members of NATO were being drawn together into more serious consideration of nuclear questions. However incomplete, this was something to be encouraged. There was, he thought, no question of the adoption of a strategy in which tactical nuclear weapons would be used for military reasons. Their purpose was political; to serve as a warning to the enemy, and to try to interpose an intermediate stage between a western conventional collapse and resort to a general nuclear holocaust. Admittedly Washington's enthusiasm for the new ideas seemed less marked than that displayed in London. If some British weapons might be used tactically, the real power of decision would still lie across the Atlantic. All that was being created were 'political guidelines', with the emphasis very much on the word 'guidelines'. Yet it was hard to see any viable alternative, given the growing pressures in America for a reduction in the American presence in Europe. Further-more, the new Social Democrat government in West Germany announced a cut-back in some military programmes from May 1970, and declared that there could be no increase in the Bundeswehr beyond the current 460,000.

If Britain could not engage by herself in a quixotic quest for a more conventional approach to the defence of western Europe in the 1970s, it was still possible to debate the wisdom of the Labour government's approach to the question of reserves. Some notable critics[32] sharply attacked a policy that concentrated on the provision of high-quality reserves to bring the Regular forces up to war establishment in an emergency, but which left virtually no nucleus for further expansion or for home defence. Sir John Hackett feared that continual Treasury pressures for economy – and he might have added political exigencies of many kinds – helped to create a rigidity and dogmatism in defence thinking that seemed to assume that all contingencies were foreseeable. The services were then forced into a strategic strait-jacket. Certainly Labour's reserve policy foresaw only a limited range of emergencies.

In 1968 the T. and A.V.R. III, recently established after much agitation, was scrapped, save for 100 tiny cadre units that might serve as the basis for any future expansion of the volunteer reserves. The commitments of 168,000 ex-National Servicemen in the Army General Reserve was extended until 1974, by which time it was hoped that the main T. and A.V.R. units, with the Regular Reservists, would be equal to all needs. The main task of the reserves would be to bring B.A.O.R. up to its war establishment of some 120,000, a matter of providing about 60,000 well-trained men. In January 1970 the T. and A.V.R. stood at 47,000, or 13,000 below strength, so that here too voluntary recruitment was encountering difficulties. The efficiency of the force was un-doubtedly very high, but critics continued to ask what Britain could do should any crisis prove long drawn out, should any emergency make heavier demands for men than expected, and should any threat to Britain's internal security develop.

Labour's qualitative solution was not enough. The Conservative response was not much more encouraging. Once in office they acknowledged the quality of the force, but to meet their complaint that the T. and A.V.R. made no provision for an uncommitted reserve, available to meet unforeseen contingencies, they initially planned an increase of no more than 10,000 men. They also added an extra T. and A.V.R. armoured car regiment to the reserves earmarked for NATO. Marginal modifications to the current reserve policy therefore alone seemed likely unless there was a dramatic change in the international situation. The Ministry of Defence had continuing cause to feel grateful in 1969–70 that the civil strife in Ulster, with the consequent despatch of troops to that province, should have occurred at a time when no other emergencies were demanding attention.[33] Indeed, the Ulster crisis appeared to be improving re-engagement rates in the army itself.

Britain was also maintaining an active Strategic Reserve whose most important element was a mobile task force of about 20,000 troops, mainly composed of 3 Divisions and the parachute brigade. This was provisionally offered to NATO as early as 10 May 1968, before the Czech crisis. Circumstances subsequently dictated that it should become essentially a NATO reserve force, with special relevance to the vulnerable flanks of the alliance in Europe, though with a general capability for Afro-Asian operations if this should be felt to be desirable. The Belfast and Hercules aircraft of Air Support Command meant that all essential equipment, save heavy tanks, could be transported by air. At sea the commando and assault ships could transport nearly 3000 reasonably well-equipped troops, and there were six new army logistic ships to provide additional capacity. According to the commander of the Army Strategic Command in 1969, Sir John Mogg,[34] his force would be able to give a useful account of itself on any front from southern Norway to the Mediterranean. Only No. 45 Royal Marine Commando was, however, as yet trained and equipped for operations in the Arctic conditions of northern Norway, a region that was felt by NATO planners to be specially in need of rapid reinforcement potential.[35] Nor were Mogg's forces truly self-sufficient logistically. They were short of armour and helicopters, which would limit their value on NATO's central front to heavily wooded terrain and country not suited to heavy tanks and vehicles.

It is also necessary to place in proper perspective the boast of the British Defence White Paper of 1969: 'We are the only European power with a role and military capabilities which cover the three main NATO fronts from the Arctic to the Caucasus on land, sea and air.' British forces, even on the flanks of NATO, could only be effective in the context of the whole alliance, especially once the carriers were withdrawn from service, and as, later in the 1970s, the longer-range strike capabilities of the R.A.F. declined. As it was, two naval exercises off Norway in 1968 were said to have underlined the dangers of relying on land-based aircraft alone, and the security of the fleet had been much enhanced by the presence of a carrier on the second occasion. Alastair Buchan argued that the redeployment of a large proportion of the American forces with NATO would be the best way to provide highly mobile reserves for all three fronts of the alliance. The British certainly possessed forces that were peculiarly suited to the role of reserves for NATO's flanks, but it was necessary to recognise their limitations, and not be misled into the belief that Britain could somehow rediscover her former strength and roles around the periphery of Europe. In any case the long history of British amphibious operations was far from being an uninterrupted success story, the Second World War alone bringing the failures of Norway, Greece and Dieppe.

Meanwhile in the Northern Army Group efforts were proceeding to fit B.A.O.R. for the strategy of flexible response that had been officially adopted by NATO. If the initial use of tactical nuclear weapons was to be carefully controlled, more effective use had to be made of the conventional forces. Manœuvres in the late 1960s placed great emphasis upon mobility, night exercises, hit-and-run tactics, and the ability of infantry to create centres of resistance behind an advancing enemy.[36] Early in 1970 Britain agreed to the return of the 6th Brigade to Europe in view of impending Canadian cuts, while West Germany agreed to meet the additional foreign exchange costs. In general Anglo-German offset agreements since 1962 had been keeping British foreign exchange costs in Germany to about £25 million a year. Other British additions to the strength of NATO included some long-range aircraft to participate in the newly-established maritime air patrol in the Mediterranean. It was stated that a carrier, or a commando or assault ship would normally be operating in the Mediterranean. The Wilson government added a Harrier squadron to British tactical air power in Europe, and the ensuing Conservative government promised four extra Jaguar squadrons. Improvements to airfield defences in Germany were to include Bloodhound missiles and aircraft shelters to lessen the risk of an aggressor's pre-emptive strike after the style of the Israeli air force in 1967. Some stores were also moved nearer the front line, and, as already noted, the Conservatives slightly increased the T. and A.V.R. reserves in Britain.

The debate concerning the desirable and feasible conventional strength of NATO continued, with statistics being deployed adjectivally – after the style of Lloyd George – to prove a variety of positions.[37] Numerical comparisons could, of course, prove hopelessly misleading, as recently underlined in the 1967 Arab–Israeli war. But by the end of 1970 it was being ominously asserted that the Soviet–NATO tank ratio had grown to four to one, and that in other respects the military strength of the Warsaw Pact was rapidly increasing. Within NATO itself there was little or no promise of expansion – rather that the United States might begin to reduce its presence in Europe from 1971. The response of both the Wilson and Heath governments in public was to argue that by greater co-ordination and co-operation with their European partners in NATO they would be able to secure much greater value for money from their defence spending. Indeed, on 18 November 1970 Britain's chief Common Market negotiator, Geoffrey Rippon, argued that once his country had been admitted to E.E.C. 'the whole setting for defence co-operation and co-ordination . . . will be transformed'. Earlier, Healey had shown great interest in encouraging the mutual procurement of military equipment, pointing out that the growth of a common tactical doctrine and common operational requirements would greatly facilitate such ventures. Common equipment would give rise in turn to major supply economies.

In the quest for common arms procurement, the outstanding British contribution lay in the realm of aircraft, with the Anglo-French Jaguar and helicopter programmes, and the joint bid with West Germany and Italy to build the M.R.C.A., or Panavia Panther, leading the way. The Jaguar project had been particularly encouraging, with such rapid progress following the start of negotiations in 1964 that the design had been frozen by November 1965. Japan was later to build its engine under licence. But a more chequered history had awaited the swing-wing undertakings. Britain and France had found it difficult to reconcile their very different needs in the A.F.V.G. programme, and in July 1967 the French had withdrawn – ostensibly for reasons of economy. It was soon noted, however, that the French firm of Dassault was making good progress with a swing-wing project of its own, the Mirage IIIG. In due course, Britain was able to make a fresh start with new partners, but further defections – including that of Canada – soon reduced the collaborators to three – Britain, West Germany and Italy. Again much initial difficulty was encountered in producing common specifications, and for a time it appeared as if two versions would have to be built – a one-seater close-support aircraft to replace the West German Starfighters, and a two-seater, all-weather strike-reconnaissance-interdictor for the R.A.F. But in the spring of 1970 the West German Social Democrat government decided to take the same version as the R.A.F., but at the price of nearly halving their probable order to about 420 aircraft. Hopes of a production run of at least 1000 planes, with consequently fairly low unit costs, were thus being rudely shaken.

In 1969 the British government spoke optimistically of a total research, development and initial production bill of some £2 billion for 1000 aircraft. Export sales at about £1·5 million per plane were being mooted. These estimates were sceptically received by many, especially since the Panther was a venture into the still unfamiliar territory of swing-wing technology. The more ambitious American F-111 was a constant reminder of the financial and technical disappointments that might lie ahead. Foreign competitors were also making an appearance in 1970, with both Dassault and Lockheed (an

American firm) hoping to offer attractive rivals in the near future. Some British critics feared that West Germany's aircraft industry would be built up as a serious competitor, profiting from British experience and expertise. On the other hand, failing a joint programme with the British, the Germans would probably have gone in search of other partners – with similar results. Other critics complained that in many respects the performance of the Panther would be inferior to that of the current generation of Phantoms, a disappointing prospect for the R.A.F. if, as was likely by the late 1970s, the Panthers, about 350–400 of them, formed two-thirds of its combat strength. On the other hand, the project had at least doubled the initial production run for Rolls-Royce's new engine, the RB-199, a crucial gain for a company whose great American rivals owed much to their vast home market.

International co-operation, therefore, was not without its problems. Agreements were not easily reached over the division of work, differing specifications, and different methods of working. The absence of a serious rival to Rolls-Royce meant almost automatic British dominance in engine development. By way of compensation prospective European partners sought leadership in airframe design. British critics, however, argued that the Labour government had so paraded its belief in international co-operation that important bargaining counters had been thrown away at the outset. Intending partners could safely raise their demands. Even the government agreed that collaborative projects were handicapped by the fact that other countries might not plan their defence policies on so long-term a basis as the British. Practical experience showed that overall costs rose by between one-quarter and one-third, though unit costs might fall by a fifth given the savings achieved from a longer production run. British aerospace jingoists had also to be reminded that even a comparatively modest military aircraft project for the 1970s could be expected to cost at least £1 billion – or more than the estimated cost of the contentious TSR-2.[38]

Other examples of international procurement included the Anglo-French helicopter programmes and the Martel air-to-surface missile; and two Anglo-German medium gun projects for their respective armies. Denis Healey had backed up this quest for economy through international co-operation with great emphasis upon efficient management at home, and the avoidance of over-ambitious operational specifications for new equipment. He hoped that such techniques would keep the cost of research and development at approximately the 1968 proportion of the defence estimates – or some 11 per cent. Even so, defence was still absorbing about a quarter of the nation's total spending on research and development at the end of the 1960s. About half the energies of the aircraft industry continued to be devoted to defence contracts: ship-building and electronics devoted about one-sixth.[39] Not all industries were pleased by the new approach. The Electronic Engineering Association told the Select Committee on Science and Technology in 1967–8 that 'such technological position as this country occupies in the world today is very largely based on military spending'. In particular they complained that there was insufficient civil demand for the micro-electronic equipment then being developed by industry. Government contracts were essential to build up production and so cut costs leading to wider civil markets. Earlier defence purchases had provided a launching-pad for civil radar, computers, and a variety of telecommunication and navigational equipment. Thus automation in industry owed much to the development of automatic anti-aircraft gun control and to guided missiles. Civil aerospace development similarly was indebted to military aircraft projects such as the Lightning, TSR-2 and Harrier.

As for government administrative procedures, there were continuing complaints in the later 1960s of the ponderousness of government departments, or so industry thought. It was agreed that the Zuckerman procedures, though imperfect, had removed many delays and brought more accurate estimates of costs. The Ministry of Technology was also welcomed as a more sympathetic authority than the Ministry of Aviation. At the same time it was widely recognised that the two main aircraft projects of the later 1960s, the Nimrod and Harrier, for all their sophistication, were both amalgams of existing technology. Difficulties must be expected whenever performance beyond the existing state of the art was sought.

Nor could industry be protected from the possibility of changes in government policy or delays in the provision of public funds. Industry for its part pointed out that it could achieve the greatest efficiency and economy only if projects followed each other in a regular sequence, so that research, development and production teams could all be kept fully employed. Industry also argued that the growing interest of government in foreign sales of armaments led logically to the earliest possible involvement of firms in the drafting of specifications. Government departments could not be so conversant with overseas sales possibilities and the type of arms most likely to be in demand as individual firms themselves. Only practical experience in the early 1970s would tell whether a more satisfactory relationship had been established between industry and government defence departments. In the meantime, in 1968, the President of the Electronic Engineering Association looked back and claimed that industry could have produced a simple piece of equipment for the army in three years, whereas government involvement had extended the period to ten! Admiralty interference was also blamed for delays in the guided missile programme.

The struggle to keep defence research, development and procurement costs within bounds thus continued to be a difficult one, and would become no easier unless the Soviet Union and the United States should themselves decide to slow the pace of military technological change. Healey had boldly cut back both the operational capabilities and the number of many new weapons. But many problems remained open in 1970. If only a few diehards refused to see that the Phantom/ Panther types must remain the ultimate in combat performance for the R.A.F. of the 1970s, there still remained the question of numbers, and of the balance to be maintained between the various types of aircraft. The new Conservative government of 1970 differed little from its predecessor in its answers. It put an end to speculation that the vast American transport plane, the C-5 Galaxy, might be purchased for the R.A.F., perhaps thereby underlining the finite character of its limited presence East of Suez. Its decision to station a few Nimrod maritime reconnaissance aircraft in that region re-opened the question of the adequacy of the original order of only 30 of those invaluable aeroplanes. More promising was the new government's decision to increase the number of operational aircraft in the order for 200 Jaguars so that four extra squadrons would be provided for the air force's close support role in NATO. A less sophisticated plane would be procured to replace the current jet-training aircraft. Even so, some uncertainties would remain. The respective merits of the Jaguar and V.S.T.O.L. Harrier in the close-support role had yet to be conclusively established. Some thought the Harrier would prove 'the Polaris of conventional warfare', but others thought the Jaguar's heavier load-carrying capability, with its ability to operate from short grass strips, would establish it as the more cost-effective plane.[40] It also remained to be seen whether the Harrier could be developed into a suitable aircraft for shipboard operation. Finally there were many critics of the current helicopter procurement programmes, questioning both the numbers and quality of the machines on order.

The long-term needs of the navy were also extensive and costly – so much so, indeed, that Neville Brown speculated on the desirability of extending the policy of international procurement more generally to this service also.[41] Notwithstanding Labour's promises in 1964 of a strong navy, the active fleet had fallen to 143 units from 181 during their six years in office. The reserve fleet had also been drastically cut back yet again. The nuclear fleet submarine programme had been slowed, so that only seven would be operational by 1972 against the twelve or fourteen that experts regarded as the minimum force. The efficacy of those completed would be diminished by the delay, at least until 1972 in the production or purchase of a modern anti-submarine torpedo.[42] Meanwhile serious delays were also being reported in the delivery of certain computers and other electronic equipment for surface ships.[43] The navy's position was to be slightly strengthened by the return of the Conservatives to office in 1970, for they decided to retain the carrier *Ark Royal* until the end of the decade, and entered into negotiations with the French in the hope of establishing a collaborative programme for the French Exocet surface-to-surface missile system. If successful, this could lead to the widespread installation of this weapon in major British surface warships in the course of the 1970s. Continuing interest was expressed in the possible development of a submarine-launched, anti-ship missile system, while the Labour programme of building a new class of through-deck cruisers[44] was to proceed. These should replace the *Ark Royal* in the late 1970s, by which time it was hoped that a suitable maritime version of a V.S.T.O.L. aircraft would be available to supplement the helicopters which these ships were originally designed to carry. It was hoped that these weapon systems would afford the fleet sufficient protection against the various Soviet missiles that could be launched from bombers, ships and submarines over distances of up to 300 miles. Land-based air cover for the fleet would be of little value beyond a radius of 250 miles.[45] But if the navy's prospects had been slightly improved, the end result was still uncertain. The new government's airy talk of undercutting the long-term projected estimates of its predecessor meant that the re-equipment process might well be a slow one. Sensible and economical as was the retention of the *Ark Royal* in some respects, she was only one ship – and a rather aged one at that. Some assistance might be required from R.A.F. personnel to man her aircraft as the navy's own fixed-wing aircrew dwindled.

The navy, meanwhile, was striving to control the cost of other re-equipment programmes. The newest destroyers in the late 1960s were priced at about £17 million each, and the general-purpose *Leander* frigates at no less than £6 million. Smaller destroyers and frigates were planned for the 1970s in the hope that their cost would not greatly exceed that of their predecessors, and major savings in operating costs were expected from the use of gas turbines as the sole propelling units in all new warships save nuclear submarines. Gas turbines could be easily and speedily replaced, and they required smaller engine-room staffs than the traditional steam-power. The Royal Navy was a world pioneer in this field, aero-engines such as the Olympus and Tyne being successfully adapted to marine requirements.[46] Even so some experts feared that such economies would not suffice in the long run, and foresaw a time when the navy might be obliged, in the interest of further savings, to order ships from shipbuilders

I

in the same way as the R.A.F. procured planes from the aero-space industry.[47] Neville Brown thought that unless Britain was prepared to collaborate with European partners in ship design and construction, either a very steep increase in naval spending or severe cuts in the size of the fleet would become inevitable.[48]

As to size, the Royal Navy had long been a poor third after that of the Soviet Union. The return of some ships to the Mediterranean from 1969 could not alter the fact that the increasingly formidable Soviet presence in that sea would be mainly offset in the near future by the American Sixth Fleet. Even in north European waters the British fleet could operate only as part of an alliance, so great was the Soviet advantage. It is interesting to find the Under-Secretary of State for the Navy, in a rare reference to naval strategy, informing Parliament on 11 March 1968 that the chief role of the navy in future would be to assist NATO in the 'deterrence of maritime aggression that could lead to all-out war'.[49] Since 1965, he observed, NATO had been discontinuing its preparations for a third Battle of the Atlantic. This extension of the strategy of flexible response to naval warfare meant that NATO would place less reliance on sheer numbers of ships. The object would be to demonstrate the seriousness of the alliance's resolve, and force an attacker to face squarely the risks of nuclear escalation. As on land, it was a policy of trying to make the utmost use of what one was prepared to maintain rather than of procuring what was really desirable – militarily. This was sensible and economical given the political impracticability of any alternative policy, but equally it meant that Britain should make an extreme effort to dovetail her naval planning into the alliance. In 1969, in contrast, Britain's naval pretensions seemed in excess of her capabilities, with promises of increased naval strength in the Mediterranean not being fulfilled, and with even home waters experiencing an embarrassing shortage of ships. There were complaints that those in commission were overworked, and that this was having a bad effect on recruiting and re-engagements.[50] Talk of meaningful British naval presences in the North Sea, the Atlantic, the Mediterranean and the Indian Ocean meant little unless properly related to the naval dispositions of Britain's allies. It was useless for the British sailor to be Jack of all seas and master of none.

In addition to certain weaknesses in ships and equipment, the navy was also short of personnel. This was a problem it shared with the other services. Government plans for the early 1970s envisaged a reduction in the naval establishment to 78,000, but it was by no means certain that even this lower figure could be attained. Early in 1970 the navy, including the Marines, had a shortfall of 3200 in their target of trained men. Officer recruitment was running about one-fifth below the number required.

The recruiting problem was common to all the services, given the steady drop in the number of young men in the fifteen-to-nineteen age-group, and as a higher percentage of that group stayed on at school or proceeded to institutions of higher education.[51] Where there had been nearly 40,000 male other rank recruits in 1966–7, the figure for 1968–9 had been a mere 28,000. This had since improved (to 34,000 in 1969–1970 and with a promise of still better things in 1970–1), but in the early 1970s the services would need to recruit over 40,000 for several years in succession to attain even the manpower projections of the Wilson government. The new Conservative government sadly conceded that it could only modify, not cancel, the reduction of major army units envisaged by its predecessor, but the viability of this policy was clearly dependent on the final outcome of the current recruiting drive. It was hoped that the prospect of some service East of Suez and the projection of a favourable service image, with the promise of long-term stability, would encourage recruiting. But the Ministry of Defence was setting itself a formidable task, especially in trying to strengthen the army. As Roy Hattersley, Labour's Minister of Defence for Administration, had bluntly pointed out on 5 March 1970, to achieve the 1974 manpower targets it would be necessary to recruit a higher percentage of the pool of possible entrants than at any time since 1957. Meanwhile, although a few voices continued to be raised in its favour, neither party, nor the services themselves, were disposed to return to any form of compulsory service. Even short regular engagements were unpopular among the service chiefs, despite the successful introduction of three-year engagements in the army in 1969. Some outside commentators thought certain units should experiment with two-year periods.

Indeed, the services might soon find that one of their strongest attractions for potential recruits would be the many specialised training facilities they had at their disposal, and which would have to be further improved to keep pace with their own future needs. A combination of short-service options with good training for post-service careers might well boost recruiting. Not all arms, of course, developed skills that would necessarily interest future civilian employers. The infantry would remain a special problem, although the technical expertise demanded of an infantryman was steadily growing. Officer recruitment too would remain a special problem, with too few candidates coming forward with the right combination of educational and personal qualifications. Too few able young men viewed the services as satisfactory, long-term careers, despite the efforts to attract graduates, and the promise of a university education or its equivalent to all suitable non-graduate entrants. There was also growing concern to improve the technical and general education of officers not suited to degree work. For the army in particular there was the further problem of attracting candidates from all sections of society, as the number of entrants from traditional sources dropped dramatically. It was not surprising that Sandhurst had vacancies in 1970 when the proportion of public-school entrants had declined from 95 per cent in 1939 to about 30.

Investigations among servicemen revealed that pay continued to be a major source of discontent. Other complaints, especially among officers, included the uncertainty of service life as a career, unsatisfactory status and promotion prospects, and family separation. Service life in general, with its discipline – albeit much relaxed since 1945 – was more readily accepted. The Ministry of Defence in 1969–70 decided to introduce a pay structure that would be more akin to civilian salaries and wages to simplify comparisons. Less pay in kind – food and accommodation – would be provided. Nevertheless the attempts of the 1960s to compete with civilian wages and salaries had been expensive. In 1970 the pay of defence personnel stood at £952,040,000 compared with the £755,600,000 spent on research, development and production. The cost of the former had risen by £243 million since 1965; that of the latter had fallen by £178 million. These were disturbing figures, since defence personnel had been falling in numbers, while the downward trend in military hardware could not continue indefinitely. The Ministry of Defence in 1970 hoped to attack some personnel costs by closing a number of old hospitals, barracks and similar establishments, and to stream-line and rationalise training and logistics.

Perhaps the least controversial aspect of British defence policy under the Wilson government was the future of the strategic nuclear forces. The keen debates of the last years of Conservative rule were seemingly forgotten.[52] Public apathy helped to silence much of the controversy surrounding 'the Bomb'. The Labour leaders, in opposition, had talked – somewhat vaguely – about the non-renewal of the British deterrent, and about renegotiation of the Nassau agreement, should they be elected to power. In office they professed to find the Polaris programme too advanced to cancel, and they were content with the gesture of not starting the fifth sub-marine. The wisdom of this step would only be confirmed or disproved after operational experience in the 1970s had shown whether a force of four would suffice to maintain two submarines on station at most times. Much would depend upon whether Rosyth dockyard could refit a nuclear sub-marine in less than a year. The government had also the task of reassuring its own rank and file concerning the mainten-ance of this potent force. Dedicated opponents of nuclear weapons could not, of course, be tranquillised, but for the sake of the party as a whole it was necessary to tread softly – just as their predecessors had had to satisfy their Right wing with repeated trumpeting of the existence of an 'independent' British deterrent. Much was made by the Wilson government of the possible use of part of the British nuclear force as an element in an international nuclear umbrella to protect India from any Chinese nuclear threat. The idea was not without interest in its own right, but New Delhi was unresponsive.

A second government move in the winter of 1964–5, again with one eye on its effects on the Labour party, was the proposal to NATO of an Atlantic Nuclear Force. Britain would contribute to such a force all the V-bombers (save any needed for extra-European roles) and the four Polaris nuclear submarines once they had been completed. It was proposed that the United States should also contribute four of her Polaris submarines, and there was to be a mixed-manned or joint force in which the non-nuclear states of Europe might participate. The whole arsenal would be under collective NATO control, each participant having the right of veto. The Atlantic Nuclear Force proposals were intended to eliminate or obscure the 'independent' elements in the British deterrent, and to replace the American plan for a European multilateral force[53] which, it was felt, offered inadequate obstacles to the emergence of West Germany as a nuclear power in her own right.

In fact interest in the American plan was already dying in Europe, so that while the new British proposals received some polite attention, essentially they too had become irrelevant. Interest was moving from 1965 towards increased participation by western Europe in the planning of the use of nuclear weapons by NATO. Formal talks began in November, and led to the establishment of two NATO nuclear planning bodies in 1967 – the Nuclear Defence Affairs Committee and the Nuclear Planning Group. With the United States devoting more of its energies to the negotiation of a non-proliferation treaty with the Soviet Union, and with de Gaulle's France showing no disposition to retreat from its own independent nuclear stance, European collaborative efforts concerning nuclear arms seemed unlikely to proceed beyond the decisions of 1967 for many years to come. The British deterrent in consequence became less of a controversial issue at home. Vietnam absorbed the energies and interests of the majority of demonstrators. The Wilson government emphasised that British nuclear forces were targeted in accordance with NATO and American plans, but, as Conservative questioners in Parliament were able to establish, ultimate sovereignty over the weapons had not been surrendered. They could always be retargeted if warranted by a change of circumstances, a change that the Prime Minister liked to limit to the collapse of NATO.[54]

The Wilson government had thus come to acknowledge, privately rather than publicly but none the less decisively, that Britain's nuclear force (since it existed and would exist for some years to come at no extreme cost to the nation) was too formidable a weapon to be cast lightly aside in an uncertain world. Even within the context of the NATO alliance and its day-to-day working, the British deterrent might not be without value, giving the nation more influence over the nuclear planning and targeting of the alliance than any other European power. Tidy-minded Americans might continue to dream of absolute control over all the nuclear arms of the alliance, and complain about Britain's delusions of grandeur. But no British government could look to the long-term future with complete confidence, and feel that the interests of the United States and western Europe would always coincide. Who could tell how introspective or cautious the United States might become in the 1970s after its harrowing experience in Vietnam, and given the probability of continuing internal racial and political divisions? A time might come when the American guarantee would be in doubt. Possibly neither Britain nor western Europe would be in a condition to provide a credible nuclear deterrent of their own if and when that time should come – nor might they feel it wise to do so – but for Britain to fall out of the nuclear race in the late 1960s would ensure that she for one had closed that option from the outset.

The actual degree of credibility and strength possessed by the current British nuclear force therefore mattered less than its existence. Future options were being kept open; scientific, industrial and operational expertise were being maintained. Should western Europe and the United States drift apart, should a European nuclear deterrent become both desirable and possible, Britain would be able to play an influential part in its creation. Britain's nuclear policy in the late 1960s should thus be viewed as primarily an insurance policy, the premiums being paid with American help. Admittedly the British share in this premium might have been used for other purposes, and if used militarily there were plenty of deficiencies within the nation's conventional forces to be rectified. But money thus applied would have secured for Britain less influence within the alliance than her current policy, and would have denied her an important option in the future.

It is true that in time this nuclear option might no longer make sense for Britain. A major Soviet A.B.M. system might erase the credibility of all but the largest nuclear forces, one beyond the capability of Britain – perhaps even beyond that of western Europe. Viable nuclear delivery systems, similarly, might become so costly and complex that Britain would be obliged to fall out of the race. A refusal of further assistance by the United States, and the absence of a European partner – or partners – might equally bring the British nuclear era to a close. Two negative decisions were indeed taken by the Wilson government. The first was to forgo the possibility of adapting the British nuclear submarines to carry the new American missile, Poseidon, with its multiple, independently targetable warheads. This modification was ruled out on the grounds of expense – one American estimate put the cost of adapting a submarine at $200 million – and because it was felt that Polaris, with improved warheads and a variety of devices to confuse an enemy's warning systems, would retain an adequate penetrative capability for several years to come. Britain could afford to wait until the early 1970s before it decided on the character of the next generation of nuclear weapons – indeed, whether such a generation was needed or desirable. Labour likewise decided that this was not the time to go in search of new nuclear partners, and consequently discouraged the various proposals for Anglo-French co-operation that were being noised abroad in the later 1960s. Fears of dissension and controversy within the Labour party itself undoubtedly encouraged both these negative decisions, but it could also be argued that circumstances in general at this time pointed to similar conclusions.

In contrast, Conservative enthusiasm for an Anglo-French nuclear partnership was rapidly mounting.[55] As their leader, Edward Heath, explained in some detail in May 1967, the creation of such a partnership might be a step towards a western European deterrent. The Anglo-French forces might be 'held in trust' for the rest of Europe until its political future became clearer. In the meantime the non-nuclear European members of NATO might join a nuclear planning committee similar to that already in existence and which gave western Europe a voice in the targeting of some American nuclear weapons. This did not seem a very promising line of thought so long as General de Gaulle remained President of France, but his resignation in April 1969 gave rise to hopes of more flexible French policies in the future. Certainly the cost of the French nuclear force (*force de frappe*) was high – between £400 and £600 million a year – and many delays and difficulties were occurring. The French, despite their progress with solid-fuelled rockets (a field in which the British relied on the Americans), were far behind the British in warhead design, guidance systems and marine nuclear technology. In public the French maintained an imperturbable and proud reserve, and displayed no interest in operational co-operation. At the level of research, development and production, however, there were reports that they might prove more sympathetic.

Any French overtures while Labour was in office were firmly discouraged. The British government contended that any Anglo–French partnership would weaken NATO, and might annoy both the United States and the rest of Europe. The American Secretary for Defence, Melvin Laird, was to explain in London on 23 June 1970 his preference for French inclusion in the existing nuclear planning organisation of NATO to any Anglo–French co-operation. Neither the American nor West German governments could view a London–Paris nuclear axis as other than a complication at a time when they were engaging respectively in strategic arms limitation talks (SALT) and negotiations for a *détente* with the Soviet Union. The Wilson government, to the last, therefore argued that priority must be given to the negotiations for Britain's entry into E.E.C. Once that had been achieved, some new thinking about the partial or complete Europeanisation of the British deterrent might become possible. Edward Heath himself agreed that any Anglo–French partnership must not be at the expense of Britain's relations with the United States or her other European allies. After the Conservative victory at the polls in June 1970, a Paris meeting of French and British Foreign Ministers on 15 July agreed that nuclear co-operation was not a matter for early decision. Many

commentators took the view, and the new government soon
appeared to be moving to the same position, that any positive
Anglo–French moves would be unpopular elsewhere in
Europe as well as in the United States, while to proceed to a
European deterrent would be impracticable without prior
political union. Even then it would be politically wise only if
relations with the United States and the Soviet Union left the
new Europe with no alternative.

Meanwhile, by 1970, the British Polaris programme had
been making excellent progress. The fourth submarine became operational in that year – the first had been commissioned in 1967. The navy took over responsibility for the
deterrent from the R.A.F. in July 1969. The estimated
annual running cost of the force in 1970 was only £32 million
compared with £45 million for the V-bombers in 1966. The
Polaris manpower requirement of 3200 servicemen and 3300
civilians was also less – only about two-thirds that required
by the V-bombers. Each submarine had two crews – 'port' and
'starboard', each about 140 strong – which would alternate
for two-month cruises. The sixteen Polaris missiles carried
by each submarine had a range of some 2500 miles (nautical).
According to American figures all but one of the missiles
were normally operational and could be fired at one-minute
intervals. Each British missile had three warheads and a
variety of penetration aids to hamper the radar system guiding
an enemy anti-ballistic missile defence. The Ministry of
Defence expressed full confidence in the ability of sufficient
of these missiles to break through any current defence system
and to destroy enough enemy cities to maintain the credibility
of the British force for some years to come.[56]

The Conservative government which took office in June
1970 was, however, likely to be presented in its lifetime with
the problem of the renewal of the deterrent. Much would
depend on the outcome of the SALT negotiations between
the United States and the Soviet Union, and on the speed,
extent and quality of their deployment of nuclear arms. The
possibility that a fifth British Polaris submarine would be
constructed was mentioned, while there was continuing Conservative interest in both an Anglo-French nuclear deterrent
and in the purchase of American Poseidon missiles. With

respect to nuclear submarines themselves the Centre for Strategic and International Studies of the University of Georgetown, Washington, D.C., was confident in 1970 that, despite the immense efforts being made by the Russians to overhaul the ten-year lead enjoyed by the Americans in anti-submarine warfare, it was unlikely that Polaris submarines could be tracked for more than short periods in the immediate future. From the British point of view, therefore, much would turn on the quality and strength of future Soviet A.B.M. systems. It remained to be seen, too, how far the United States would continue to assist in the maintenance of the British deterrent. Any obvious American reluctance might well strengthen the case for attempted co-operation with France. Or circumstances might persuade Britain to treat the current Polaris force as the last of her nuclear forces. Only one thing was clear. Any quest for a new generation of nuclear arms would be hideously expensive without American assistance.

Meanwhile military science and technology were advancing remorselessly in other directions. Experimental work at Porton Down on chemical-bacteriological warfare became a centre of controversy from February 1968, with twenty-one members of the Royal Society supporting a campaign against the secrecy and mystery that surrounded this establishment, and its exchanges of information with the United States. Some of its work was said to have been put to practical use by the Americans in Vietnam. Some relaxation of the secrecy enveloping Porton Down followed, but the value of the American connection was re-emphasised. Lord Shepherd, the Minister of State for Foreign and Commonwealth Affairs, told the House of Lords on 5 February 1969 that the United Kingdom was not manufacturing or stockpiling chemical and bacteriological weapons. The research was solely for the purpose of gaining knowledge concerning these awful threats, and of exploring the possibility of defence against them. The Commons Select Committee on Science and Technology reported on 7 May 1969 in favour of continuing control of Porton Down by the Ministry of Defence for reasons of security. By 1970 it seemed as if this controversy, like the one over the British deterrent, was joining the ranks of forgotten causes, save for a small minority of enthusiasts.

Indeed, no defence issue was to figure prominently in the 1970 election. A few Labour cries concerning the danger of conscription under a Conservative government, and a few Conservative protests over the retreat from East of Suez, were drowned by the uproar over the state of the economy. Nor could one quarrel unduly with this sense of priorities. For if the British gross national product continued to grow at a mere 2 or 3 per cent a year,[57] and given the rising expectations of the population concerning private consumption, more and better social services, and greater educational opportunities, only a dramatic change in East–West relations in Europe would enable any British government to increase markedly its spending on defence. Any government's choices in defence policy would similarly be limited by the numbers of servicemen who could be raised by voluntary enlistment. Even a readiness or ability to spend more money was unlikely to have more than a marginal effect here, though it might prove possible to strengthen the second-rank reserves for home defence, or perhaps even for foreign service should an emergency last long enough to complete their training. In any case, there would be plenty of other claimants for additional funds, whenever they became available. As Charles Douglas-Home noted in *The Times* on 14 February 1970:

> If an emergency now overtook us we would have little or no spare supplies of ammunition, of vehicles, of tanks or guns, of medical stocks or any other defence equipment. Our present military capability is more or less a confidence trick based on the bluff of a nuclear weapon which politicians say they would use but know they could not do so.

The return of the Conservatives to office in June 1970 was welcomed with great hopes by all who took the view that Labour defence policy had been short-sighted, too cost-conscious, too susceptible to Left-wing pressures, too indifferent to Britain's place in the world and the realities of international politics. It was noticeable, however, that as the election approached, and the possibility of office drew nearer, so leading Conservatives became more cautious in their pronouncements on defence. Given the continuing slow growth of the national product, the public's expectations of lower taxes and a check to inflation, not to mention the service man-power problem, there existed no room for drastic changes. International and internal circumstances were combining in 1970 to make 5 per cent, or thereabouts, of the gross national product seem a politically expedient level of defence spending. Yet such a level of spending, without a sharp rise in the gross national product, would leave little margin, if any, in which to expand the defence plans of Denis Healey. Service salaries, the cost of the Panther and of new warships could all outstrip expectations, while each of the three services could produce expensive shopping-lists for new and additional equipment merely to meet the defence commitments accepted by the Wilson government.

For instance, the navy was interested in more fleet nuclear submarines, and in the provision of improved armaments for these and surface ships. Both interim and long-term provision was needed to protect the fleet from missile attack. With respect to the R.A.F., many were troubled by its steady decline in overall numbers, and they hoped for an enlargement in the procurement programmes. Some, too, continued to hope that a longer-range type of aircraft might yet be authorised to fill the gap left by the TSR-2 and F-111 cancellations, or at the very least that a stretched version of the Panther might be developed. For the army it was said that more anti-tank weapons and helicopters were required; no replacement for the obsolescent Honest John missiles was in prospect, while the Soviets were two years ahead in night-fighting equipment. There were hopes that the army's over-stretch in manpower – especially in the infantry – would receive some consideration, and that in the process some famous regiments due for extinction might be saved. On the one hand, too, there were pleas for more reserves, whereas some experts thought that priority should be given to expanding the stocks of existing armaments, since these had fallen to a precariously low level. So extensive a list meant that many would be disappointed unless a totally new defence philosophy were to be adopted.

That Conservative innovations were likely to be marginal was indicated by the announcement in August 1970 that several regiments destined for early disbandment or fusion

with others would be given the option of surviving for the
time being as independent companies. This was a doubtful
expedient, though one that might prove its utility should
army recruiting improve sufficiently for some of these companies to be reconstituted later at battalion strength. The
approach, however, could hardly commend itself to radicals
such as Liddell Hart, General Ward-Harrison or Correlli
Barnett who favoured the creation of a corps of infantry, or
the fusion of infantry and tank units.[58] All military men,
whatever their feelings on the regimental question, could
nevertheless welcome the new government's less rigid
approach to the problems of manpower.

In August 1970 the Heath government also decided to
remove the uncertainty left by their predecessors concerning
the future of the Brigade of Gurkhas. Four or five infantry
battalions were to be retained for the foreseeable future, a
decision that fitted in well with the announcement that
Britain was to maintain indefinitely a small presence East of
Suez. The *Supplementary Statement on Defence Policy*, published on 27 October 1970, included promises of continuing
support for both SEATO and CENTO, of British entry into
a five-power defence arrangement relating to Malaysia and
Singapore, and of further British participation in local discussions concerning the future of the Persian Gulf. In
practice, however, the degree to which previous Labour policy
was to be modified was likely to remain very limited. The
envisaged defence arrangement with Malaysia, Singapore,
Australia and New Zealand, which would replace the existing
Anglo-Malaysian defence treaty with its firm commitments,
would be no more than 'a political commitment of a consultative nature' to be undertaken by each of the five members
equally. Some British forces would remain in the region, but
these were designed to complement the units provided by the
other four partners. Thus the British naval contribution
would consist of no more than five frigates or destroyers, with
Hong Kong and the Rhodesian blockade among their responsibilities. There would be a British battalion group, including
an artillery battery. The air force would provide up to four
Nimrod aircraft and some Whirlwind helicopters. Other
units of all three services would visit Singapore and Malaysia

for training purposes. The extra annual cost of this presence, including overseas expenditure, was not expected to exceed £10 million per year.

Welcome as this new policy undoubtedly was to Britain's four Commonwealth partners, it was doubtful whether it represented a very significant advance in military terms on the intentions of the Wilson government. Its advantages were mainly political, educative and psychological. It might facilitate and encourage co-operation between those uneasy neighbours, Malaysia and Singapore. The stronger the international flavour of the defence arrangement, the easier the local Chinese and Malays might find it to sink their many differences. The larger number of British personnel would be especially valuable for the development of a wide spectrum of military skills in the local defence forces, especially of the most sophisticated kind, and also embracing logistics. British expertise in jungle warfare, air defence and maritime reconnaissance would be particularly valuable. Yet the fact remained that Britain would find herself in a highly embarrassing situation should a major threat develop in the region. If internal, it might find Chinese ranged against Malays. If external, the outcome would be determined by the reactions of all the major powers interested in this region. At most it might be said that the new Conservative policy was a slightly better way of doing what Labour had planned from January 1968 – a matter of encouraging certain local trends that were making for greater regional stability, but whose success and failure would be essentially conditioned by regional circumstances. So long as the government recognised these limitations in its policy, all might yet be well.[59]

Experience of office seemed to persuade the new government that their predecessors' policy in the Persian Gulf was irreversible. The island of Masirah, conveniently sited in the Arabian Sea, would remain an important R.A.F. base within easy reach of the Gulf. Similarly, in certain circumstances, the Royal Navy might still have a role to play. Britain might also be able to help Bahrein and the Trucial States in the creation of viable local defence forces. But Britain's part in the future military balance in the Gulf would clearly be marginal. The Gulf states themselves, or failing them the

Soviet Union and the United States, would call the tune. Already the United States was displaying a discreet strategic interest in the region, though for the time being Iran was likely to prove the most influential state.

More controversial was the new policy of the Heath government towards South Africa. Labour, despite some dissension in the Cabinet, had decided to end all arms sales to South Africa in protest against that country's racial policies. But the Conservative Foreign Secretary, Sir Alec Douglas-Home, announced on 21 July 1970 that the new government wished to maintain the Simonstown Agreement of 30 June 1955 which had provided for mutual Anglo–South African co-operation in defence of the sea routes around South Africa. Britain should therefore be prepared to consider 'applications for the export to South Africa of certain limited categories of arms, so long as they are for maritime defence directly related to the security of the sea routes'. The expectation that some arms would be sold to South Africa led to a great outcry in Britain and in the Commonwealth, not all of which was devoted to the strategic aspects of the question. The matter was furiously debated at the Commonwealth Conference held in Singapore in January 1971. An outright rift was avoided, but the British government announced on 22 February that it was to sell seven helicopters to South Africa in fulfilment of a legal obligation to that state arising out of the Simons-town Agreement. These legal obligations had been set out in a white paper of 4 February, the new Attorney-General and Solicitor-General differing from the conclusions of the previous government's legal advisers that no such obligations existed. It was emphasised, however, that few arms (mostly helicopters for anti-submarine purposes) were thus covered, and the government would have to defend more extensive sales on grounds of national interest.[60]

The strategic debate over the wisdom and desirability of these arms sales centred upon the appearance of a permanent Soviet naval presence in the Indian Ocean.[61] Was this the start of a large Russian naval build-up similar to that achieved in the Mediterranean in the 1960s, and if so, what would be the wisest western response? Some experts thought they detected the emergence of tougher and more ambitious trends in Soviet foreign policy. Once the Suez Canal had been re-opened the Russian navy would be able to reinforce its units in the Indian Ocean at short notice. These and other arguments persuaded many that no opportunity should be lost to strengthen pro-western forces in the vicinity of the Indian Ocean, and that South Africa's maritime forces in particular should be built up to that end. Critics of this view – and they came not merely from the Left – contended that arms sales to South Africa would prove counter-productive, alienating many in 'Black' Africa, and forcing them to turn to the Soviet Union for aid. Precipitate British action could help to create a second Arab–Israeli imbroglio, a repeat of a situation in which Arabs had often found themselves reluctant supplicants in the Kremlin. Some defence commentators also questioned whether the Soviet Union was likely, of its own volition, to seek a major crisis with the West in that region. The Indian Ocean was remote from the main Soviet bases and power centres; the Soviet navy had yet to eradicate all its weaknesses as a long-range ocean-going force; and finally there were many other parts of the world where the Soviet Union could more conveniently test its strength against the West. It was further argued that on the worst possible assumptions arms to South Africa were not necessarily the right response. It was not certain that South Africa wished to make more than marginal additions to her maritime capabilities. Facilities at Simons-town were unlikely to be withheld in an emergency, or should at most be retained by minimal arms sales. Certainly in any East–West competition in 'showing the flag' or in some late twentieth-century variant of 'gunboat diplomacy', South African warships would be more of an embarrassment than a help.

Sea power, in any case, was but one among the many expensive instruments required by a power to extend its influence. This had been true even in the nineteenth century, though many Britons had cherished illusions about the efficacy of gunboats.[62] One hundred years later the Soviet navy could be sure of the warmest welcome in those parts of the world where the people felt most aggrieved against the West, or most fearful of its friends and associates – notably Israel. Should the Soviet navy in the Indian Ocean become a real strategic threat to the West, the chief response could only be provided by the United States. If, early in 1971, the American government was strangely silent on this question, the American navy was beginning to express concern, though naturally there was a tendency for it to exploit any argument that might facilitate the replacement of the many over-age units in its fleet. For the moment, in the winter of 1970–1, Anglo–American co-operation in the Indian Ocean seemed likely to be confined to the construction of a naval communications centre on Diego Garcia, part of the British Indian Ocean Territory. Circumstances could, of course, soon change.

Finally the Heath government launched yet another attempt to improve the administration and control of arms procurement. The merging of the short-lived Ministry of Technology with the Board of Trade to form a new Department of Trade and Industry meant that aviation was in need of yet another home. A temporary Ministry of Aviation Supply was set up, with full responsibility for civil work, and inheriting the Ministry of Technology's special responsibility to the Secretary of State for Defence for military aerospace projects. It proved possible, however, by May 1971 for 'all defence research and development and procurement activities' to be fully integrated under the responsibilty of the Secretary of State for Defence. Once this was achieved the dream of the air force to control military aerospace procurement could at last be broadly realised, an aim which successive governments had frustrated since the war, and which many still feared would lead to the undue subordination of civil aerospace interests to considerations of defence. In theory these interests might be protected by the government's new 'central capability unit', a small staff of experts based in the Cabinet Office, whose task it would be to question and challenge departmental policy proposals. It remained to be seen how influential and effective this body would prove to be.

As the first post-war generation of British defence policy draws to a close some obvious conclusions stand out. Above all, there has been the remorseless pressure of circumstances that, step by step, have forced succeeding governments – Conservative and Labour – to adopt less and less ambitious defence policies. Britain's own economic problems, coupled with ever-rising domestic expectations concerning private consumption and the social services, the emergence of the super-powers and of Afro–Asian nationalism, the development of nuclear weapons and the ever-increasing cost and sophistication of arms – all have diminished her freedom of choice. True, Britain has remained a strong military power of the second rank. In all-round professional skill and in the quality of their equipment her forces in 1971 are probably as good as they have ever been in time of peace. The numerous foreign students at her staff colleges are striking evidence of the high standing of Britain's armed forces in world opinion. Britain's experience of and expertise in most forms of conflict from civil disturbance upwards are outstanding.

Yet the complaint persists that Britain's forces are, in truth, essentially schoolmasters and parade-ground performers, with too little quantitative strength to engage in a serious or at least more than a brief major struggle. Lord Wigg insisted to a radio audience on 17 August 1970 that Britain possessed a 'very well-disciplined, beautifully dressed, gloriously turned-out stage army'. The Air League, in the same month, thought that the nation should aim at an air force with a combat strength of 1000 planes compared with the 700 available then and the 400–500 that might be available in 1975. Correlli Barnett sweepingly asserted:

> The cumulative historical evidence therefore suggests to me that in fact we ought to replace our present small, all-regular army with some kind of national service, so that in the event of crisis or war we could put into the field an army large enough, and with sufficient reserves, to fight a prolonged campaign with conventional weapons on a major scale. The concomitant of this would be an air force whose reserves would also enable it to withstand the wastage of a long battle, and a navy equally able to fight another battle of the Atlantic.[63]

Interestingly, the service audience he was addressing at the time seemed more intent upon the old controversy over the value of the air force's strategic bombing offensive against

Germany in the Second World War. It would have been more rewarding had a serious discussion of Correlli Barnett's proposals taken place. In any case it is important to note that his thesis took no account of the reluctance of any of Britain's European allies to think in terms of a long conventional conflict. France, by the end of 1970, was planning to reduce her defence expenditure to no more than 3 per cent of the national income by 1975, with consequent cuts in her conventional forces. There were signs that some other European states were becoming disturbed by the difficulty of instructing short-term conscripts properly in the use of modern sophisticated weapons. It was possible that in time conscription would be reserved for militia or territorial-type forces if sufficient volunteers could be found for the first-line units. Interest in all-volunteer forces was also growing in the United States.[64] In such circumstances any British move towards conscription would have but a marginal effect upon the strength of NATO.

Some new thinking might, of course, become necessary in western Europe and Britain should the United States begin to make serious cuts in its forces assigned to NATO, or if the deterrent value of nuclear weapons were to be seriously questioned. Although President Nixon in his 'State of the World' message to Congress on 25 February 1971 promised that the United States would make no cuts in its forces in Europe save as part of a reciprocal arms agreement with the Soviet Union, one could not view this as an indefinite guarantee. However predetermined western defence policy might seem in the light of current circumstances and considerations, it was essential to maintain an open mind as to the future. If there is any lesson to be learned from the military history of the first half of the twentieth century it is the degree to which most pre-war assumptions have been confounded.[65] Few experts before 1914 expected a long war, or understood that the contemporary military arts and technology, coupled with modern industry, the remarkable organising powers of twentieth-century bureaucracy, and the great emotional drives provided by nationalism would result in a bloody stalemate for so many years. Events after 1939 gradually proved that the new methods of the *Blitzkrieg* were not infallible, and it was only in the closing stages of the war that strategic bombing (largely through the exhaustion of the enemy's air defence) began to fulfil some of the expectations of the inter-war enthusiasts. Past failures to divine the future of war have been so widespread that one might even be tempted to conclude that current defence policy is more likely to be wrong than right, especially when, as we have repeatedly seen, it has been guided so often by political and economic considerations rather than military ones.

Nevertheless the reasoning behind British defence policy of recent years remains remarkably persuasive. The doubtful utility, the political difficulty and the economic cost of any alternative – unless of unilateral disarmament – would seem to constitute overwhelming objections. From the standpoint of the early 1970s one would seem to have more reason to complain of the slowness with which the current policies have been adopted than to lament their inadequacies. The latter, it is true, are manifold, yet, in many instances, inescapable. Common sense would seem to dictate that Britain recognise that her heroic past may not be a sound guide, that her contribution to the defence of the West will continue to decline rapidly unless her economy can be rejuvenated, that she can no longer expect to maintain the full range of modern weapon systems, or act effectively in northern Europe, the Mediterranean, the Atlantic and the Indian Ocean simultaneously. Even in her days of greatest strength Britain was too often tempted to act beyond her means – or at least her capabilities. There is a quixotic streak in the national character that has served her both ill and well. But in the future if Britain wishes to play an influential military role in the world it can only be as a conscientious and responsible member of a team. Individually she must face the future of a retired soldier.

Notes

Chapter 1

1. As long as France stood undefeated the need for such a force seemed unnecessary. Only in 1939 did Britain adopt compulsory military training and begin the slow build-up of a large army. It was still believed that ample time remained. Probably the most pessimistic note to be struck in the early months of 1940 was the calculation that British gold and dollar reserves would, at best, last no more than three years – the time expected to be spent in preparing the nation's forces to take the offensive and to exploit the slow strangulating effects of the blockade and bombing of Germany.

2. For R.A.F. neglect of tactical air power, note A. Verrier, *The Bomber Offensive* (1968) pp. 62–3 and chaps i–ii *passim*. British rearmament in general was handicapped by the massive run-down of the armaments industry since 1919.

3. H. Duncan Hall, *North American Supply* (1955) pp. 424–6, 432.

4. W. S. Churchill, *The Second World War*, vol. vi: *Triumph and Tragedy* (1954) p. 500. See also A. Bryant, *Triumph in the West: 1943–6* (1959) pp. 470–1.

5. Lord Avon, *The Eden Memoirs: The Reckoning* (1965) pp. 545–7.

6. Sir Llewellyn Woodward, *British Foreign Policy in the Second World War* (1962) pp. 272, 464, 469–70; for 1945, see chaps xxix–xxxi.

7. *The Economist*, 8 Feb 1947 and 27 Mar 1948. Alanbrooke's ideas are to be found in *Royal United Service Institution Journal* (hereafter *RUSIJ*) (1947) pp. 182–6; see also pp. 378–9.

8. Considerable back-bench criticism achieved comparatively little, though National Service was cut to one year in 1947 under such pressure. Note M. R. Gordon, *Conflict and Consensus in Labour's Foreign Policy: 1914–65* (1969) chaps iv–vii. Alanbrooke (Bryant, pp. 530–2) got on well with the new Cabinet, especially Bevin, who had already warned a Party Conference in December 1944 that National Service would be needed after the war at least until the United Nations had demonstrated its potential. Note A. Bullock, *Ernest Bevin*. vol. ii: *Minister of Labour* (1967) pp. 205, 279, 283.

9. As the Labour leaders argued in *Cards on the Table* (1947) p. 18: 'A nation which puts domestic comfort before its own security and independence is condemned to a foreign policy of appeasement leading inevitably to capitulation or to a war under unfavourable circumstances.' (Cited by Gordon, p. 127.)

10. E. J. Kingston McCloughry, *The Direction of War* (1955) p. 241; Bryant, pp. 496–502, 532–3.

11. For the role of British forces in south-east Asia after Aug 1945, see S. Woodburn Kirby, *The War against Japan* (1969) vol. v, part 3. On commitments in general, see Bryant, pp. 489–91, 530.

12. H. Dalton, *Memoirs, 1945–60: High Tide and After* (1962) pp. 101, 105; Bryant, p. 491. *The Economist* (23 Nov 1946) also took a sceptical view of a continuing British presence in the Middle East.

13. Bryant, pp. 491–532; Viscount Montgomery of Alamein, *Memoirs* (1958) p. 436.

14. There is a useful essay on Bevin and the Middle East by E. Monroe in A. Hourani (ed.), *Middle Eastern Affairs*, no. 2 (1961) pp. 9–48. See also Montgomery, pp. 420–2, 435–6; Piers Dixon, *Double Diploma: the Life of Sir Pierson Dixon* (1968) pp. 214–15; L. Hollis, *One Marine's Tale* (1956) p. 154.

15. W. Millis, *The Forrestal Diaries* (1952) p. 185.

16. Hollis, pp. 155–7.

17. Millis, pp. 489–90.

18. F. Williams, *The Triple Challenge* (1948) p. 20.

19. Royal Institute of International Affairs (hereafter R.I.I.A.), *United Kingdom Policy* (1950) pp. 51–4.

20. Montgomery, pp. 418 ff.

21. Montgomery, pp. 435–6, 499–502, 510–12. See below, pp. 45–7.

22. Dalton, pp. 193–8. According to R. Maudling's statement to the Commons on 16 Apr 1953, British forces overseas between 1946 and 1952 cost £1158 million in foreign exchange: however, in the same period Britain received more than twice as much in various forms of foreign aid.

23. Montgomery, pp. 480–2.

24. Montgomery, pp. 480–1.

25. See, for example, *RUSIJ* (1967) p. 132.

26. Montgomery, pp. 480–2; Hollis, pp. 152–4.

27. On recruiting problems, see important parliamentary statements by E. Shinwell, 16 Mar and 26 July 1950, and by J. Strachey, 20 Mar 1950. Note Sir Godfrey Ince on service manpower in *RUSIJ* (1947) pp. 390–402. For R.A.F. recruiting problems, see *Brassey* (1950) pp. 282–91, and Sir Basil Embry, *Mission Completed* (1957) pp. 287–9. Embry was Assistant Chief of Air Staff for Training (1945–8) and he concluded that National Service should be used as little as possible in peacetime for the R.A.F. (ideally, not at all) since the heavy training burden reduced the morale and efficiency of the Regulars, and therefore of the service as a whole.

28. Note interesting articles on officer recruitment by Major J. P. Corbally and Wing Commander S. G. Walker, *RUSIJ* (1946) pp. 204–8 and (1948) pp. 177–86.

29. E. Shinwell, *Conflict Without Malice* (1955) p. 194.

30. For the early history of British nuclear policy, see especially M. Gowing, *Britain and Atomic Energy: 1939–45* (1964); R. G. Hewlett and O. E. Anderson, *The New World, 1939–46: A History of the United States Atomic Energy Commission* (1962); R. N. Rosecrance (ed.), *The*

Dispersion of Nuclear Weapons (1964) chaps ii–iii; R. N. Rosecrance, *Defense of the Realm* (1968) chaps ii–iv; F. Williams, *A Prime Minister Remembers* (1961) pp. 113–19; F. Duncan, 'Atomic Energy and Anglo American Relations, 1946–54', *Orbis* (winter 1969) pp. 1188–1203; and articles by A. Goldberg in *International Affairs* (1964) pp. 409–29 and 600–18. Note also Bryant, pp. 477–8, 487–9.

31. G. R. Strauss, who was Minister of Supply in 1948, briefly explained the process in a letter to *The Times*, 23 Mar 1969. See also J. P. Mackintosh, *The British Cabinet* (1968) p. 496 and note.

32. R.I.I.A., *British Security* (1946) pp. 19–20.

33. See the relevant volumes of *Jane's Fighting Ships* and *Brassey's Naval Annual*. Also Sir P. Gretton, *Maritime Strategy* (1965).

34. Millis, p. 490.

35. See below pp. 72–3, 110, 141–2.

36. *The Navy League Year Book* (1947) p. 34.

37. Note Lord Tedder's views in his *Air Power in War* (1948) and his article in *RUSIJ* (1946) pp. 59–68. I am indebted to the 2nd Baron Tedder and to Wing Commander G. H. Wiles, who worked closely with Tedder when he was Chief of the Air Staff, for further impressions. McCloughry (pp. 157 ff.) has an interesting pen portrait of Tedder; his feeling that the latter should have pressed the claims of the R.A.F. harder than he did in the later 1940s probably does less than justice to Tedder. Embry (pp. 283 ff.) gives a brief glimpse of the service painfully and slowly adjusting itself to post-war conditions.

38. See O. Thetford, *Aircraft of the R.A.F. since 1918* (1968) or *Jane's All the World's Aircraft* (1946 ff.). For general comment, see Sir R. Fedden, *Britain's Air Survival* (1957) and R. Worcester, *Roots of British Air Policy* (1966). Much of interest is to be found in *The Supply of Military Aircraft* (1955, Cmd 9388). For the early history of jet-engines note Sir Frank Whittle, *Jet* (1953), and Hayne Constant, *Gas Turbines and Their Problems* (1953), Whittle's successor as head of Power Jets after its nationalisation in 1946.

39. A four-jet interim bomber, the SA-4, was begun late in the 1940s as an insurance policy, but was cancelled before reaching production.

40. For the history of post-war defence organisation, see F. A. Johnson, *Defence by Committee: The British Committee of Imperial Defence, 1885–1959* (1960); *Central Organisation for Defence* (1946, Cmd 6923); H. Daalder, *Cabinet Reform in Britain: 1914–63* (1964) chap. xii; McCloughry, chaps xi and xiii; Hollis, pp. 147–50; L. W. Martin, 'The Market for Strategic Ideas in Britain', *American Political Science Review* (1962) pp. 23–4; Bryant, pp. 487–8, 533–4.

41. Montgomery, pp. 489–96.

42. McCloughry, p. 249.

43. For Tizard's views see *RUSIJ* (1946) pp. 333–46, and R. W. Clark, *Tizard* (1965) pp. 368–402. See also M. M. Postan, *Design and Development of Weapons* (1964) chaps xv–xix.

44. McCloughry, p. 199.

45. Sir M. Dean, Permanent Under-Secretary of State for Air, 1955–

1963, thought (*RUSIJ*, June 1969, pp. 53–9) Labour favoured the Ministry of Supply because it fitted in with their economic thinking in general. Alanbrooke (Bryant, p. 489) came to believe that the Ministry of Supply would prove more efficient than separate service procurement. It would also protect the army and navy from dominance by the Air Ministry in the supply of aircraft.

Chapter 2

1. Duff Cooper, *Old Men Forget* (1955) pp. 372–4; Dalton, p. 269.
2. Montgomery, pp. 510–12. See above, pp. 21–2.
3. K. Knorr (ed.), *NATO and American Security* (1959) p. 14; Montgomery, pp. 509–12.
4. Millis, pp. 162, 185, 198; Montgomery, pp. 440–3; Rosecrance, *Defense of the Realm*, pp. 50–1.
5. H. G. Nicholas, *Britain and the United States* (1963), p. 50; Millis, pp. 455–6, 460, 480, 488–90, 500–1; Rosecrance, *Defense of the Realm*, pp. 74–5; R. Dawson and R. Rosecrance, 'Theory and Reality in the Anglo–American Alliance', *World Politics* (Oct 1966) p. 31; R.I.I.A., *Atlantic Alliance: NATO's Role in the Free World* (1952). Note also *The World Today* (Aug 1960) pp. 319–25.
6. Montgomery, pp. 480–7.
7. E. Shinwell, House of Commons, 23 Sep 1948.
8. *The Times*, 4 July 1949. But see also Embry, pp. 289 ff., for a brief account of the earlier reduction of Fighter Command to an experimental 'development area' covering only part of Britain, and of the gradual expansion that took place from 1948. The 1948 exercises highlighted the vulnerability of control centres to air attack, with many other weaknesses. A brief account of the modernisation of air defence is to be found in P. Wykeham, *Fighter Command: 1914–60* (1960) pp. 273 ff. For the modernisation of the British radar screen, see Select Committee on Science and Technology (1967–8), *Defence Research* (Feb–Oct 1968) 139–xviii 388–9: Marconi Co. was invited by the Ministry of Supply early in 1948 to study the possibility of achieving much higher interception rates through the development of a new radar system in anticipation of Russia becoming a nuclear power in the near future.
9. C. Attlee, House of Commons, 19 Nov 1947; Clark, *Tizard*, p. 390.
10. *Brassey* (1951) p. 5; R. E. Osgood, *NATO, the Entangling Alliance* (1962) pp. 30–7, 61, 67.
11. President Truman was ready to use America's nuclear power in defence of Europe from Sep 1947, but even by 1950 it is doubtful if the U.S. had more than 100 bombs. See Rosecrance, *Defense of the Realm*, pp. 74–5, 102, and chap. iv; Millis, pp. 455–6, 466 ff., 500–1; S. P. Huntington, *The Common Defense* (1961) pp. 33–59. Forrestal, in Oct 1948, believed that a $14.4 billion defence budget would provide little more than an air reprisal strategy based on Britain. Many American defence experts argued for more, but extra funds were not forthcoming

until 1950. On the other hand, it would appear from Soviet figures released in Jan 1960 that in some respects the West had exaggerated Russian strength in 1948, putting their armed personnel at 4 million plus against the 2,870,000 admitted later by Moscow.

12. *The Times*, 14 Sep 1951; *The Economist*, 20 Nov 1949.

13. Rosecrance, *Defense of the Realm*, chap. iv; Dean Acheson, *Present at the Creation* (1970) pp. 314–21.

14. *RUSIJ* (1950) pp. 41–51.

15. *The Times*, 15 and 28 July 1949.

16. For the Korean War see D. Rees *Korea: The Limited War* (1964); C. N. Barclay, *The 1st Commonwealth Division* (1954); R. C. W. Thomas, *The War in Korea: 1950–3* (1954); and T. Carew, *Korea: The Commonwealth at War* (1967). See also the contemporary analyses in *Brassey* and *RUSIJ* (1950–4).

17. H. C. Hinton, *Communist China in World Politics* (1966) p. 213, citing the *Manchester Guardian*, 18 Nov 1950. British efforts to restrain the U.S.A. are also mentioned by General Douglas MacArthur, *Reminiscences* (1964) pp. 370–1, and Major-General C. A. Willoughby and J. Chamberlain, *MacArthur: 1941–51* (1956) p. 357.

18. J. Callaghan, House of Commons, 12 Mar 1951.

19. Montgomery, p. 510. See also Lord Ismay, *NATO: The First Five Years, 1949–54* (1954) pp. 29–30, 103; Liddell Hart, *Defence of the West* (1950), and R.I.I.A., *Defence in the Cold War* (1950).

20. Sir J. Slessor, *The Central Blue* (1956) pp. 20–1. But for the strengths and weaknesses in Soviet air power in the early 1950s, see Asher Lee, *The Soviet Air Force* (1961) pp. 106–9, 131–3, 166–8; and R. F. Futrell, *The United States Air Force in Korea, 1950–3* (1961) pp. 471–3, for praise of Soviet air defence systems supplied to Communist China.

21. *RUSIJ* (1950) pp. 221–31.

22. Ibid. pp. 405–23.

23. *Brassey* (1951) p. 113, and P. M. S. Blackett, *Studies of War* (1962) p. 16. For NATO thinking, see Osgood, *passim*; H. A. Kissinger, *The Troubled Partnership: A Reappraisal of the Atlantic Alliance* (1965); Rosecrance, *Defense of the Realm*, chap. v.

24. For the evolution of British rearmament during the Korean War see, J. Mitchell, *Crisis in Britain, 1951* (1963); C. R. Attlee, *As It Happened* (1954) p. 199; R. Dawson and R. Rosecrance, 'Theory and Reality in the Anglo–American Alliance', *World Politics* (Oct 1966) p. 30; J. C. R. Dow, *The Management of the British Economy, 1945–60* (1964) pp. 55–65. Shinwell recalled to the House of Commons on 9 Mar 1960 that the services had been hoping in 1950–1 for £6000 million over three years. *The Economist* also argued at this time in favour of more defence expenditure, to be achieved at the expense of personal consumption. According to S. Pollard, *The Development of the British Economy, 1914–67* (1969) p. 473, an increase of £150 million in taxes on consumption had little effect, the 'real cut' coming in investment. Adverse effects of rearmament on British exports were noted some time

after the Korean War (S. Brittan, *Steering the Economy* (1969) pp. 110–111), and Brittan concluded that the government had been far too optimistic concerning the nation's ability to afford the 1950–1 programmes. In general it is difficult to see how the government could have undertaken more rearmament than it did: as it was they failed to strike a proper balance between defence, production and consumption.

25. *The Times*, 21 Aug 1950; Slessor, p. 162.

26. For the debate within the Labour party, see Gordon, chap. viii; H. Macmillan, *The Tides of Fortune* (1969) pp. 335–7, gives Attlee the highest credit for his management of this issue. Shinwell emphasised to Parliament on 6 Dec 1951 the circumstantial nature of the £4700 million figure, and in practice Churchill noted to the Commons on 5 Mar 1952 that spending for 1951–2 was likely to turn out at some £120 million below the announced figure of £1250 million. He also stressed that the expected American aid was only just beginning. One hint, however, of the sort of military alarmism to which Labour had been subjected is to be found in a War Office circular of 4 Feb 1951 (unpublished Dalton papers, cited by S. Haseler, *The Gaitskellites* (1969) p. 121): 'war possible in 1951, probable in 1952'.

27. T. Geiger and H. van B. Cleveland, *Making Western Europe Defensible*. For a comparison of industrial production among the various states of western Europe, see the Economic Commission for Europe's *Economic Survey of Europe* (1955). In 1952 Britain was spending much more of her gross national product on defence (over 10 per cent) than in 1938–9 (7½ per cent). A common pre-war calculation was that the economy could not bear more than about a 5 per cent defence burden for any length of time – short of war.

28. See House of Commons Select Committee Reports on the Estimates of 28 May 1951, 31 Aug 1951 and 27 Feb 1952; the *Economic Surveys* for 1951 (Cmd 8195) and 1952 (Cmd 8509); debates in the Commons of 23 and 26 July 1951; articles in *The Times* of 29–30 Mar 1951, and *The Economist*, 28 July and 15 Sep 1951. Note also the chapters on machine tools and electronics in D. L. Burn, *The Structure of British Industry* (1958), and for steel see Burn, *The Steel Industry, 1939–59* (1961) pp. 320–39.

29. Statement by Selwyn Lloyd, House of Commons, 2 Mar 1955.

30. For contemporary concern over the weakness of British production engineering, see *Aircraft Engineering* (Feb 1953) pp. 35–42; (Mar 1953) pp. 74–86; (May 1954) pp. 137, 168–9. G. Turner, *Business in Britain* (1969) pp. 360–9, noted that in the 1950s the British aircraft industry was interested in sophisticated aircraft, not sophisticated management: even Rolls-Royce paid little attention to cost control, and much of its administration was described as 'inspired chaos'. For the lack of co-ordination between government departments and industry, and the consequent ignorance of each other's problems, see G. Williams (ed.), *Crisis in Procurement* (Royal United Service Institution, 1969) pp. 14–15. On the problem of aircraft procurement as a whole, see the reports of the Select Committee on Estimates of 9 June 1953; the

Commons debates of 1 Mar 1954 and 28–9 Feb 1956; Professor Keith-Lucas touches on many interesting points in *RUSIJ* (1967) pp. 120–31; the Select Committee on Science and Technology (1967–8), *Defence Research* (Feb–Oct 1968) 139–iii 27–33, includes references to the neglect of cost control in the 1950s, to operational requirements that asked 'for the moon' and hoped for 75 per cent, while costs were allowed to 'balloon'. For other references see above, note 38 of the previous chapter.

31. As late as 16 Mar 1950 Churchill, despite his repeated complaints about British weakness in the air, thought British jet-fighters superior to those of Russia, and the equal of the Americans. Merlyn Rees, in a written answer to the Commons, 2 July 1968, while stating that it was not government policy to reveal the number of operational aircraft, gave the overall strength of the R.A.F. as 4510 in 1950; 6338 in 1952 (the peak in post-war numbers); 4730 in 1956; and a little over 2000 throughout the early 1960s. For an analysis of the strategic bombing capabilities of the Soviet Union, see Asher Lee, pp. 131–3, who notes that the several hundred TU-4s had a radius of action of 2000 miles, and lacked bad-weather and night-flying navigational and radar bombing aids. The vulnerability of the roughly comparable American B-29s in Korea suggested good shooting prospects for British jet-fighters, even of pre-Hunter vintage.

32. Slessor, p. 169.

33. See, for example, *The Economist*, 9 Mar 1957. Twenty-five Valiant bombers were also ordered in Apr 1951 before the first flight of the prototype (J. D. Scott, *Vickers*, 1962, p. 343).

34. For an unfavourable comparison of British as opposed to American methods of aircraft procurement, see P. B. Lucas, House of Commons, 5 Mar 1956.

35. For contemporary naval thinking, see Gretton, *passim*; Rose-crance, *Defense of the Realm*, pp. 173–5. For accounts of Soviet naval policy, see A. Buchan, *NATO in the 1960s* (1963) p. 15; Commander M. K. MacGuire, 'The Background to Russian Naval Policy', *Brassey* (1968) pp. 141–58; and R. W. Herrick, *Soviet Naval Strategy* (1968).

36. *Brassey* (1952) pp. 142–56.

37. *RUSIJ* (1951) pp. 61–4; (1965) pp. 254–61.

38. See government statements to the Commons of 26 July and 12–14 Sep 1950; 29 Jan, 14–15 Feb and 8 Mar 1951. John Strachey later told Parliament (9 Mar 1960) that whilst at the War Office he had prepared plans for 11 active divisions, 14 readily mobilisable, with the possibility of 20 more for a long war. More economical use of manpower also meant that whereas in Jan 1950, 363,500 soldiers produced only $7\frac{1}{2}$ divisions, in 1953, 437,500 produced $11\frac{1}{3}$ according to Antony Head, House of Commons, 9 Mar 1953.

39. Churchill, House of Commons, 5 Mar 1952.

40. Slessor, p. 232. Lord Avon, *The Eden Memoirs: Full Circle* (1960) pp. 32–3, refers to talks with Eisenhower in Nov 1951 in which the latter appeared to hope that in due course the Anglo–American armies could be drawn back into reserve once the continental armies had been built

up. European fears of an Anglo-Saxon withdrawal are to be seen in
D. Stikker, *Men of Responsibility* (1966) pp. 303–4. British advocates of
the integration of British forces into a western European defence
organisation were rare, but note Woodrow Wyatt, House of Commons,
6 Dec 1951; and Air Vice Marshal Yool, *Brassey* (1951) pp. 1–9.

Chapter 3

1. Macmillan, pp. 362, 486, 548–9, 560; Lord Moran, *Winston
Churchill: The Struggle for Survival, 1940–65* (1966) p. 627. McCloughry
(pp. 211–12), recalling his experience of three Ministers of Defence,
thought that only Churchill made much impact on the services.
Viscount Chandos (*The Memoirs of Lord Chandos*, 1962, pp. 343–4)
recorded that Churchill toyed with the idea of offering him the post of
Minister of Materials and Rearmament, but Chandos argued that the
other departments would not co-operate sufficiently in time of peace.

2. Macmillan, p. 497.

3. Churchill, House of Commons, 5 Mar 1952 and 2 Mar 1954. Liddell
Hart thought the Soviet military chiefs should give priority to a paratroop attack on Britain, but according to Asher Lee (pp. 106–9, 193–4)
Russia was giving only second-class priority to airborne forces, and
was developing only a short-range capability.

4. Macmillan, pp. 378–91.

5. Christopher Soames informed the Commons (1 Mar 1960) that
British expenditure on defence research, development and production
equalled £652 million in 1952 and £745 million in 1953. P.E.P., *Growth
in the British Economy* (1960) p. 143, notes that defence absorbed 7 per
cent of the metal-using industries in 1950, 14 per cent in 1953, and 10
per cent in 1957; exports took 33 per cent, 29 per cent and 32 per cent
respectively; gross domestic fixed capital formation took 30 per cent,
27 per cent and 31 per cent respectively. For the Churchill ministry's
alarm at the financial situation in 1951–2, see Macmillan, pp. 379 ff.,
and Chandos, p. 343.

6. For the evolution of NATO in the early 1950s, see Osgood, chap. iv;
Rosecrance, *Defense of the Realm*, chap. vi; NATO Information Service,
NATO (1962), and R.I.I.A., *Atlantic Alliance* (1952) *passim*.

7. Nigel Birch (Parliamentary Secretary, Ministry of Defence) told the
Commons on 5 Mar 1953 that four active divisions (three of them
armoured) would be Britain's normal commitment; the navy was meeting its NATO goals save in minesweepers, while the R.A.F. was falling
a little below its planned contribution to the tactical air forces.

8. See Commons debates on 5 and 20 Feb, 5 and 26 Mar 1952. About
three-quarters of a Venom order of 1000 and one-third of a Canberra
order of about 1000 were cancelled. See also *The Economic Survey for
1952* (Cmd 8509).

9. Antony Head, House of Commons, 11 Mar 1954.

10. Britain seems to have hoped to develop supporting bases and
communications in British Africa, with African troops to ease the man-

power strain. This was discussed at the Nairobi Conference in Aug 1951. Egypt, however, refused to attend, and South Africa opposed the use of black troops (W. C. B. Tunstall, *The Commonwealth and Regional Defence*, 1959, pp. 47–8).

11. Dalton, pp. 377–8; H. Morrison, *An Autobiography* (1960) pp. 281–2; Attlee, pp. 175–6.

12. Avon, *Full Circle*, p. 234.

13. *RUSIJ* (1963) p. 29.

14. Something of the nature of this debate can be gleaned from Rosecrance, *Defense of the Realm*, chap. vi; Lord Avon, *Full Circle*, p. 256; Moran, pp. 478, 482, 580, 585; Dwight D. Eisenhower, *Mandate for Change: 1953-6* (1963) pp. 150–9; Macmillan, pp. 504–6, 574; R. M. McClintock, *The Meaning of Limited War* (1967) pp. 94–5; and see the Commons debate of 29 July 1954.

15. *The Times*, 5 Oct 1953.

16. *RUSIJ* (1953) pp. 98, 216–17.

17. See Lieutenant-General H. G. Martin's contribution in *Brassey* (1953) pp. 38–9.

18. *RUSIJ* (1953) pp. 228–36.

19. McClintock, pp. 94–5.

20. House of Commons, 2 Mar 1964.

21. J. G. Starke, *The ANZUS Treaty Alliance* (1966).

22. R.I.I.A., *Collective Defence in South East Asia: A Report by a Chatham House Study Group* (1956).

23. There are many studies of this 'emergency'. Note especially R. Clutterbuck, *The Long, Long War* (1967); Sir Robert Thompson, *Defeating Communist Insurgency* (1966); Brigadier M. C. A. Henniker, *Red Shadow over Malaya* (1955); Lieutenant-Colonel J. Paget, *Counter-Insurgency Campaigning* (1967); and the *War Office Statement accompanying the Army Estimates for 1955* (Cmd 9395).

24. Moran, p. 363. On the background to Templer's appointment, see Chandos, chap. xix.

25. J. P. L. Thomas, House of Commons, 9 Mar 1954.

26. *The Times*, 11 Jan 1955. For an interesting overall critique of counter-insurgency operations in Kenya, see Paget, pp. 83–113. Above all he questions the value of large sweeps after Operation Anvil, and especially into 1955, when the killing of each Mau Mau was costing some £10,000. Small, highly-trained *élite* forces should have been used earlier. The purposeless, indiscriminate violence in which the Mau Mau frequently engaged helped to isolate them from the mass of the population. Nevertheless, the emergency forces, despite their ponderousness, followed the sound principles established in Malaya, denying secure bases to the enemy, cutting their food supplies, and finally eroding their strength by a variety of offensive tactics.

27. See R.I.I.A., *Survey of International Affairs, 1954* (1957) part V, section 2, for a useful introduction to the Cypriot question, and especially pp. 178–9 for British motivation. Attlee emphasised the deficiencies of the island as a base in a speech to the Commons of 29 July

12. *The Times*, 11 Oct 1957 and 20 Dec 1958.

13. Interesting criticisms of British policy are to be found in *Brassey* (1957) pp. 46–51; (1958) pp. 200–5, 214–25. For the German reaction, see D. C. Watt, *Britain Looks to Germany* (1965) p. 133.

14. By 1961 Transport Command was capable of flying about 150 million passenger-miles a year compared with about 55 million in 1956.

15. Rosecrance, *Defense of the Realm*, pp. 241 ff.; Gretton, esp. pp. 36–8, 89–94; Snyder, chaps vii and viii; note useful articles in *RUSIJ* (1956) pp. 351–63, and *Brassey* (1958) pp. 210–13. Montgomery argued (*The Times*, 22 Oct 1957) that the future Soviet challenges were most likely to occur at sea, in the Middle and Far East, rather than in Europe. British servicemen overseas, however, were to be halved between 1957 and 1967, most of the 150,000 reduction being provided by the army and air force. See also P. Kemp (ed.), *History of the Royal Navy* (1969) p. 294.

16. See *The Times*, 28 Sep 1957, for the complaints of the two commanders, Admiral Sir John Eccles and Air Marshal Sir Bryan Reynolds.

17. Cf. Gretton, pp. 89–94, 142–3, and F. Mulley, *The Politics of Western Defence* (1962) pp. 166–7. Gretton thought that the dangers he envisaged would demand a British strength of some 100 destroyer-frigate type ships.

18. They were completed at a cost of £40 million, only to see little service in their original guise.

19. The Wolfenden Committee on the Employment of National Servicemen (Cmnd 35, 17 Dec 1956) reached some critical conclusions concerning the employment of National Servicemen.

20. See below, pp. 158, 172. Lord Head in a letter to *The Times* (5 Nov 1970) stated that he was unable to accept Macmillan's offer that he should remain at the Ministry of Defence in Jan 1957 since the new Prime Minister insisted on unacceptable cuts in defence spending and manpower.

21. An Army League pamphlet, *The Army Britain Needs* (1964), advocated selective service, entailing an entry of some 15,000–20,000 per year and serving for 18–24 months. For a general survey of the raising of service manpower by all leading states, see M. R. D. Foot, *Men in Uniform* (1961).

22. Aircrew shortages persisted into 1961.

23. Thus Lieutenant-Colonel J. D. Lunt (*Brassey*, 1960, pp. 54–61) thought officers' pay broadly adequate, but that much else would be needed to attract sufficient candidates. See also the Army League's *A Challenge to Leadership: An Examination of the Problems of Officer Recruitment for the British Army* (1962).

24. Rosecrance, *Defense of the Realm*, pp. 239–42.

25. From remarks made by Duncan Sandys and Lord Mountbatten when interviewed on Independent Television, 12 Mar 1969.

26. For this debate see Rosecrance, *Defense of the Realm*, chaps viii and ix; Martin, *American Political Science Review* (Mar 1962) pp. 27, 33–7; S. King-Hall, *Defence in the Nuclear Age* (1958); Liddell Hart, *Deterrent or Defence* (1960); C. Driver, *The Rise and Fall of C.N.D.*

(1964); F. Parkin, *Middle Class Radicalism* (1968); R. Goold-Adams, 'Those against the H-bomb', *Brassey* (1958) pp. 90–7; Bertrand Russell, *Common Sense and Nuclear Warfare* (1959). For the debate in the Labour party, see M. R. Gordon, chap. ix, and S. Haseler, *The Gaitskellites* (1969) pp. 189–208. Haseler argues that the Labour debate really revolved around personal rivalries, and the question of party leadership, rather than detailed questions of strategy. Experience of office from 1964 led the Labour leadership to rely almost as heavily on nuclear arms as their predecessors. Contemporary sceptics among the press include *The Times* and *The Economist*; note articles in the latter, e.g., for 1 Feb 1958 and 31 May 1958, and a correspondence in *The Times* initiated by P. M. S. Blackett, 27 Jan 1962 ff.

27. Blackett, pp. 31–45, 54 ff.

28. *Brassey* (1959) p. 70.

29. *RUSIJ* (1957) pp. 473–82. For other pleas to increase the conventional elements in Britain's armed strength, see R. Goold-Adams and A. Buchan, in *Political Quarterly* (1960) pp. 26–45.

30. See the Anglo-American *Agreement for Co-operation on the Uses of Atomic Energy for Mutual Defence Purposes* (1958, Cmnd 537). Note also W. T. R. and A. B. Fox, *NATO and the Range of American Choice* (1967) pp. 92–3, 129, 137–8; M. Howard (ed.), *The Theory and Practice of War* (1965) p. 303; C. Bell, *The Debatable Alliance* (1964) pp. 56 ff. General Power, commander of the American Strategic Air Command, described Bomber Command as 'an essential element of the Western deterrent', especially since it would form part of the 'first wave of the allied retaliatory force'. Further light is thrown on American thinking by M. H. Armacost, *The Politics of Weapon Innovation* (1969) pp. 190–198, and note his reference (pp. 59–60) to an American study (1955) of the possibility of leaving the development of an Intermediate Range Ballistic Missile to the British.

31. See Commons debates of 26–7 Feb 1958; 25–6 Feb 1959; 5 and 9 Mar 1959; 29 Feb 1960; 27 Apr 1960; 27–8 Feb 1961. See also Sir Frederick Brundrett's R.U.S.I. lecture of 16 Mar 1960.

32. *The Times*, 7 May 1958.

33. *Sunday Times*, 8 Dec 1963.

34. *Foreign Affairs* (Jan 1962) pp. 196–212.

35. F. O. Wilcox and H. H. Field, *The Atlantic Community* (1964) p. 106.

36. See especially W. W. Kaufmann, *The McNamara Strategy* (1964); L. Hart, *Deterrence or Defence*, chaps ix and xvi, notably pp. 45, 93, 166–7, 172; T. W. Stanley, *NATO in Transition* (1965) pp. 243–305; O. Heilbrunn, *Conventional Warfare in the Nuclear Age* (1965) esp. pp. 63–83; A. Buchan, *NATO in the 1960s* (1963) chap. vi; Mulley, chaps v, viii, x, xiii; A. Buchan and P. Windsor, *Arms and Stability in Europe* (1963).

37. See the discussion in *RUSIJ* (1962) pp. 122–9, 244–5, 350. See also Mulley, pp. 145–6; M. Howard (ed.), *Theory and Practice of War*, p. 324; Zuckerman, *Foreign Affairs* (Jan 1962), pp. 196–212.

38. Cmnd 1639.

39. *Survey of International Affairs, 1961* (1965) pp. 73, 87 ff. Note also *The Times*, 6 and 11 May 1963, 17 Oct 1963.

40. See for instance, Tunstall, pp. 51–68; and K. Younger, *Changing Perspectives of British Foreign Policy* (1964) pp. 59–67.

41. But according to Mountbatten (*The Times*, 2 Oct 1969) the Admiralty had not been unduly worried over the possible loss of Singapore and other bases, given their growing faith in the highly mobile task force, and its protecting aircraft carrier.

42. Statement made during a B.B.C. television interview on 14 Sep 1967.

43. Tunstall, see above note 40.

44. Lieutenant-Colonel De Witt C. Armstrong, *RUSIJ* (1959) pp. 423–432. Air Vice-Marshal W. Carter (*Brassey*, 1967, pp. 180–8) was another who thought that the British services had clung uncritically to their overseas bases.

45. *The Times*, 22–3 Aug 1961; 8–9 Feb 1962; Liddell Hart, *Deterrence or Defence*, pp. 35–6. See also the Commons debates of 5 Mar 1959, 29 Feb 1960 and 27–8 Feb 1961.

46. D. D. Eisenhower, *The White House Years: Waging Peace, 1956–61* (1966) II 273, 279–82.

47. *Brassey* (1959) pp. 137–47, 162–3, contains interesting analyses of British needs in the Middle East. Note also 2nd Report from the Estimates Committee, session 1963–4, *Transport Aircraft* (H.M.S.O., 1963).

48. Useful analyses of this emergency are to be found in *RUSIJ* (1961) pp. 307–8, 461–2, and *Brassey* (1962) pp. 34–8, 171. See also *Survey of International Affairs, 1961* (1965) chap. xi; M. A. Fitzsimons, *Empire by Treaty* (1965) pp. 217–19; M. Howard (ed.), *Theory and Practice of War*, pp. 327–8; H. Trevelyan, *The Middle East in Revolution* (1970) pp. 182–92; and U. Dann, *Iraq under Qassem* (1969) pp. 349–52.

49. Note the parliamentary exchanges between George Wigg and John Profumo, 23 Nov 1962, on this question.

50. *RUSIJ* (Dec 1969) p. 20.

51. Compare the speeches in the Commons by Patrick Gordon Walker, Harold Wilson and Emanuel Shinwell (5–6 Mar 1962) and D. Healey, 26 Feb 1964.

52. For an interesting examination of British needs for amphibious warfare in the later 1960s, see Major-General J. L. Moulton, R.M., *RUSIJ* (1962) pp. 19–28.

Chapter 6

1. Thus A. C. L. Day asked (*Political Quarterly*, 1960, pp. 57–65) whether the national image was still not distorted, excessive defence spending meaning 'that we are not really capable of any useful military effort at all'. Investment had repeatedly suffered to the advantage of

defence and personal consumption. For other analyses of the British economy, see S. Brittan, *Steering the Economy* (1969) pp. 245–52, and S. Pollard, *The Development of the British Economy: 1914–67* (1969) pp. 480–3.

2. C. J. E. Harlow, *The European Armaments Base* (Institute for Strategic Studies, 1967) part 2, pp. 9–10.

3. Manpower costs were rising sharply: thus 846,000 servicemen (including those conscripted) had cost £286 million out of the £1640 million spent on defence in 1954–5 whereas 485,000 were costing £351 million out of £1656 million in 1961–2. *The Economist* (17 Dec 1960) estimated that each Regular cost four times as much as a conscripted man in pay, and twice as much in keep.

4. D. Healey, House of Commons, 27 June 1967. *The Economist* (4 Feb 1967) thought that the pre-confrontation aim of the Conservative government had been a Middle–Far Eastern defence posture costing some £123 million in foreign exchange.

5. *RUSIJ* (1966) pp. 119–21.

6. The Secretary of State for Air informed the Commons on 27 Feb 1964 that of a total R.A.F. spending on new aircraft and equipment between 1959 and 1964, 43 per cent had been on Bomber Command, 28 per cent Fighter Command, and 13 per cent Transport Command. See also statements by the Under-Secretary of State for Air on 7 Mar 1963 and 3 Mar 1964. The V-bomber force alone had cost £1100 million between 1950 and 1964. Lack of government support compelled the Hawker and Bristol companies to begin the V.T.O.L. P-1127 and its engine as private ventures, with 75 per cent of the funds for the engine being provided by the American Mutual Weapon Development Programme Agency. For a full history of the resultant aircraft, the Harrier, see *Aircraft Engineering* (Dec 1969–Feb 1970).

7. Kaufmann, *passim*; L. Beaton, *The Western Alliance and the McNamara Doctrine* (Institute for Strategic Studies, 1964) *passim*; *The Times* defence correspondent (13 Dec 1962 and 2 Aug 1963) believed that many American authorities found British nuclear pretensions 'ridiculous'.

8. For the Skybolt crisis, see Kaufmann, pp. 124–6; A. J. R. Groom, *The Year Book of World Affairs* (1964) pp. 73–95; T. C. Sorensen, *Kennedy* (1965) pp. 564 ff.; A. Schlesinger, *A Thousand Days: John F. Kennedy in the White House* (1965) pp. 731 ff. See also *Sunday Times*, 8 Dec 1963, and R. Neustadt, *Alliance Politics* (1970) chap iii.

9. British naval interest in Polaris dated back to at least 1958. The whole British programme cost about £350 million.

10. See the Commons debate of 30–1 Jan 1963; *RUSIJ* (1963) pp. 4–11; Sir John Slessor's criticism of Britain as a nuclear power in K. H. Cerny and H. W. Briefs (eds), *NATO in Quest of Cohesion* (1965) pp. 239–56. E. J. de Kadt, *British Defence Policy and Nuclear War* (1964) chaps ii–iv, and Rosecrance, *Defense of the Realm*, esp. pp. 23–4, were other critics. Defenders of the deterrent included C. Bell, *The Debatable Alliance* (1964), D. K. Palit, *War in the Deterrent Age* (1966) and Sir Michael

Wright, *Disarm and Verify* (1964). Note, too, the multinational discussion of nuclear strategy in *Foreign Affairs* (Oct 1963) pp. 49–106.

11. See J. L. Moulton, *RUSIJ* (1962) pp. 19–28.

12. To modernise a large British carrier in the 1960s cost about £30 million. One effort at economy by equipping both the R.A.F. and navy with the P-1154 failed, studies of the cost of adapting it for naval use suggesting that this would be out of proportion to the numbers involved.

13. Younger, pp. 62–3.

14. E. Monroe, *Britain's Moment in the Middle East* (1963) pp. 214–217; C. Mayhew, *Britain's Role Tomorrow* (1967) p. 145.

15. Note D. Healey's belief (see his *A Labour Britain in the World*, 1964) that Britain must remain a world power. For differences in the Labour party, note the Commons debates of 5–6 Mar 1962. For a general review of its defence thinking in and out of office, see C. Stevenson, *RUSIJ* (1966) pp. 52–7.

16. Comments on this operation are to be found in *Brassey* (1963) pp. 77–84 and (1965) p. 30.

17. For the Aden crisis, see Tom Little, *South Arabia: Arena of Conflict* (1968); J. Paget, *Last Post: Aden, 1964–7* (1969), and G. King, *Imperial Outpost: Aden* (1964). Two useful accounts of operations in the Radfan are to be found in *Brassey* (1965) pp. 129–36 and in *RUSIJ* (1966) pp. 30–40. For the Tanganyikan operation, see Lieutenant-Colonel T. M. P. Stevens, ibid. (1965) pp. 48–55. British pretensions East of Suez were also shaken by the successful defiance of the Southern Rhodesians from 1965. Military intervention does not seem to have been contemplated by the government, and in any case would have been a considerable gamble (unless only minimal resistance had been encountered) given the concurrent crises in Aden and Malaysia. Few transport aircraft were available, the region was remote from the sea, while the airfields, roads and railways in neighbouring Zambia were all of limited value. See *The Times*, 30 Oct 1965; *New Statesman*, 15 Oct 1965; and *Spectator*, 16 Dec 1966. For the Rhodesian question in general, see K. Young, *Rhodesia and Independence* (1969).

18. On 'confrontation', see Sir R. Allen, *Malaysia: Prospect and Retrospect* (1968); Peter Boyce, *Malaysia and Singapore in International Diplomacy* (1968); Sir Walter Walker, 'How Borneo was Won', *Round Table* (Jan 1969) pp. 8–20 or *Survival* (Mar 1969) pp. 79–87. Note also the references to Borneo in a R.U.S.I. report, 12 Feb 1969, *Lessons from the Vietnam War*. M. Elliott-Bateman, *Defeat in the East* (1967) pp. 157–161, criticises the military handling of the emergency, and R. Hilsman, *To Move a Nation* (1967) chaps xxvi–xxvii, is critical of British policy as a cause of the crisis.

19. D. Healey, House of Commons, 4 Mar 1970, estimated that about one-quarter of the 1964–5 estimates were devoted to the presence East of Suez. 'Confrontation' in 1966 absorbed about 10,000 naval personnel, for instance, or more than one-quarter of those serving afloat. Total British service manpower deployed in this crisis reached over 50,000.

20. A SRN-5 hovercraft could carry 20 troops or 2 tons of supplies.

Among the aircraft used, the tiny Beaver was especially useful with its ability to use tiny jungle strips.

21. *Public Expenditure, 1963/4–1967/8* (Cmnd 2235); R. Maudling, House of Commons, 14 Apr 1964.

22. See, for instance, *Observer*, 17 Jan 1965. Note also the *10th Special Report from the Estimates Committee* (H.M.S.O., 1963) and the *9th Report from the Estimates Committee* (H.M.S.O., 1964).

23. Sir S. Zuckerman, *Scientists and War* (1966) p. 45.

24. For the reorganisation of the Ministry of Defence, etc., in the 1960s, see D. N. Chester (ed.), *The Organisation of British Central Government: 1914–64* (1968), in which F. M. G. Wilson describes the 1964 reorganisation as 'almost certainly the largest administrative merger ever to take place in British central government' (p. 387). See also the *Central Organisation for Defence* (Cmnd 2097); Daalder, chap. xii and pp. 332–6; and especially M. Howard, *The Central Organisation of Defence* (R.U.S.I., 1970).

25. *Brassey* (1968) pp. 220–5. M. Howard (*The Times*, 1 May 1970) and Dr D. Owen (*The Times*, 27 July 1970) also urged an extension of the functional approach. For the views of Healey's successor on the reorganisation of the Ministry of Defence, see Lord Carrington, 'British Defence Policy', *RUSIJ* (Dec 1970) pp. 3–10.

26. House of Commons, 10 Mar 1969.

27. *RUSIJ* (June 1969) pp. 53–9.

28. Lord Kilmuir, *Political Adventures* (1964) p. 321.

29. See the *Report of the Committee on the Management and Control of Research and Development* (the Gibb-Zuckerman Committee, 1958–61) (H.M.S.O., Dec. 1961); the *1st and 2nd Reports of the Inquiry into Pricing of Ministry of Aviation Contracts* (Cmnd 2428, 2581); see also note 51 below for references to reports concerning the Bristol-Siddeley engine contracts. For civil service reform, see the *Report of the Fulton Committee, 1966–8* (Cmnd 3638).

30. *1st and 2nd Reports of the Committee of Public Accounts*, part 1, sess. 1966–7, pp. xv–xvii, 114, 117.

31. See, for instance, *The Economist*, 12 Dec 1959, 5 Mar 1960 and 18 Mar 1961.

32. For criticism of civil service expertise and its relations with experts, see A. Sampson, *Anatomy of Britain* (1962) pp. 227–41, 511, 523–9; W. A. Robson, 'The Fulton Report on the Civil Service', *Political Quarterly* (Oct–Dec 1968) pp. 397–414; R. Worcester, *Roots of British Air Policy* (1966) chap. iii; F. Ridley (ed.), *Specialists and Generalists* (1968). Note also *RUSIJ* (1964) pp. 100–1, (1965) pp. 347–9, (1967) pp. 120–31, 304; *Brassey* (1963) pp. 85–91; *New Scientist*, 24 Oct 1968. Difficulties also arose with service officers, in part because of insufficient scientific and technical knowledge on their part in many instances, and also from the shortness of their tours of duty in connection with advanced projects. Finally the Institution of Professional Civil Servants thought that the Ministry of Defence had done less well than, for instance, the Ministry of Technology in integrating scientists and engineers into

general management, save at the highest levels. Engineers were less well treated than scientists. See Select Committee on Science and Technology (1967–8), *Defence Research*, 139–xiii 284–7.

33. See above, pp. 153–4, cf. Zuckerman, pp. 41–4, and S. Hastings, *The Murder of the TSR-2* (1966) pp. 129 ff.

34. Cmnd 4236. Much of interest is to be found in the minutes of evidence taken by the Select Committee on Science and Technology (1967–8), *Defence Research*, 139–i–xxii. Its enquiries concerning the Gibb–Zuckerman government decision-making procedures suggested that the profligate practices of the 1950s had been checked to some extent — some thought the new restrictions excessive (139–ii 21, 25; iii 27–33). Relations between military staff (operational requirements), technical directors in the Ministry of Technology, and R. & D. establishments were now claimed to be 'terribly close' (139–iv 63), and contacts with industry were improving (139–ii *passim*; xx 417 ff.; xxi 447). Among the Wilson government's innovations was the National Defence Industries Council, chaired by the Secretary of State for Defence, and with government representatives sitting beside top industrialists.

35. *Aircraft Engineering* (Sep 1969) pp. 8 ff.; *Engineering* (29 Aug 1969) pp. 212–13.

36. See John Simpson, *RUSIJ* (Mar 1969) pp. 46–50; *The Economist*, 20 Apr 1968, which noted that the exacting American specifications for Polaris had been a great stimulant to British contractors. Similar British gains have been claimed for Phantom and Hercules sub-contracting. On project management, see Select Committee . . . *Defence Research*, 139–xxi 450 ff.

37. G. Williams (ed.), *Crisis in Procurement*, chap. viii. In contrast *Military Aircraft Procurement* (R.U.S.I., 23 Oct 1968) adds little of importance.

38. The twentieth century has not been the only victim of escalating costs. The original Great Western Railway exceeded its initial estimates by 100 per cent in the 1840s.

39. *RUSIJ* (Mar 1969) pp. 29 ff.

40. Note the claim of D. Healey (4 Mar 1969) that at current prices Labour's defence policy was costing £700 million less than that envisaged under the Home government (a cut of 25 per cent). The Conservatives rejected such claims as purely hypothetical, J. Ramsden conceding on 4 Mar 1969 that they might have had some meaning only if *all* the Conservative plans, as they stood in 1964, had been implemented without any delays. For doubts concerning the feasibility of the 1964 air programme, see Williams, *Crisis in Procurement*, p. 35. Three major projects would have reached fruition roughly together, unless the P-1154 and HS-681 had again been delayed in favour of the TSR-2. The Royal Aircraft Establishment, Farnborough, was overstretched by these projects, while the estimated cost of the HS-681 had risen 100 per cent (1961–4) and of the P-1154 by more than 300 per cent (Select Committee . . . *Defence Research*, 139–iii 41; xxi 449–50).

41. *The Times*, 11 Feb 1965. *The Economist* (16 Jan 1965) cryptically

remarked that future inquiry would reveal government preference for the advice of civil servants and senior officers concerning expensive new arms rather than that of research staff.

42. House of Commons, 1 May 1967.

43. R. Beaumont, an ex-test pilot, fiercely defended the quality of British aircraft in his *Phoenix into Ashes* (1968), but one cannot escape the superior sales appeal of certain foreign aircraft, notably the Mirage III, of which by 1970 France herself had bought 400 and eight foreign buyers another 700. Aubrey Jones foresaw bleak foreign sales prospects for the Lightning and TSR-2 as far back as 27 Apr 1960. Suggestions that the U.S., disappointed by the F-111, would have bought the TSR-2 seem unlikely. Export sales of the Lightning totalled £60 million by 1970, a fairly modest record.

44. Note for instance R. Jenkins, House of Commons, 9 Feb 1965; J. G. Crowther, *Science in Modern Society* (1967) pp. 358–9; *The Economist*, 5 Sep 1964 and 16 Jan 1965, which favoured a 25 per cent cut in the size of the aircraft industry. The Working Group on Migration, *The Brain Drain* (Cmnd 3147, para. 143), concluded, however, that the 1965 cancellations increased the 'brain drain' to the U.S.A.

45. See *Flight International*, 11 and 18 Feb 1965, for a discussion of the aircraft cancelled and their replacements. See also the Commons debate, 9 Feb 1965.

46. *1st, 2nd and 3rd Reports from the Committee of Public Accounts*, sess. 1967–8, pp. xxviii–xxx, 467–8.

47. See House of Commons, 6 and 13 Apr 1965; 4 and 7–8 Mar 1966; 1 May 1967. Respective costs were continually disputed by both parties, and Julian Amery (House of Commons, 9 Feb 1965) interestingly illustrated some of the difficulties of making fair comparisons between British and American aircraft, especially over any length of time. A Conservative party publication, *Notes on Current Politics: Defence 1966–7* (11 Apr 1966) pp. 163–4, cited the editor of an American periodical, *Missiles and Rockets* (28 Feb 1966), who declared that the TSR-2 cancellation was 'virtually a death knell' of the British aircraft industry, and that McNamara's salesmanship and influence in this instance were 'worthy of the Marquis de Sade'. This claim, to say the least, was premature.

48. *Treasury Minute on the 1st and 2nd Reports from the Committee of Public Accounts*, sess. 1966–7 (Cmnd 3137) p. 4. See also Hastings, *passim*, who, though a defender of the aircraft, agreed that the Air Staff had insisted on ambitious specifications without due regard to costs (pp. 59–60). The best account of the TSR-2 is given by Williams, *Crisis in Procurement*, who shows how increasing costs led to increasing doubts as to the value of the aircraft in possible conditions of the later 1960s. But he also questions the government claims concerning the cheapness of the F-111 substitute: these he thought at best non-proven.

49. *The Times* (21 Dec 1967) claimed that an Air Staff memorandum drafted early in 1965 agreed that the case for the TSR-2 rested heavily on needs East of Suez. The British Aircraft Corporation's defence of the

TSR-2 was similarly based on its East of Suez role – see *The Economist*, 20 Feb 1965. Slessor supported the F-111 option in a letter to that journal, 24 Apr 1965.

50. L. R. Beesley (Director General of Aircraft Production, Ministry of Aviation), *Aircraft Engineering* (Oct 1966) pp. 26–36. For other analyses of aircraft problems, note D. W. G. L. Haviland (ex-Deputy Secretary of the Ministry of Aviation), ibid. (Dec 1965) p. 358; E. M. Ellis (Director and General Manager Engineering, Aero-plane Division of Rolls-Royce), ibid. (Jan 1967) pp. 22–3; Handel Davies (Technical Director, British Aircraft Corporation), ibid. (July 1970) pp. 20–3; Professor D. Keith-Lucas, *RUSIJ* (1967) pp. 120–31; G. Turner, *Business in Britain* (1969) pp. 360–9; and *Report of the Committee of Inquiry into the Aircraft Industry* [Plowden Report] (Cmnd 2853).

51. *Productivity of the National Aircraft Effort* [Elstub Committee] (H.M.S.O., Oct 1969). Note also the *2nd Special Report from the Committee of Public Accounts, session 1966–7, Bristol Siddeley Engines Ltd*, pp. xix, 117–19; and *3rd Report . . . session 1967–8 . . .* pp. xii. Bristol-Siddeley claimed that from 1959 to 1965 it had been struggling to integrate two firms and establish the new company on firm foundations. The merger had been necessary to secure the contract for the Olympus 320 (the TSR-2 engine), and the company felt that it was emerging from its troubles when the 1965 cancellations cost it two of its four main projects, the possible loss of £300 million over the next seven years, and 2000 workers had had to be sacked. Government criticism of its efficiency and management should be viewed in this context.

52. Christopher Soames, House of Commons, 13 Apr 1965.

53. The Hawker-Siddeley Nimrod, a Spey-engined development from the Comet airliner, was designed for maritime reconnaissance, and was to replace the ageing Shackletons. The Air Staff had been looking for a successor since 1958; both the American Lockheed Orion and the French Breguet Atlantique had been considered. The Nimrod choice was a good one. See Select Committee . . . *Defence Research*, 139–xix, 405, 410–11, 413.

54. For this controversy, see Commons debates, 4 Mar 1965 and 4 Mar 1970 (esp. Hugh Fraser); 22 Feb 1966 (esp. C. Mayhew); 7 Mar 1966 (esp. D. Healey); and 9 Mar 1970 (esp. I. Orr-Ewing). The key place of the carrier in naval thinking is well illustrated by Gretton, chap. vii. The *Observer* (3 Mar 1966) thought that the carrier school was weakened when Sir Richard Hull succeeded Mountbatten as Chief of the Defence Staff. Note L. W. Martin, *The Sea in Modern Strategy* (1967) pp. 123 ff., who thought that if the modernisation of Asian navies continued, even a medium naval power would feel menaced by them unless able to use politically unacceptable weapons.

55. *RUSIJ* (1966) pp. 95–8. But see also the remarks of D. C. Watt in the same vol., pp. 128–31.

56. *Spectator*, 19 July 1968. Note also the continuing R.N.–R.A.F. debate on the role of air power in a seminar at the R.U.S.I., reported in *The Times*, 21 Nov 1968.

57. See *The Times*, 14 and 16 Dec 1965; *The Economist*, 20 Mar 1965; Montgomery, House of Lords, 23 Nov 1965. See also the Commons debates, 16 Dec 1965, 10 May 1966, and *Reorganisation of the Army Reserves* (H.M.S.O., Dec 1965 Cmnd 2855). Michael Howard (*Sunday Times*, 19 Dec 1965) broadly supported the new approach, though he thought some purely home defence force was needed to try to meet the problems of 'a post-nuclear environment'. An account of the subsequent development of the T. and A.V.R. is to be found in *RUSIJ* (Feb 1968) pp. 12–19 by Lieutenant-General Sir Geoffrey Musson, and great praise for the increased efficiency of the new force in the same journal (Sep 1969) p. 81 by Major J. C. M. Baynes.

Chapter 7

1. For a survey of British dilemmas in defence, see N. Brown, *Arms without Empire* (1967). Note also A. Verrier, *An Army for the Sixties* (1966). For an American view, see W. Goldstein, *The Dilemma of British Defense* (1966).

2. Note, e.g., J. Critchley, *Spectator*, 9 Apr 1965.

3. *International Affairs* (Apr 1966).

4. *Spectator*, 18 Feb 1966 and 14 Apr 1967.

5. See *The Times*, 23 Oct 1969.

6. For the emergency in Aden and South Arabia, see Tom Little, *South Arabia: Arena of Conflict* (1968); J. Paget, *Last Post: Aden, 1964–7* (1969); H. Trevelyan, *The Middle East in Revolution* (1970). Note also W. P. Kirkman, *Unscrambling an Empire* (1966) pp. 152–62, and Major P. de la Billière, 'The Changing Pattern of Guerrilla Warfare', *RUSIJ* (Dec 1969) pp. 42–4.

7. For a forceful attack on the government's Gulf policy, see A. Verrier, *RUSIJ* (Nov 1967) pp. 349–55. See also Centre for Strategic Studies, Georgetown University, Washington D.C., Special Report Series, *The Gulf: Implications for Withdrawal* (1969).

8. See articles in the *New Scientist*, 8 June and 23 Nov 1967; Healey's account to the Commons, 27 Nov 1967; and T. Beamish, *Aldabra Alone* (1970).

9. P. Gordon Walker, *The Cabinet* (1970) pp. 122–33.

10. B.B.C. television interviews of 12 Jan 1970 and 5 Mar 1970.

11. *Observer*, 11 Feb 1968, and *The Times*, 24 Apr 1968.

12. *Daily Mail*, 9 Apr 1970; and the press in general, 10 and 14 Apr 1970. Note also Gordon Walker, pp. 138 ff., and a variety of articles in *RUSIJ* and *Brassey* for 1968–9.

13. Healey gave the cancellation costs as £13·5 million, House of Commons, 10 June 1969. A fortnight later he told reporters in Bangkok that no British forces would be available for SEATO's contingency planning after 1971 (P. Darby, *International Affairs*, Oct 1970, p. 657). This decision was reversed by the Heath government.

14. *Survival* (June 1969) pp. 186–92.

NOTES287

15. On Civil Defence, see Major-General R. F. K. Goldsmith, *Brassey* (1968) pp. 43–53 and *Financial Times* (supp.), 4 Mar 1970.

16. *The Economist,* 29 Dec 1962, refers to the impact of the Cuban missile crisis on civil defence.

17. *The Times,* 23 Oct 1969.

18. K. Gordon (ed.), *Agenda for the Nation* (1968) pp. 550–1, 569–73.

19. See *RUSIJ* (Sep 1969) pp. 55–8, and Hackett's letter to *The Times,* 6 Feb 1968 (note the ensuing comment of A. Buchan, 10 Feb 1968). Note also Lord Monckton's article in *RUSIJ* (Feb 1968) pp. 27–33.

20. J. J. Baritz, 'The Soviet Strategy of Flexible Response', *Bulletin (Institute for the Study of the U.S.S.R.)* (Apr 1969) pp. 25–35.

21. *Survival* (Apr 1969) pp. 110–19. Note the estimate in *Brassey* (1969) p. 59 that the Northern Army Group could resist a major attack for only 2–3 days; the Central Army Group should be able to hold out for 6–7 days with its powerful American components. Note R. Paget's more pessimistic estimate, based on a war game with Liddell Hart, as related to the Commons, 4 Mar 1970.

22. *RUSIJ* (Sep 1969) pp. 5–17.

23. See Hackett's letters to *The Times,* 27 Feb 1970, and the *Sunday Times,* 1 Mar 1970.

24. Letter to *The Times,* 24 Feb 1970.

25. *The Times,* 23 Feb 1970. See also Healey's statement to the Commons, 4 Mar 1970 (see above, p. 160).

26. Letter to *The Times,* 27 Feb 1970.

27. *Observer,* 1 Mar 1970.

28. *The Economist,* 21 Feb 1970.

29. Letter to *The Times,* 26 Feb 1970.

30. *The Times,* 25 Feb 1970.

31. *Spectator,* 28 Feb 1970.

32. Correlli Barnett, *Britain and her Army* (1970) pp. 493–4; C. Douglas-Home, *Britain's Reserve Forces* (R.U.S.I., 1969); *The Times,* 29 Nov 1968, 20–1 Feb 1969. See also the Commons debate of 16 Dec 1968. Healey argued (*RUSIJ,* Dec 1969, pp. 19–21) that Britain's European allies preferred professional forces on the spot to larger and less efficient forces arriving over an uncertain period after the start of a crisis.

33. Thus up to 11,000 troops were stationed in Ulster in July 1970, a great strain on the already over-stretched infantry.

34. *RUSIJ* (June 1969) pp. 14–24. The army's six Landing Ships (Logistic) could each carry about fifteen Chieftain tanks and 400 troops. The navy's assault ships and commado ships could carry various mixes of men and equipment, depending on the distance to be covered. Together they could lift a lightly equipped brigade.

35. General Lemnitzer (see *Orbis,* spring 1969, pp. 106–7) described Soviet exercises near northern Norway in mid-1968 as defensive in the main, but Soviet strength on the Kola Peninsula (and in the Baltic) remained disturbingly strong. The only immediate available NATO reinforcements were the ACE Mobile Force and the Standing Naval

Force (Atlantic). See also *NATO Letter* (Sep 1969) pp. 16–19; C. G. M. Koran in *Brassey* (1969) pp. 62–72; and Sir Walter Walker, *RUSIJ* (Sep 1970) pp. 13–23.

36. *Spectator*, 19 July 1968. Unfortunately few British helicopters were available for B.A.O.R., which had to borrow from the Americans for exercises. Nor did the number and type of British helicopters on order promise much improvement in the future. For the overall state of B.A.O.R., see *The Economist*, 28 Nov 1970 – a very convenient brief analysis.

37. Compare the estimates given by Healey (*Survival*, Apr 1969, p. 115), T. W. Stanley (ibid., Nov 1969, pp. 342–8 and May 1970, pp. 152–160), and by A. C. Enthoven and K. W. Smith (*Foreign Affairs*, Oct 1969, pp. 80–96). Stanley also contributed to a report by the Atlantic Council of the United States that urged a unilateral cut of 10 per cent in American forces in Europe to test the possibility of later agreed and reciprocal cuts in conjunction with the Warsaw Pact (*The Times*, 23 Mar 1970).

38. On international aircraft procurement, see M. Edmonds, *International Affairs* (Apr 1967) pp. 252–64; C. Layton, *European Advanced Technology* (1969) pp. 144–7; and W. T. Gunston, 'Aviation: Collaborate or Perish', *Science Journal* (July 1970) pp. 74–7. But note also the complaints of the Electrical Engineering Association, *Formula for Success* (Apr 1970), that France had gained much British electronic know-how and expertise as a result of the Jaguar collaborative project. Sir George Edwards of B.A.C. complained that the British aircraft industry had been badly let down over the A.F.V.G. He understood that the Jaguar and A.F.V.G. had together formed a package deal, Britain having design leadership of the airframe of the latter. But the French had nevertheless been allowed to withdraw from the A.F.V.G. project. The aircraft industry had been let down in other international deals, though he recognised the importance of co-operative projects. A useful history of the Jaguar is to be found in *Flight International* (29 Oct 1970) pp. 675–686. In the winter of 1970–1 there were disturbing rumours about escalating costs in both the Jaguar and Panther programmes.

39. *Financial Times* (supp.), 4 Mar 1970. On the interaction of the services and industry, see Select Committee . . . *Defence Research*, 139 – esp. ii 18–25; iii 27–33; vi 118; x 186–7, 191–2, 195–6; xv 324; xvi 348; xviii 379–80. Overall the proportion of expenditure on research and development in Britain devoted to defence fell from over one-third in 1961–2 to under one-quarter for the years after 1966.

40. For a full technical analysis of the Harrier, see *Aircraft Engineering* (Dec 1969–Feb 1970). On the future of air warfare, especially for its effect on tactical aircraft, see, e.g., I. M. D. Wray, ibid. (Dec 1968) pp. 28–9; Air Vice-Marshal L. D. Mavor (Assistant Chief of the Air Staff, Policy), *RUSIJ* (Feb 1967) pp. 6–15; Air Marshal Sir Christopher Hartley, Adelphi Papers no. 46, *The Implications of Military Technology in the 1970s* (1968) pp. 28–37; Air Marshal Sir Christopher Foxley-Norris, *RUSIJ* (Sep 1969) pp. 5–17; and Air Vice-Marshal

P. de L. le Cheminant, ibid. (Sep 1970) pp. 39–46. Controversies over the future of tactical air power also extended to its control. The R.A.F. was reluctant to deploy Harriers so well forward as the army wished. Foxley-Norris insisted that the establishment of air superiority must come first, but Pasti Nino (*Orbis*, spring 1969, pp. 130 ff.) feared that crucial losses might occur on the ground while air forces fought their private battles. Certainly if only a brief land battle was envisaged, there might be insufficient time for western air forces to establish air superiority in the orthodox way. At least this was a controversy that should not be settled simply by resort to traditional dogma. The battle for air superiority would be complicated by the introduction by both NATO and the Warsaw Pact of aircraft shelters, dispersal of airfield facilities, and of aircraft that did not require concrete runways. For the belated modernisation in the British contribution to the 2nd Tactical Air Force, see *The Economist*, 28 Nov 1970.

41. *New Scientist*, 28 Aug 1969.

42. *The Times*, 22 July 1969. See the Commons debate, 9 Mar 1970, for important exchanges on torpedo development between P. Wall, Rear-Admiral Morgan-Giles and Dr Owen (Ministry of Defence).

43. *The Times*, 31 Oct 1968 and 20 Feb 1970.

44. At an estimated cost of £35–£40 million in 1970, and displacing some 25,000 tons, these ships were almost small carriers, having escalated dramatically in cost and size during their ten-year design period. Without effective V.S.T.O.L. aircraft (another expensive development) they might well prove unduly expensive ships. With effective V.S.T.O.L. aircraft, they might be better ships if built as genuine and unashamed small carriers.

45. At a high-level conference at Greenwich it was stated that it would be exceptional in any case for a naval commander to have tactical control of supporting aircraft (*Glasgow Herald*, 1 June 1970). For a defence of Labour policy with respect to the security of the fleet from long-range missile attack, see the speeches by the Minister of Defence for Equipment, House of Commons, 13 Nov 1967 and 4 Mar 1968.

46. For a comparison of types of ship propulsion, see Rear-Admiral R. G. Raper (Director-General of Ships), *RUSIJ* (Aug 1968) pp. 221–7. On possible developments, see Rear-Admiral T. T. Lewin (Assistant Chief of the Naval Staff, Policy), ibid. (Aug 1968) pp. 202–9.

47. Select Committee . . . *Defence Research*, 139–x 195–6.

48. *New Scientist*, 28 Aug 1969.

49. Compare the accounts of NATO naval strategy given to the Commons by the Minister of Defence for the Navy on 11 Mar 1965 and the Under-Secretary of State for Defence for the Navy on 11 Mar 1968. For the development of Soviet maritime strategy, see M. Edmunds and J. Skitt, *International Affairs* (Jan 1969) pp. 28–43; W. Laqueur, *Foreign Affairs* (Jan 1969) pp. 296–308, and his book, *The Struggle for the Middle East* (1969), esp. pp. 142–4, 181, 186–7; R. W. Herrick, *Soviet Naval Strategy* (1968); and Admiral Sir John Frewen, *RUSIJ* (Dec 1969) pp. 24–30. Walter C. Clemens, Jr, 'Soviet Policy in the Third World

in the 1970s', *Orbis* (summer 1969) pp. 476–501, makes an interesting attempt to divine the future, arguing that against many 'forward' Soviet policies in the Third World the most effective western responses were likely to be political and economic rather than military. Extreme Soviet moves could be self-defeating, dangerous and expensive, just as western military presences could often prove provocative rather than tranquillising among the local peoples. He thought any future British military action in the Third World would be dependent on the existence of friendly air bases, since Britain was unlikely to possess sufficient carrier strength – even if her carrier force were retained in the 1970s – to be effective on their own.

50. See *Spectator*, 13 Dec 1969, and *The Times*, 5 Jan 1970.

51. On recruiting problems, see the National Board for Prices and Incomes, *Standing Reference on the Pay of the Armed Forces* (2nd Report, H.M.S.O., June 1969, Cmnd 4079); Brigadier A. J. Wilson, *Brassey* (1969) pp. 260–7.

52. See above, pp. 147–9.

53. The multilateral force (M.L.F.) was to consist of mixed-manned Polaris-armed merchant-ships, a political rather than a military force.

54. See D. Healey, House of Commons, 4 Feb 1970, and H. Wilson, 26 Feb and 12 Mar 1970.

55. See, e.g., the Conservative Monday Club pamphlet, *A Europe of Nations: a Practical Policy for Britain* (1965), and the Conservative Political Centre pamphlet by Eldon Griffiths and M. Niblock, *Towards Nuclear Entente* (Mar 1970). For the debate on the pros and cons of an Anglo-French joint nuclear policy, see also Vice-Admiral Sir Arthur Hezlet, *Brassey* (1968) pp. 29–30; N. Brown, *The World Today* (Aug 1969) pp. 351–7; M. J. Brenner, *Bulletin of the Atomic Scientists* (Nov 1969) pp. 4–6; A. Buchan, *The Future of Nato* (1967); *Financial Times* (Defence Supplement), 4 Mar 1970 (which thought no one in NATO took the idea seriously); *The Times*, 27 June 1969 and 23 Mar 1970 (which argued the need for one European state before a European deterrent could even be considered); Adelphi Papers, no. 46, *The Implications of Military Technology in the 1970s* (Mar 1968) esp. pp. 5–6, 41–2; G. Hugo, *Britain in Tomorrow's World* (1969); and J. Lambert, *Britain in a Federal Europe* (1969).

56. See, e.g., *The Times*, 11 Feb 1969 (report of an interview given by D. Healey to *Der Spiegel*); ibid. 14 Aug 1969 (where L. Beaton thought that the British Polaris force would retain its credibility for most of the 1970s); and N. Brown, *Survival* (June 1970) pp. 194–8.

57. Projections of the economic trends of the 1960s by H. Kahn, *The World of 1980* (Hudson Institute, 1969), and by *The Economist*, 5 Sep 1970, suggested that real product per head of the population could be 40 or 50 per cent higher in West Germany and France than in Britain by 1980. More immediately D. Greenwood, *RUSIJ* (Nov 1968) pp. 328–330, doubted whether the necessary industrial capacity could be found for a much larger British effort in the near future. On the other hand, a service audience responded enthusiastically to a euphoric

lecture by Julian Amery (*RUSIJ*, June 1969, pp. 5–14) which belittled economic considerations. More soberly Sir Alec Douglas-Home as Foreign Secretary was to warn the Conservative Party Conference on 9 Oct 1970 that a nation's international credibility depended on its economic base. The Conservative *Supplementary Statement on Defence Policy* (28 Oct 1970) itself placed great emphasis on restraint in defence spending, even claiming that its own projected estimates for 1974–5 would be £130 million less than those of its Labour predecessors had all the programmes of the latter been implemented. Indeed, projected Conservative defence spending down to 1975 was so miserly that its targets were likely to prove unrealistic unless the pace of service re-equipment proved very slow indeed.

58. For the regimental controversy, see C. Barnett, *Britain and her Army* (1970) pp. 488–90; Peter Young, *The British Army* (1967) p. 273; numerous articles and letters in *RUSIJ* from 1966 (including some radical suggestions from Lieutenant-Colonel Colin Mitchell, ibid., 1966, pp. 225–9); and a stout defence by Field-Marshal Sir Gerald Templer in *The Times*, 29 June 1968.

59. A well-reasoned plea for a continuing mobile British presence East of Suez is provided by P. Darby in *International Affairs* (Oct 1970) pp. 655–69. Interesting articles on Soviet naval ambitions and strategy East of Suez are to be found by D. W. Mitchell, *Orbis* (spring 1970) pp. 129–53, and T. B. Millar, *Foreign Affairs* (Oct 1970) pp. 70–80. See also D. W. Mitchell's forthcoming book, *The History of Russian Sea Power*.

60. *Legal Obligations of H.M. Government arising out of the Simonstown Agreements* (1971, Cmnd 4589). For differences in the Wilson Cabinet over arms sales to South Africa in December 1967, see Lord George-Brown, *Sunday Times*, 11 Oct 1970, and *The Times*, 4 Feb 1971.

61. Of particular interest on the South African arms-base controversy are G. Rippon, *Survival* (Sep 1970) pp. 292–7; L. Martin, ibid. (Oct 1970) pp. 347–51; J. Spence, *The Strategic Importance of South Africa* (R.U.S.I., 1970); and *The Times*, 13 Oct 1970.

62. C. J. Bartlett (ed.), *Britain Pre-eminent: Studies in British World Influence in the Nineteenth Century* (1969) pp. 186–91.

63. *RUSIJ* (June 1970) pp. 13–20. See also C. Barnett, *Britain and her Army* (1970) pp. 493–4.

64. D. C. Watt, *RUSIJ* (June 1970) p. 43; and *The Economist*, 23 May 1970.

65. For an outstanding example of rigid military planning with almost fatal consequences, see S. R. Williamson, *The Politics of Grand Strategy: Britain and France Prepare for War 1904–1914* (1969). A R.U.S.I. seminar in 1971 is rightly posing the question, 'Does the Strategy of Flexible Response in Europe Need Modifying?'

Index